LEGENDARY LOCALS

OF

MOUNT CLEMENS

MICHIGAN

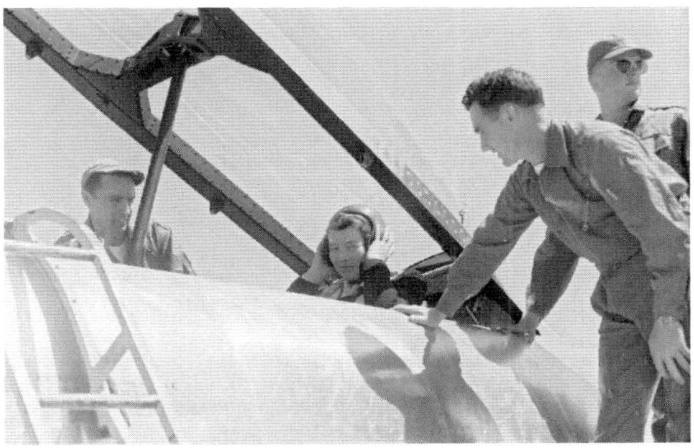

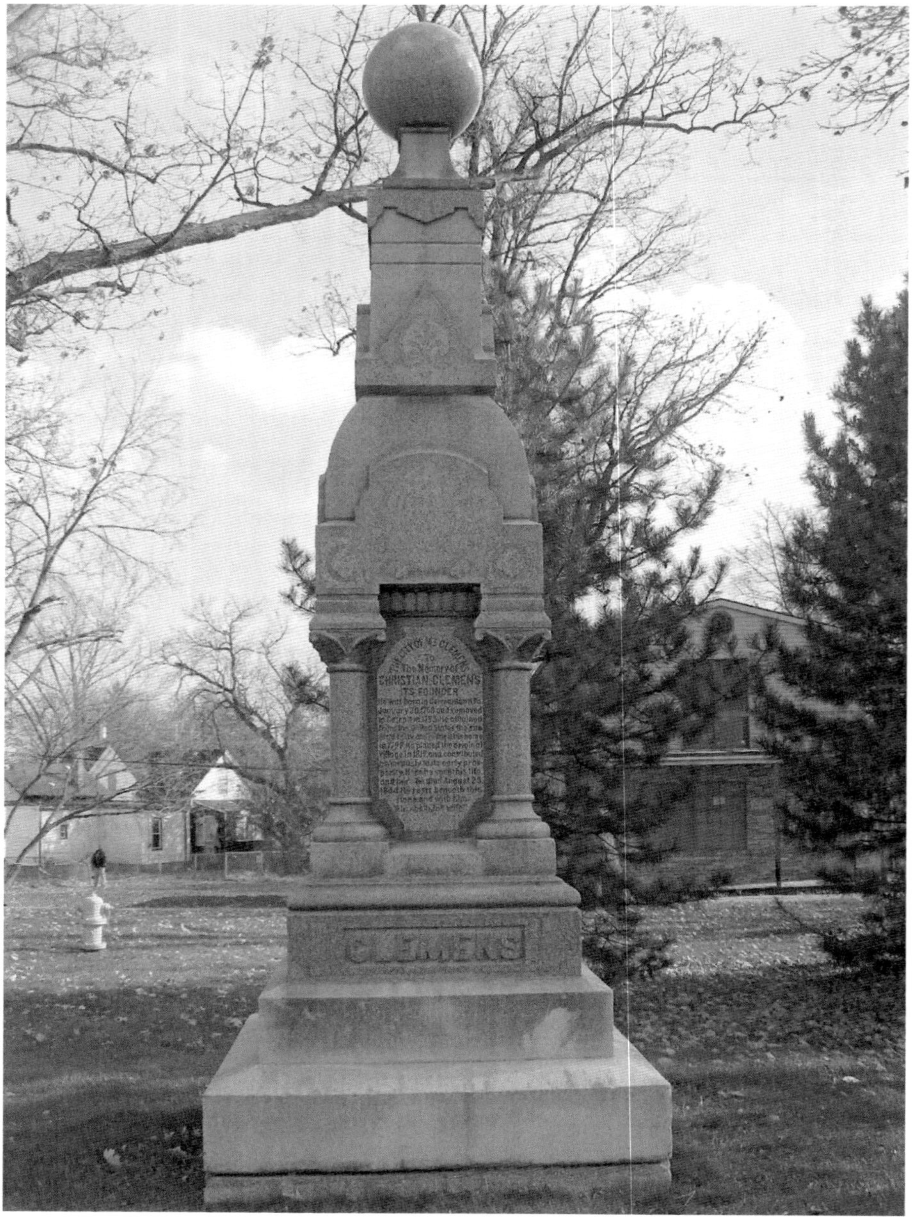

Page 1: Dorothy McPherson Magee
See page 105

Page 2: The Founders
Originally used as the town cemetery, tiny Clemens Park now contains only two graves—those of founder Christian Clemens and his wife, Elizabeth Talmadge Allen. This granite monument honoring Clemens was raised in 1897 when the former burying ground was rededicated as a public park. (Photograph by Deborah J. Larsen.)

LEGENDARY LOCALS

OF

MOUNT CLEMENS

MICHIGAN

DEBORAH J. LARSEN

LEGENDARY LOCALS

ISBN 978-1-4671-0012-0

Published by Legendary Locals, an imprint of Arcadia Publishing
Charleston, South Carolina

Printed in the United States of America

Library of Congress Control Number: 2011962630

For all general information, please contact Arcadia Publishing:
Telephone 843-853-2070
Fax 843-853-0044
E-mail sales@arcadiapublishing.com
For customer service and orders:
Toll-Free 1-888-313-2665

Visit us on the Internet at www.arcadiapublishing.com

Dedication

To the Macomb County Genealogy Group, without whose tireless indexing and record preservation efforts the research for this book would not have been possible.

On the Cover: From left to right:
(TOP ROW) Desmond A. Arnsby, journalist (Courtesy of the *Macomb Daily*; see page 101), Rylma Strevel Marquardt, golfer (Courtesy of the *Macomb Daily*; see page 90), Alger F. Graham, pilot (Courtesy of the *Macomb Daily*; see page 13), Ivan J. Harris, community leader (Courtesy of the *Macomb Daily*; see page 33), Robert George Peltier, showman (Courtesy of the *Macomb Daily*; see page 85).
(MIDDLE ROW) Bonner C. Upshaw, police officer (Courtesy of the *Macomb Daily*; see page 17), John M. Emerson Sr., local historian (Courtesy of John M. Emerson Sr.; see page 41), Ruth Phyllis Westover, city commissioner (Courtesy of the *Macomb Daily*; see page 16), Austin William Heine, physician (Courtesy of the *Macomb Daily*; see page 62), George William Priehs, businessman (Courtesy of the *Macomb Daily*; see page 64).
(BOTTOM ROW) Ada Davis Eisenfeld, mayor (Courtesy of the *Macomb Daily*; see page 18), Harley Bertrum Ensign, sheriff (Courtesy of the *Macomb Daily*; see page 25), Jennie Clawson Fenton, community volunteer (Courtesy of the *Macomb Daily*; see page 28), George Alfred Merifield, pastor (Courtesy of the *Macomb Daily*; see page 24), John R. Murphy, businessman (Courtesy of Mount Clemens Public Library; see page 51).

CONTENTS

ACKNOWLEDGMENTS

The author gratefully acknowledges the work of all prior historians of Mount Clemens, whose efforts serve as a foundation for this volume. For sharing their personal photographs for this project, I thank Gebran S. Anton, Deanna Black, Mark Brewer, Ross Champion, Barb R. Dempsey, John M. Emerson Sr., Mrs. John C. Lee, John F. MacArthur, Betty Lou Morris, Donald E. Odell, JoAnne Roskopp, George C. Steeh III, and Ruthie M. Stevenson.

I also wish to thank Salvatore D'Angelo of the Martha T. Berry Medical Care Facility; Kim Parr, director of the Crocker House Museum, as well as members of the museum volunteer staff; Laura Cutting of the Mount Clemens Community School District; and Mayor Barb R. Dempsey and the City of Mount Clemens for sharing materials from their institutional collections. For permission to publish images from their archival holdings, my thanks go to the Michigan State University Archives and the New York Public Library for the Performing Arts. For lending encouragement and support, I thank library director Donald E. Worrell Jr. and the staff and board of trustees of Mount Clemens Public Library, as well as my husband, Gerald S. Larsen, who always listens patiently to my research stories.

Finally, my immeasurable gratitude goes to Ken Kish and the management of the *Macomb Daily* newspaper, for granting permission to publish many outstanding photographs from the *Macomb Daily/Daily Monitor-Leader* archive.

INTRODUCTION

In 1795, Judge Christian Clemens founded a settlement north of Detroit on the high bank of the Huron River (known today as the Clinton River) that would one day become the town of Mount Clemens. The village was platted in 1818 and was established as the seat of Macomb County in the same year. Early Mount Clemens was fairly unremarkable as a small inland port on the Great Lakes waterway system with an economy based on a modest shipbuilding and cooperage trade. Her fortunes took a dramatic turn after the end of the Civil War, when prospectors drilling for oil discovered not the black gold that they were seeking, but abundant mineral springs.

From there, legend has it, the serendipitous cure of a lame horse who was exposed to the mineral water led local residents and physicians to use the brackish liquid to treat a variety of human ailments, including rheumatism, eczema, and arthritis. In 1873, two Mount Clemens physicians erected the first bathhouse in town, began offering mineral bath treatments to the public, and gave birth to a new industry. By the turn of the twentieth century, nine bathhouses and scores of hotels had sprung up in what was by then being called the "Bath City of America." The population of Mount Clemens soared to over 50,000 in the high summer season with visitors from the world over, all of whom were willing to spend the three weeks required for the full 21 treatments in the dark and sulfurous water.

Guidebooks proclaimed that patients arrived with wheelchairs, crutches, and canes, and after a course of baths, departed walking on their own two feet. The city's hotel registers boasted, at various times, names such as Alice Roosevelt Longworth, William Jennings Bryan, Helena Rubinstein, Jerome Kern, George M. Cohan, Babe Ruth, and Jack Dempsey. A 1912 promotional guide published by the Grand Trunk Railway system described the booming mineral bath town thus:

> Sickness flees at Mount Clemens. Rest comes, health returns, and with health new hopes, new courage and contentment. The curative waters bathe annually an unending pilgrimage, whose members in the aggregate are from the ends of the world, and which gives the Mineral Bath city a cosmopolitan character not found in other towns the size of Mount Clemens, yet all the more interesting on account of the surprise with which the activities, the restless current of life, must be viewed by him who visits the baths for the first time. In all the hotels, boarding houses and private houses will be found patients and tourists from all over the world, who have come to Mount Clemens for health and happiness. The elixir of life, the bubbling springs highly charged with mineral constituents, insure this city's fadeless renown.

That "elixir of life," so readily available for exploitation to anyone with a plot of ground and a well, attracted not only the infirm, but also the energetic entrepreneur. Mount Clemens blossomed with adjunct businesses, including bottled table waters, patent medicines of various kinds, recreational venues, and breweries. Some came for a cure, and seeing opportunity, stayed to partake of the prosperity that the health resort offered. Among the part-time residents were a variety of actors and entertainers who sought off-season respite in the Bath City, creating a theatrical colony of sorts; they included the American musical stage actress Sadie Hasson Dowling, juggler James DeWitt Cook, the Nelson family of circus aerialists, and burlesque dancer Amelia "Millie" Price Churchyard.

As the automobile age roared to life in the mid-1920s, the fortunes of the Mount Clemens mineral bath industry began to decline. Fewer people were willing to invest in the three-week stay necessary for a full course of baths, and medical science had begun to offer other treatment options that required far less time and effort. Furthermore, the Great Depression wiped out any capital that might have otherwise been available to proprietors to modernize their hotels and bathhouses, and by the beginning of World War II, the bath industry in Mount Clemens had all but ceased to exist.

The bath industry may have been down for the count, but the city of Mount Clemens was not. As the seat of government for a well-populated suburban Detroit county with strong ties to the automobile business, Mount Clemens was transformed into a governmental and light industrial center. Local leaders had to navigate the sometimes choppy waters of a changing tax base, urban renewal, population shifts, and evolving forms of government. During the postwar era, Mount Clemens saw African Americans appointed to prominent positions in local government for the first time, elected its first woman mayor, reinvented its waterfront, and expanded its cultural institutions.

Today's Mount Clemens looks vastly different than the bath town of old, but here and there one still finds artifacts of bygone days peeking through the fabric of the physical landscape. More abundant testimony to its history is found in the stories of the people who have called Mount Clemens home. Among their number are those who took fearless first steps to breach physical, racial, gender, or economic barriers; the teachers and scribes who handed knowledge and wisdom from one generation to the next; the business leaders and professionals whose vision fueled the economic engines; the community builders who created a place where newcomers could settle and be welcomed; the entertainers who brought acts to the local stage that would have otherwise never been seen in a small Midwestern town; the innovators and rebels who tried the risky, unexpected, or outrageous; and finally, the heroes of every generation who placed service above self.

CHAPTER ONE

First and Fearless

After Christian Clemens was first to formally establish and plat the settlement of Mount Clemens in 1818, many others followed him with the courage, vision, or foresight to take the necessary first steps to propel the community forward. Joshua B. Dickinson stepped forward to serve as the very first mayor of Mount Clemens when the city was incorporated in 1879, and 102 years after Dickinson, Ada Davis Eisenfeld broke a gender barrier when she became the first woman to sit in the mayor's chair.

Being first is not always easy, comfortable, or even safe. Bonner C. Upshaw certainly did not take the comfortable option when he became the first African American police officer in Mount Clemens, nor did Alice Louise Tucker follow the path of least resistance when she became the first woman elected official in Macomb County government. The trailblazers always had to swallow fear, resist the temptation to flee from detractors, obstructionists, and naysayers, and keep their eyes on the ultimate goal, even when insults were flying.

Sometimes being first means having the vision to walk an untried path, as Dor Kellogg did when he experimented with a mineral water cure, or as Alger F. Graham did when he flew into the arctic reaches of the Alaskan wilderness. Taking a risk to prove what was possible also sometimes meant facing down impossible odds.

Those first and fearless—whether by accident or design—created the foundation upon which all other advancements in Mount Clemens have stood. Whether by breaking a racial or gender barrier, altering a traditional course, or by looking at something as commonplace as water in a new and creative way, they opened doors of opportunity for everyone who came after them.

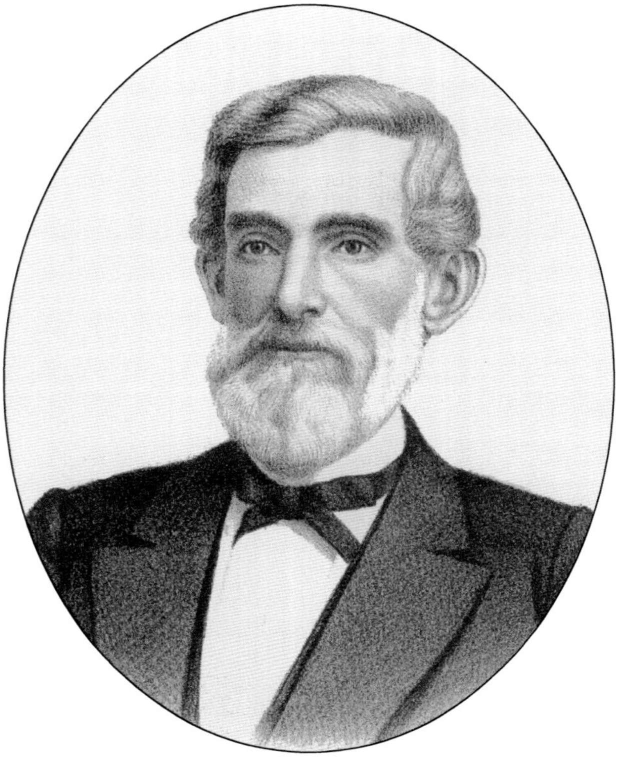

Joshua B. Dickinson

As the newly incorporated city of Mount Clemens was on the verge of becoming a renowned health resort in 1879, businessman Joshua B. Dickinson was honored to be elected its first mayor. No stranger to public service, the staunch Democrat had served as county treasurer and register of deeds and was dedicated to civic improvement. In 1869, Dickinson built this impressive Italianate Victorian house, where his daughter Katherine, and her husband, George M. Crocker, resided after their marriage in 1870. Joshua B. Dickinson died suddenly in May 1879, scarcely a month after taking his oath as mayor, and was succeeded by his son-in-law, George M. Crocker. Dickinson's house, later known as the Crocker House, became a historical museum in 1976. (Courtesy of Mount Clemens Public Library.)

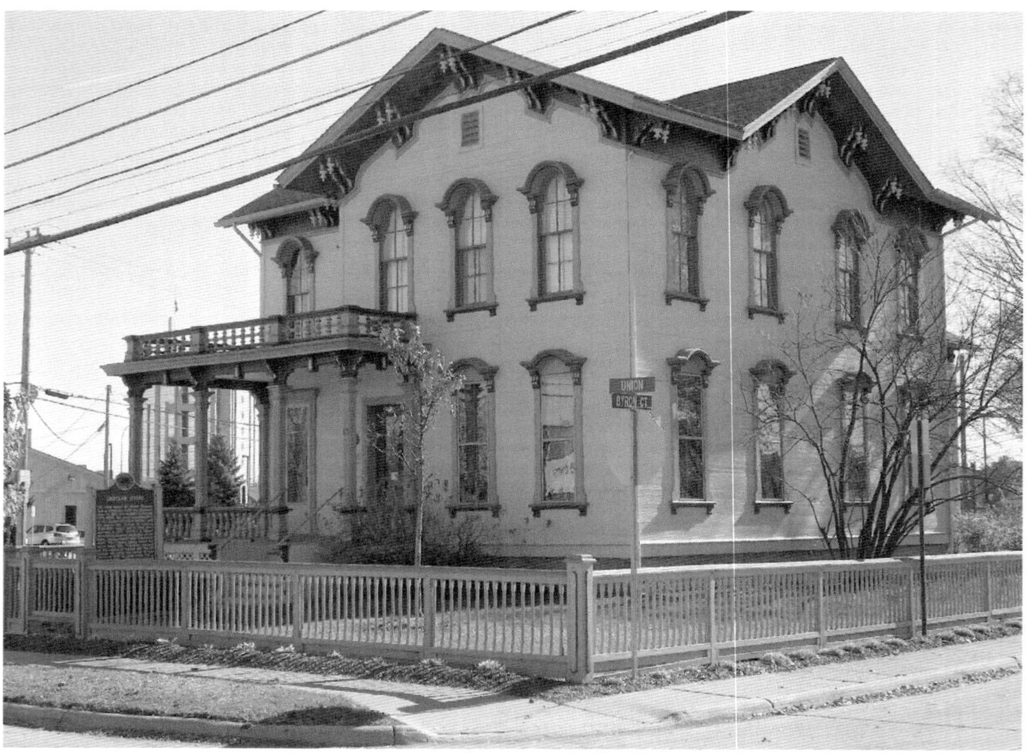

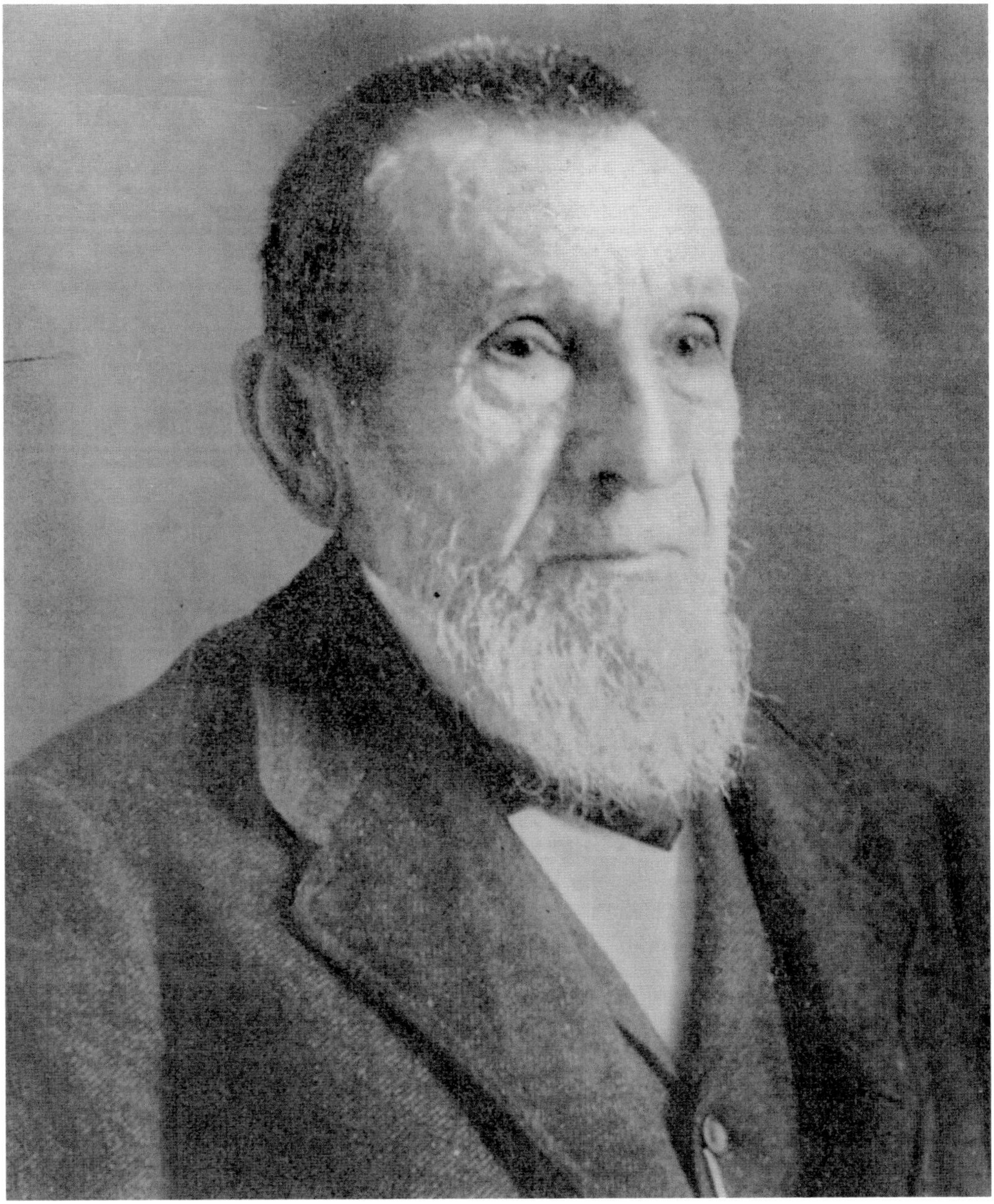

Dor Kellogg

One of the greatest legends in Mount Clemens history surrounds Kellogg, a miller who came to town in 1870 from Cayuga County, New York. In that year, according to colloquial accounts, Kellogg observed the activities of an old horse that had been turned out on its own and had taken shelter near a brine tank from an old salt well. The horse suffered from sores on its legs and hooves and was apparently cured by standing in the water dripping from the tank. Intrigued, Kellogg fashioned a bathtub and successfully treated his eczema with the same water, thus discovering its healing powers. Three years after Kellogg's experiment, the first public bathhouse was opened in Mount Clemens, and Kellogg himself went to work in the local mineral bath industry. (Courtesy of Mount Clemens Public Library.)

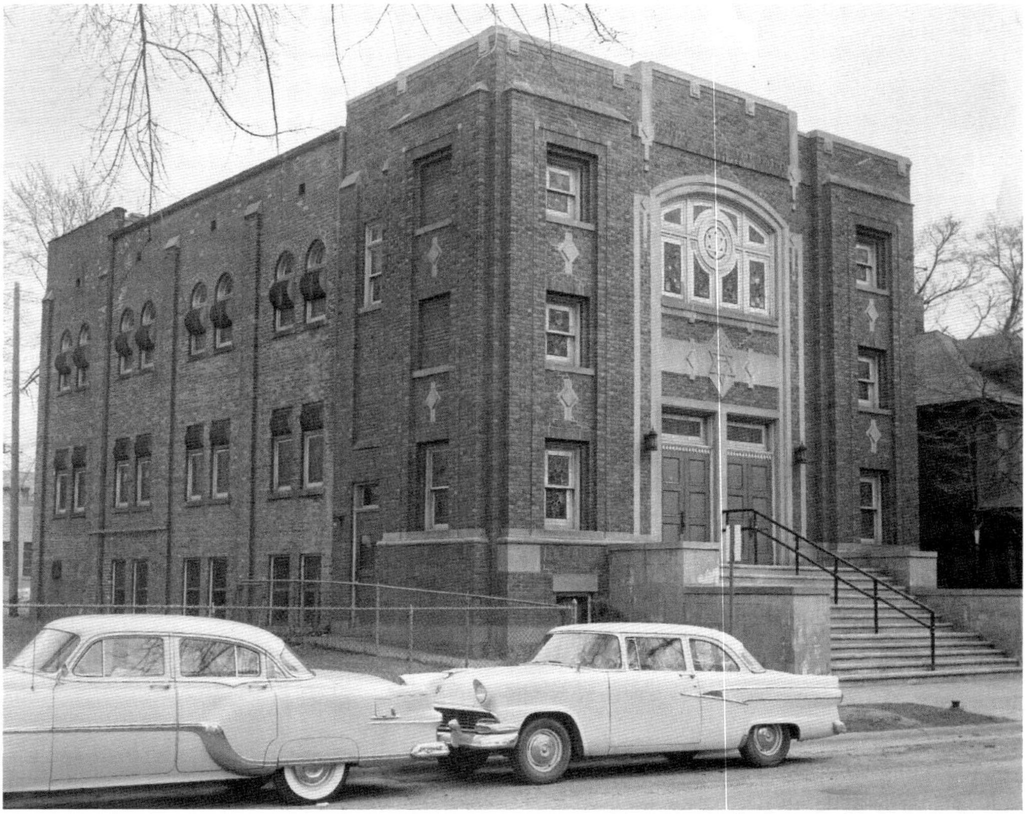

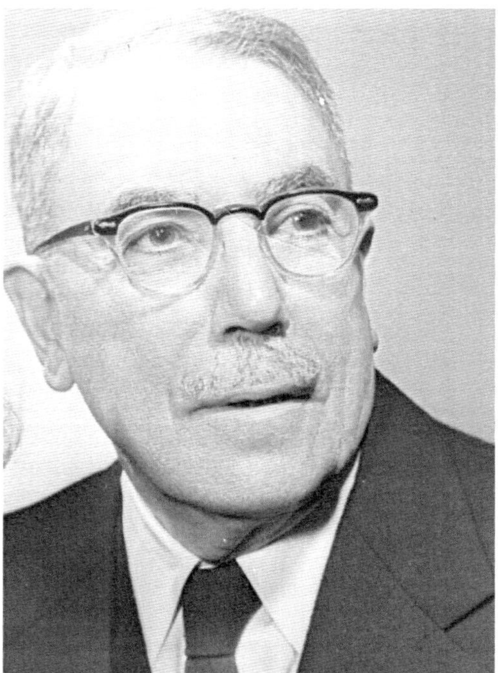

Meyer Davis
When the Lithuanian-born Davis came to Mount Clemens in 1907, there was no place of worship in town for persons of Jewish faith. The 22-year-old Davis helped hotel operator Moses Reh form a congregation and served as its religious leader. In 1912, under Davis's leadership, the Jewish faithful established a synagogue and adopted the name Beth Tephilath Moses. (Courtesy of the *Macomb Daily*.)

Alger F. Graham (RIGHT)
World War I veteran Alger F. Graham left Mount Clemens to fly a Stinson biplane in the Wilkins Arctic Expedition of 1927, and in 1928, when the Wilkins party was stranded on the frozen tundra, Graham searched the polar ice cap for the lost explorers. After that adventure, he flew with the pioneering Alaskan Airways, mapping air routes in uncharted territory. (Courtesy of the *Macomb Daily*.)

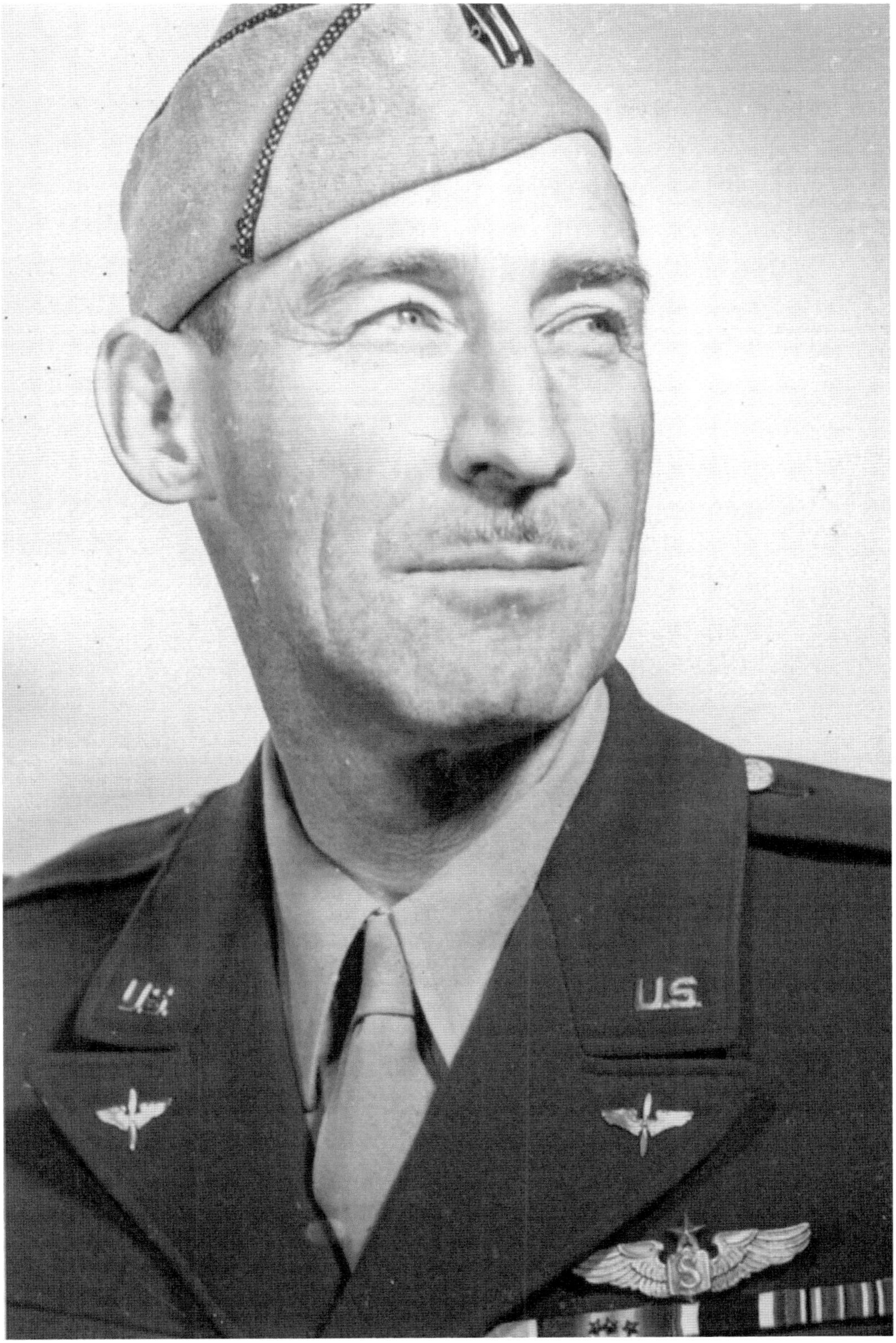
U.S.
U.S.

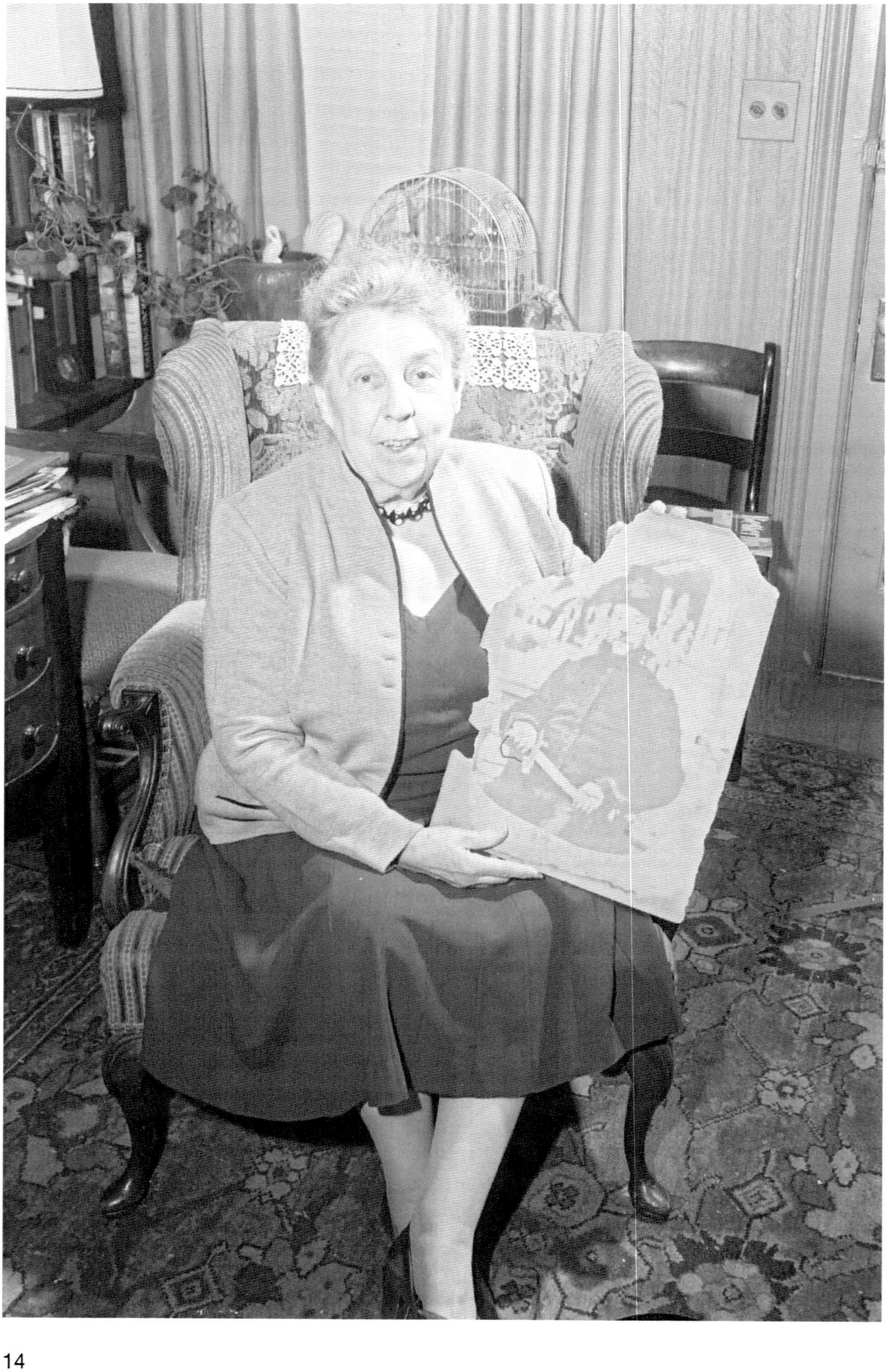

Alice Louise Tucker (LEFT)
When Macomb County's Democratic Party chairman, Varnum J. Bowers, approached Tucker in 1931 and asked her to run for public office, her brother, Albert, told her to "go ahead, because no woman can ever get elected." Tucker would prove otherwise to her brother—and to many other skeptics—when she became the first woman to be elected to county office in Macomb County, 114 years after its founding.

Born in Mount Clemens in 1881, the oldest child of coal merchant and lake captain John N. Tucker, Tucker was descended from one of the first white settlers of Macomb County and was surrounded by a large extended family as she grew to adulthood. She attended the local public schools, but left before graduation to study music in Detroit. An accomplished pianist and music teacher, Tucker traveled abroad in 1908 to study piano in Paris with celebrated musician Wager Swayne.

After returning home to Mount Clemens, Tucker threw herself into a variety of civic organizations, including the Red Cross and Salvation Army. She was a tireless worker in home front activities during World War I, and Michigan governor Albert E. Sleeper rewarded her with an appointment to the Macomb County War Board, where she served as the only woman member.

During the war years, Tucker's interests turned toward politics and she became a strong advocate for women's suffrage. After women won the right to vote, she served as the first president of the Mount Clemens League of Women Voters and set an example for her peers by taking an active role in Democratic Party politics at the local level.

At age 50, Alice Louise Tucker won the office of register of deeds in the election of 1932, unseating a 10-year incumbent in the process. She went on to earn re-election four times before finally retiring from office voluntarily in 1944. In retirement, she devoted herself to music, antique collecting, and travel. It would be two more decades before another woman would follow Alice Louise Tucker through the door that she had opened in Macomb County. (Courtesy of the *Macomb Daily*.)

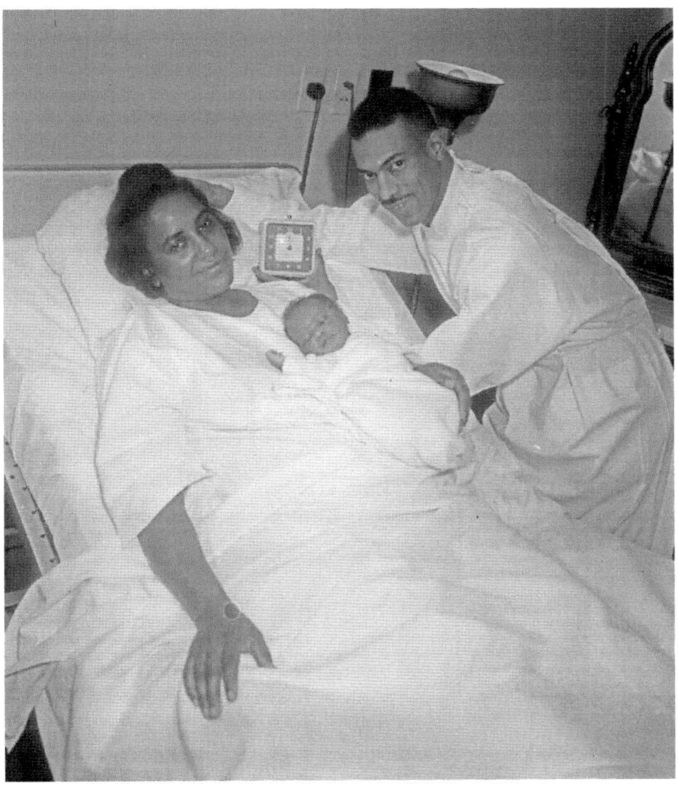

Lewis D. Rickman
Rickman earned degrees from Wilberforce University and Meharry Medical College before coming to Mount Clemens in 1949. The general practitioner and surgeon became the first African American physician to practice in Macomb County and was also a member of the staff of St. Joseph Mercy Hospital. Dedicated to the cause of improving public education, Rickman also served on the Mount Clemens Board of Education for 24 consecutive years. Here he is shown with patient Addie McGlown after delivering her child, who was celebrated as the "New Year's Baby" of 1951. (Courtesy of the *Macomb Daily*.)

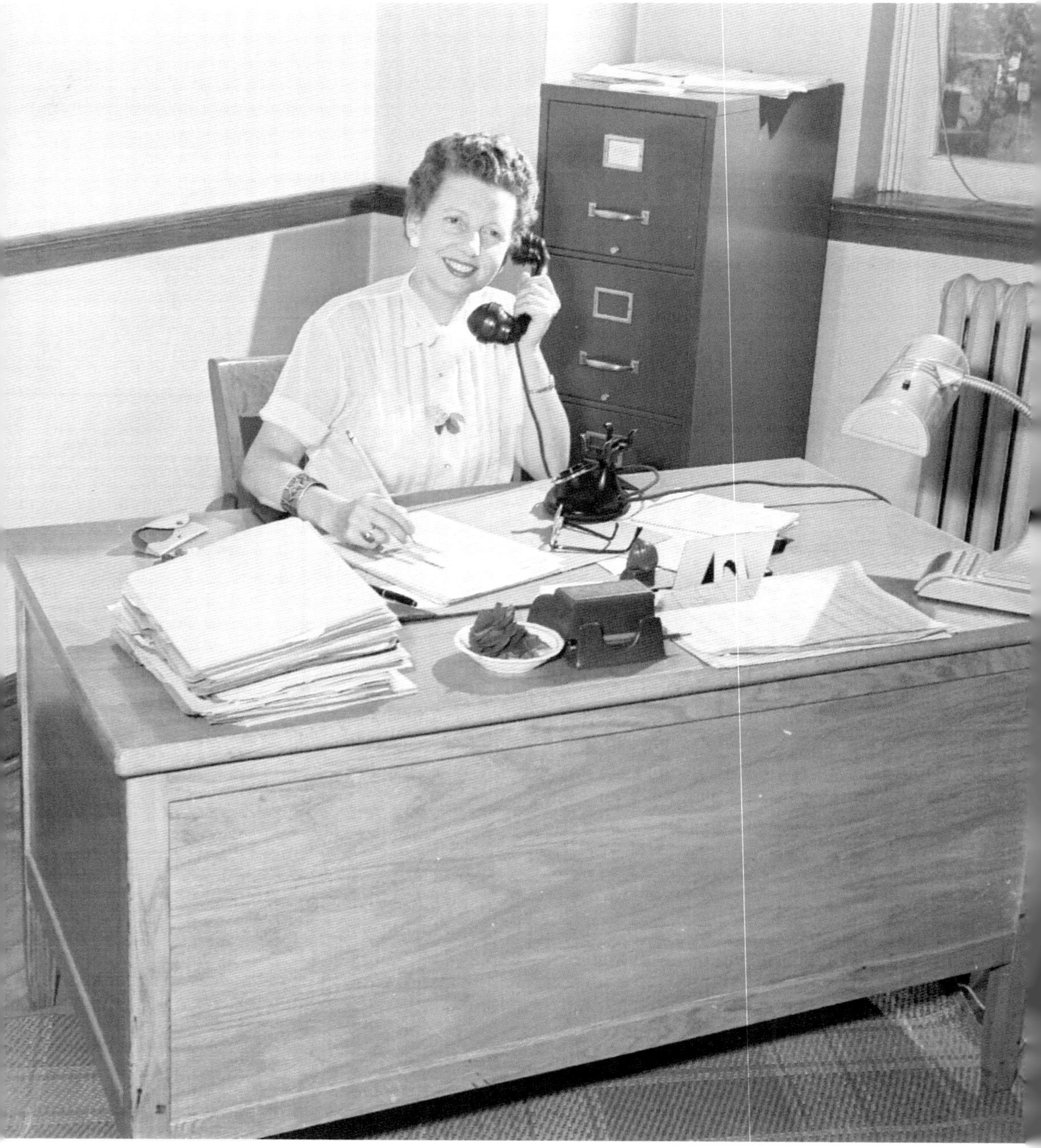

Ruth Phyllis Westover

Despite Alice Tucker's groundbreaking entry into Macomb County politics in 1932, no woman had ever served on the Mount Clemens City Commission until Ruth Phyllis Westover won a seat on the panel in 1954. The popular guidance counselor and history teacher from Mount Clemens High School led a field of 12 candidates—all of them male—by inspiring an overwhelming female turnout at the polls. In addition to her work in education and city government, Westover was a writer who had numerous stories and articles printed in journals and periodicals. (Courtesy of the *Macomb Daily*.)

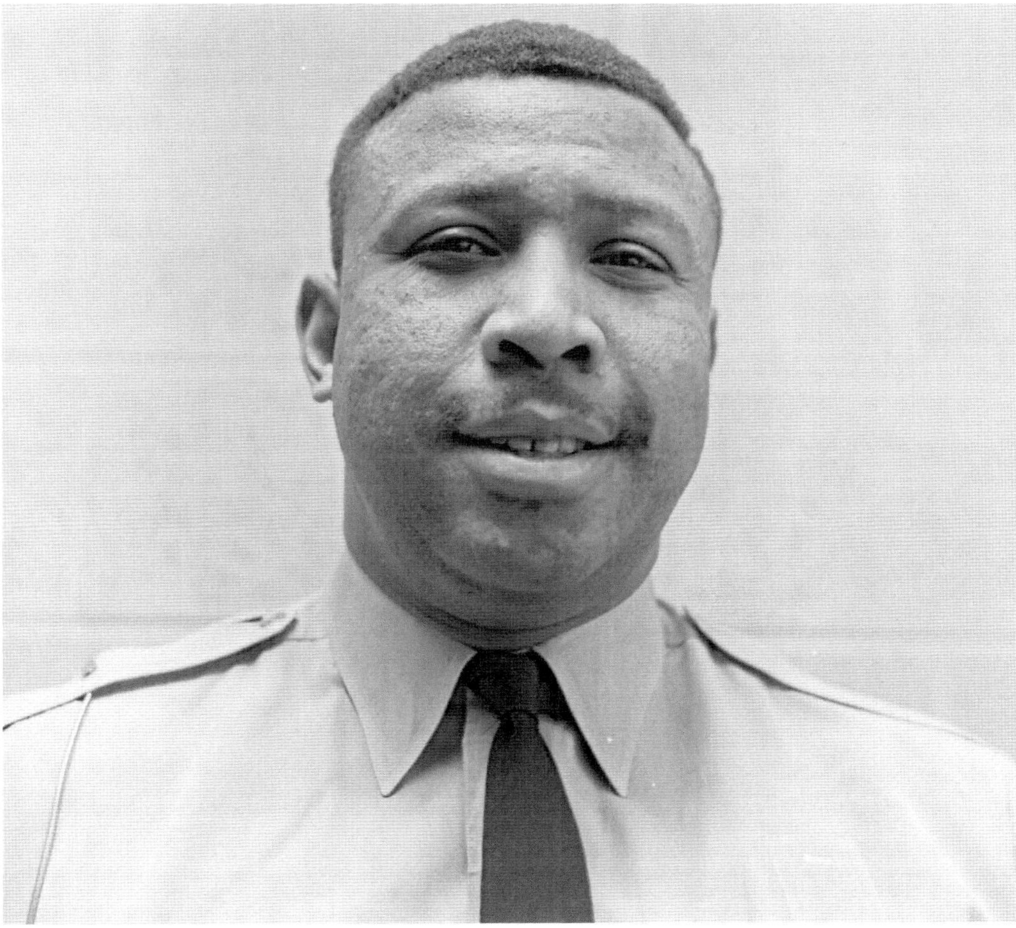

Bonner C. Upshaw

According to Upshaw's obituary, he loved a challenge, and challenges definitely stood before the man who was Mount Clemens's first African American police officer. The Mount Clemens High School graduate was an outstanding athlete in his early years, playing semi-professional football and baseball, and earning tryouts with the Detroit Tigers and Cleveland Indians. He was a postal worker in Mount Clemens after returning from a tour of duty with the US Navy during the Korean War, and in 1960 he was hired by the Mount Clemens Police Department, where he served with distinction for 24 years. Upshaw's first years on patrol were difficult ones as he dealt with mistrust from the public as well as from fellow officers. Upon his retirement in 1985, Upshaw recalled in a newspaper interview the hurdles he faced as the city's only African American patrol officer. "I had black people call me an 'Uncle Tom' and white people say I was prejudiced," he remembered. "I got it from both sides. I'd come home at night and I would be so keyed up. Finally people would see me as I really am. I never took sides. If you were wrong, you were wrong. It paid off for me. I think I gained respect from anybody I dealt with." Although he earned respect on the streets of Mount Clemens, Upshaw did not receive a promotion to a command position while less experienced officers moved ahead of him in rank. In 1978, he and another African American officer filed a lawsuit that resulted in the establishment of an affirmative-action program to ensure opportunities for minorities within the police department. Following his death at the age of 68 in 2000, the Mount Clemens City Commission passed a resolution honoring the memory of the man who had blazed a trail, in spite of adversity, for people of all races in public service. (Courtesy of the *Macomb Daily*.)

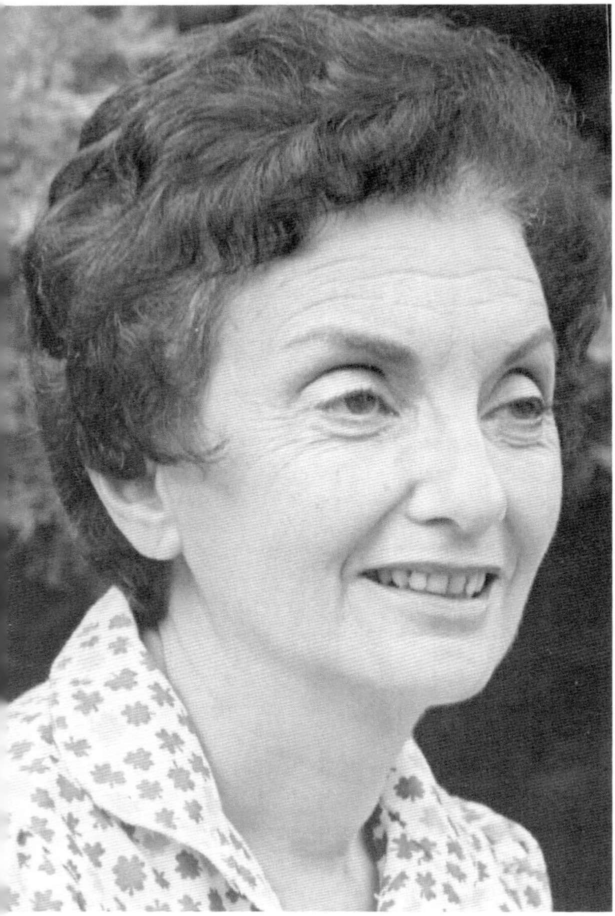

Ada Davis Eisenfeld

The first woman mayor of Mount Clemens was Ada Davis Eisenfeld, who was elected in 1981 after serving two terms as a city commissioner. Eisenfeld, who had been trained as an economist, took the helm during a challenging era in which the city was reeling from the loss of major downtown retailers and struggling to reinvent itself. (Courtesy of Mount Clemens Public Library.)

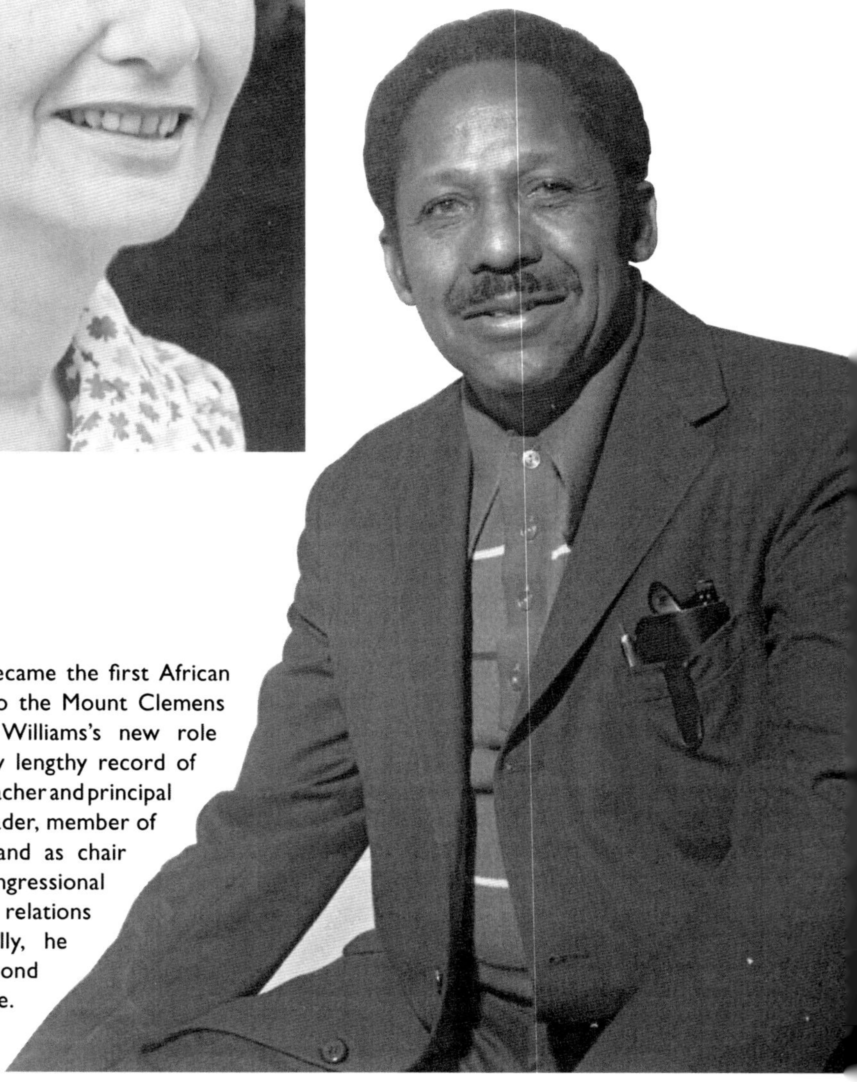

Lee J. Williams

In 1967, Williams became the first African American elected to the Mount Clemens City Commission. Williams's new role extended an already lengthy record of public service; the teacher and principal served as a scout leader, member of the zoning board, and as chair of the 12th Congressional District's human relations committee. Tragically, he died during his second term of office. (Courtesy of the *Macomb Daily*.)

CHAPTER TWO

Community Builders

Dr. Martin Luther King Jr. once said, "Everyone can be great because everyone can serve." Communities are built through service of all kinds, and Mount Clemens has blossomed under service offered by people from varied walks of life. Some efforts were widely publicized and drew great attention, such as the Military-Community Relations Committee's initiative to provide creature comforts for soldiers stationed at nearby Selfridge Air Force Base, or the Old Crowd's annual parade to foster kinship and camaraderie. Others helped to build up educational, cultural, and recreational institutions that made the town liveable and welcoming, and their contributions are commemorated on monuments or plaques.

Much of community building, however, happens in small, quiet ways. It happens when people like Ivan J. Harris encourage neighbors to set aside differences and work together, or when someone like Norman O. Lorway shares his love of local history with audiences of all ages. Many of these contributions go unheralded during the lifetimes of those who make them; it falls to historians to reveal how small gestures of goodwill produced great things such as historical museums, art centers, and revitalized neighborhoods.

Not all of Mount Clemens's community builders have their names engraved over the doorways of her institutions. Most received scant notice when they volunteered for committees at just the right time, extended a hand in friendship when it was desperately needed, or made telephone calls to marshal support for an important cause. Scattered here among the stories of those who were well known are the stories of those who contributed quietly, and without fanfare, to a better community for themselves and their descendants.

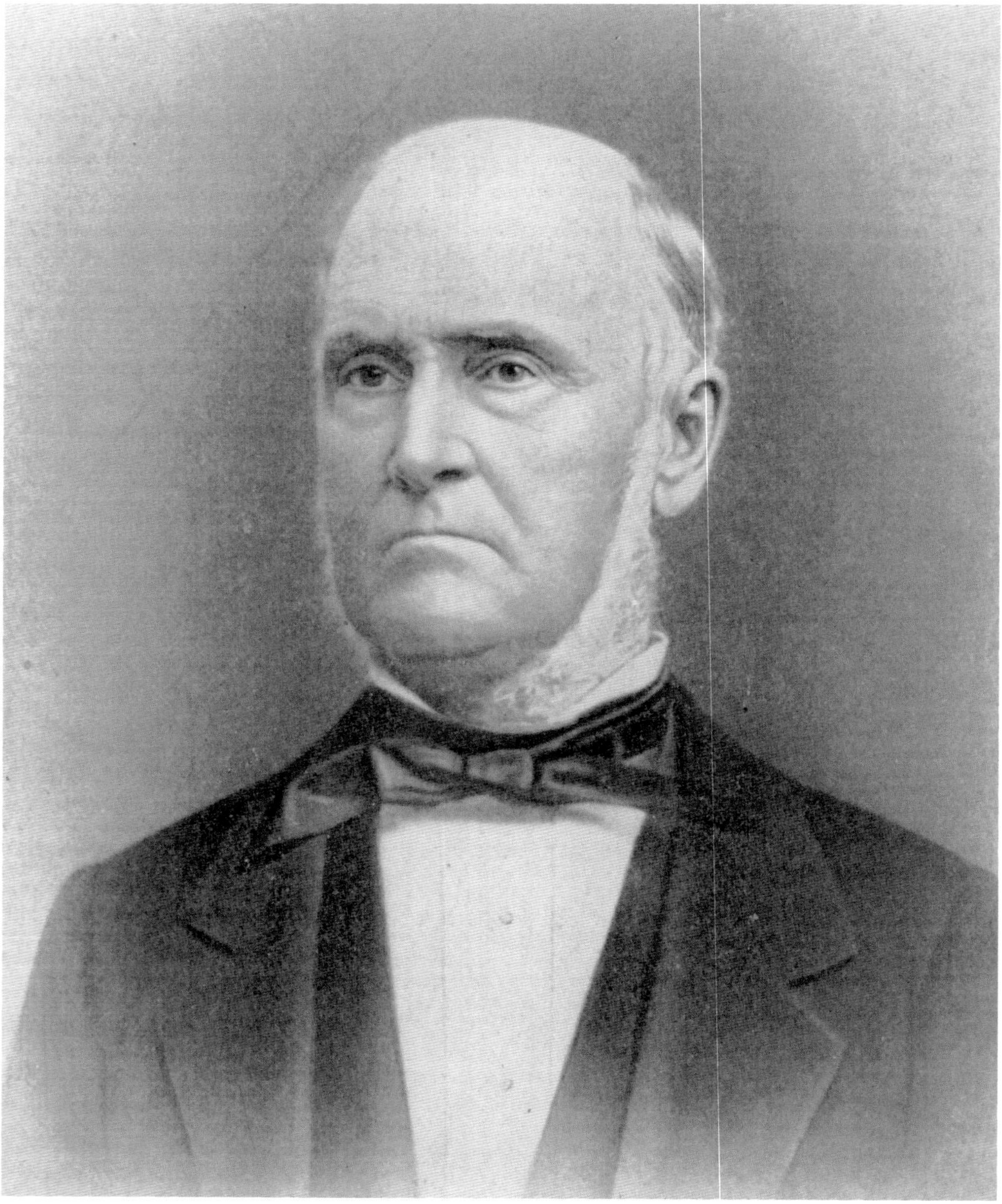

Robert P. Eldredge

In 1827, Eldredge walked from Pontiac to Mount Clemens in search of an opportunity to further his study of law. The following year, after he was admitted to the bar at Detroit, he became the first lawyer to establish a practice in Macomb County. As the dean of his profession in Mount Clemens, Eldredge was involved in nearly every important legal case in the county for the next half century. He served as prosecuting attorney for two years, and was then appointed to a four-year term as Michigan secretary of state; he was also twice elected to the Michigan Senate. Robert P. Eldredge established a legal dynasty of sorts in Macomb County in which several of his descendants followed in his footsteps to serve as attorneys and judges. (Courtesy of Mount Clemens Public Library.)

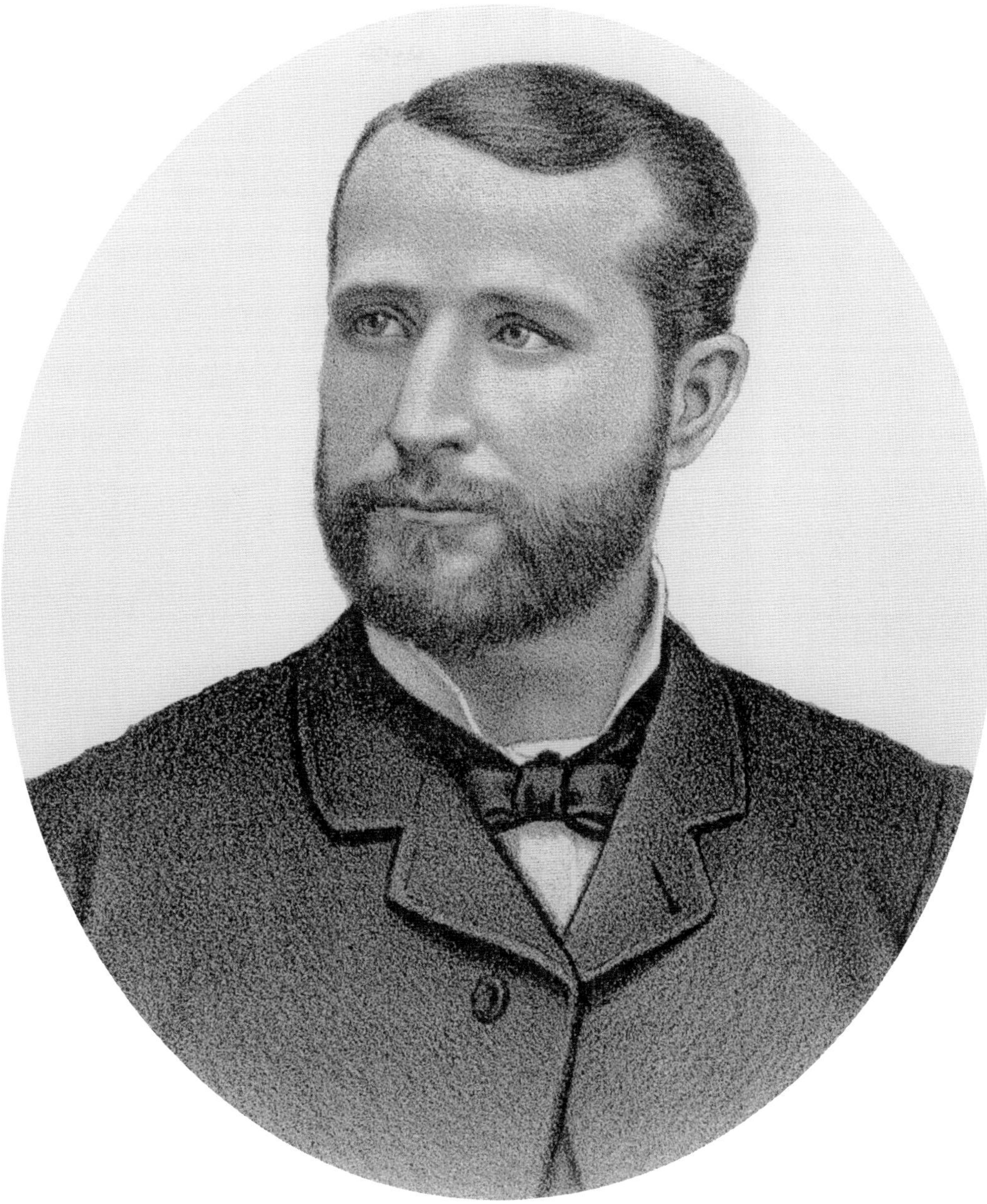

Edgar Weeks

Weeks, descendant of Jonathan Atwood, who commanded a unit of Minutemen at Lexington during the Revolutionary War, spent a lifetime in public service. He was born in Mount Clemens in 1839 and began learning the printer's trade at the age of 15, but turned to the study of law and was admitted to the bar in 1861. During the Civil War, Weeks served in two Michigan infantry regiments and was commissioned a captain. In 1864, with W.J. Lee, he established the *Mount Clemens Monitor*, one of the predecessor newspapers of the *Macomb Daily*. He continued to pursue the practice of law, and served two terms as Macomb County prosecutor, almost six years as probate judge, and was twice elected to Congress from the seventh district of Michigan. (Courtesy of Mount Clemens Public Library.)

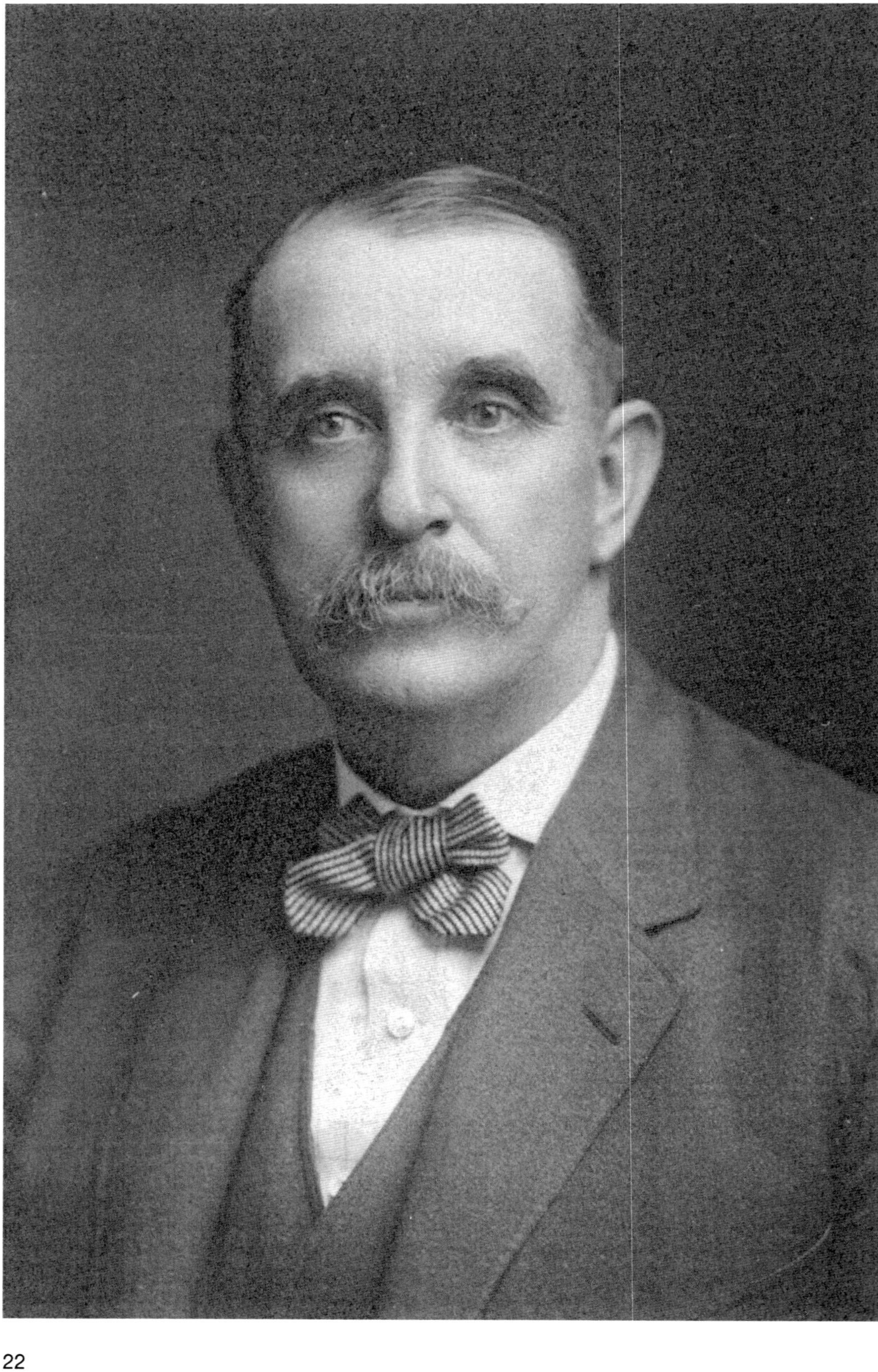

George Martin Crocker (LEFT)
Crocker's political career was launched soon after he came to Mount Clemens in 1867 to study in the law office of his uncle, Thomas M. Crocker. After being admitted to the bar in 1870, he served as justice of the peace and then held the offices of prosecuting attorney and probate judge of Macomb County. In June 1879, a special election named Crocker as mayor of Mount Clemens to fill the unexpired term of his late father-in-law, Joshua B. Dickinson, who had died after serving only one month in office. Crocker was mayor during the time that the newly incorporated city was experiencing tremendous growing pains generated by the emerging mineral bath industry. He was an advocate for infrastructure improvements, and argued successfully for a second bridge over the Clinton River to facilitate the development of the east side of town. Later, when the city was in desperate need of a new post office facility, the site of Crocker's home was selected as the ideal site for the new building. Crocker obligingly sold his property—but not his residence—to the federal government. The Crocker house was then moved to another lot several blocks to the west to make way for the construction.

George Crocker was married three times and widowed twice. With his first wife, Katherine Lee Dickinson—a great-granddaughter of Mount Clemens's founder, Christian Clemens—he had six children. Left with a large family to rear after Katherine's death in 1882, Crocker then married Harriett L. Steele, who survived their wedding by only one year. Harriett's sister, Cecilia Tarleton Steele, married Crocker in 1888 and had three more children with him. He died in 1918 after a nearly half-century career in public service. (Courtesy of Macomb County Historical Society.)

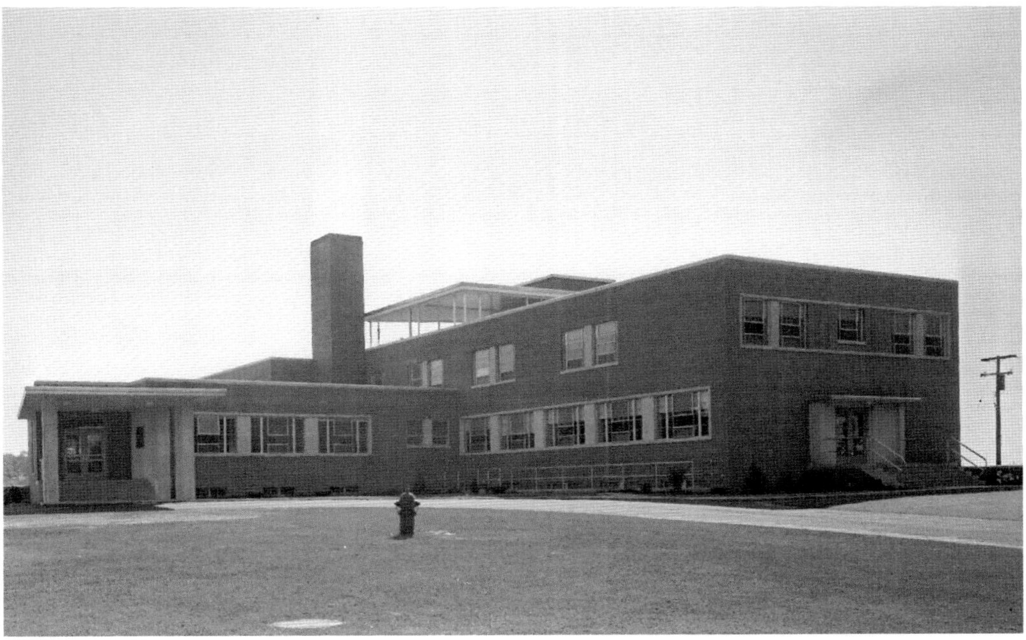

Martha Taylor Berry
It was said of Berry that "her cheerful, happy nature drew people to her and no one in trouble ever came to her without receiving help and sympathy." The wife of beloved Mount Clemens physician Dr. Henry G. Berry was a selfless volunteer and a tireless worker for the Red Cross, among other organizations. She died unexpectedly in 1942 while sitting at the hospital bedside of her husband, and when he died three years later, his will revealed a plan that the couple had devised to use their estate to fund a county hospital to serve the needy. Dr. Berry's will stipulated that the facility be named in honor of his wife, and in 1950 that wish was realized when Macomb County officially dedicated Martha T. Berry Memorial Hospital. (Courtesy of the *Macomb Daily*.)

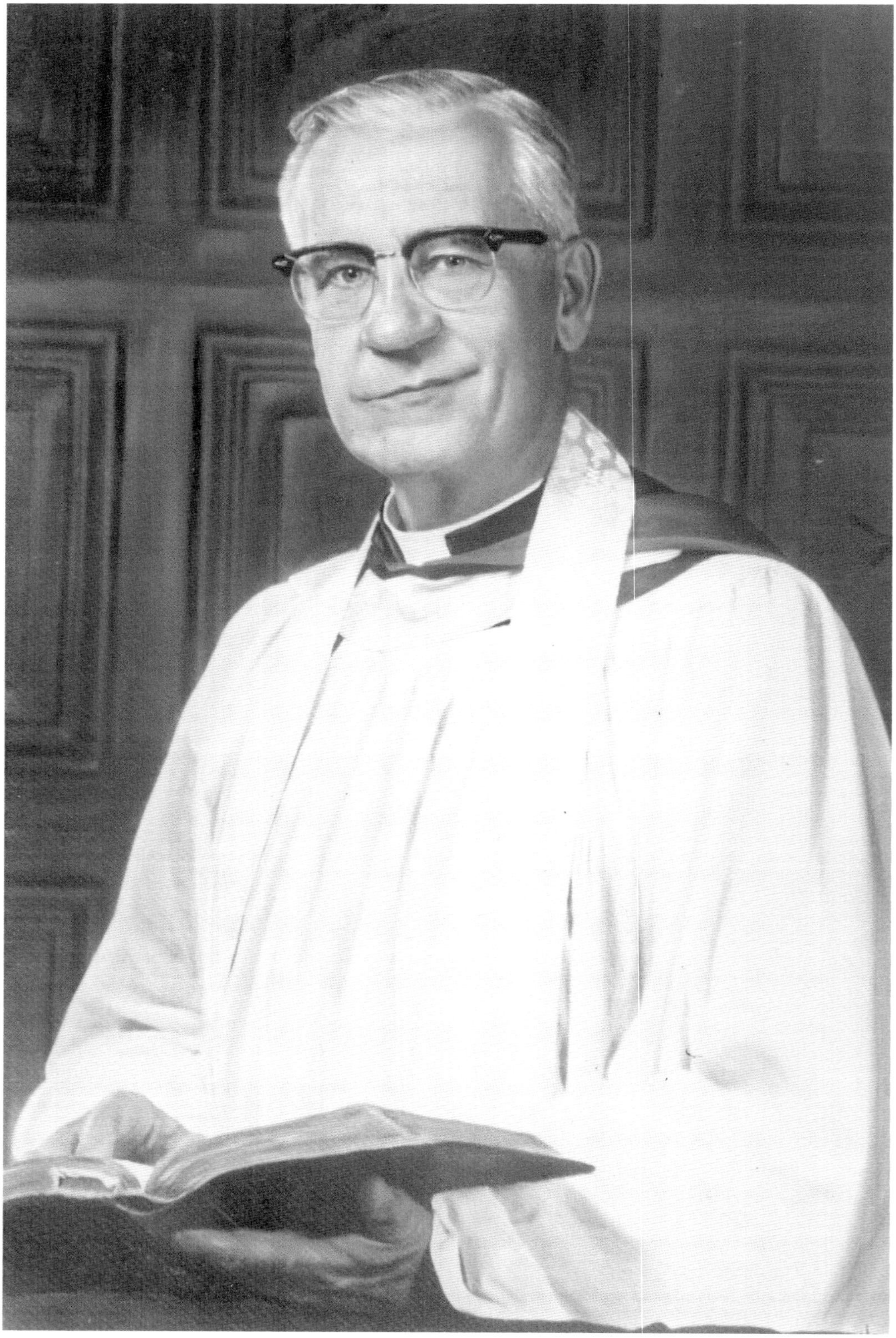

George Alfred Merifield (LEFT)
Born in Plumstead, England, in 1901, Merifield was ordained a priest at All Saints Church in Windsor, Ontario, in 1926, on the same day that his brother, Harry, was ordained a deacon there. Installed as rector of Grace Episcopal Church of Mount Clemens in 1937, Merifield led the congregation as it renovated and expanded its facilities and planted a mission church in the nearby community of Utica. He was a respected leader among the Episcopal clergy in Michigan and was named to a diocesan post in 1952. Merifield was the longest-serving pastor in the congregation's history at the time of his death in 1967. (Courtesy of the *Macomb Daily*.)

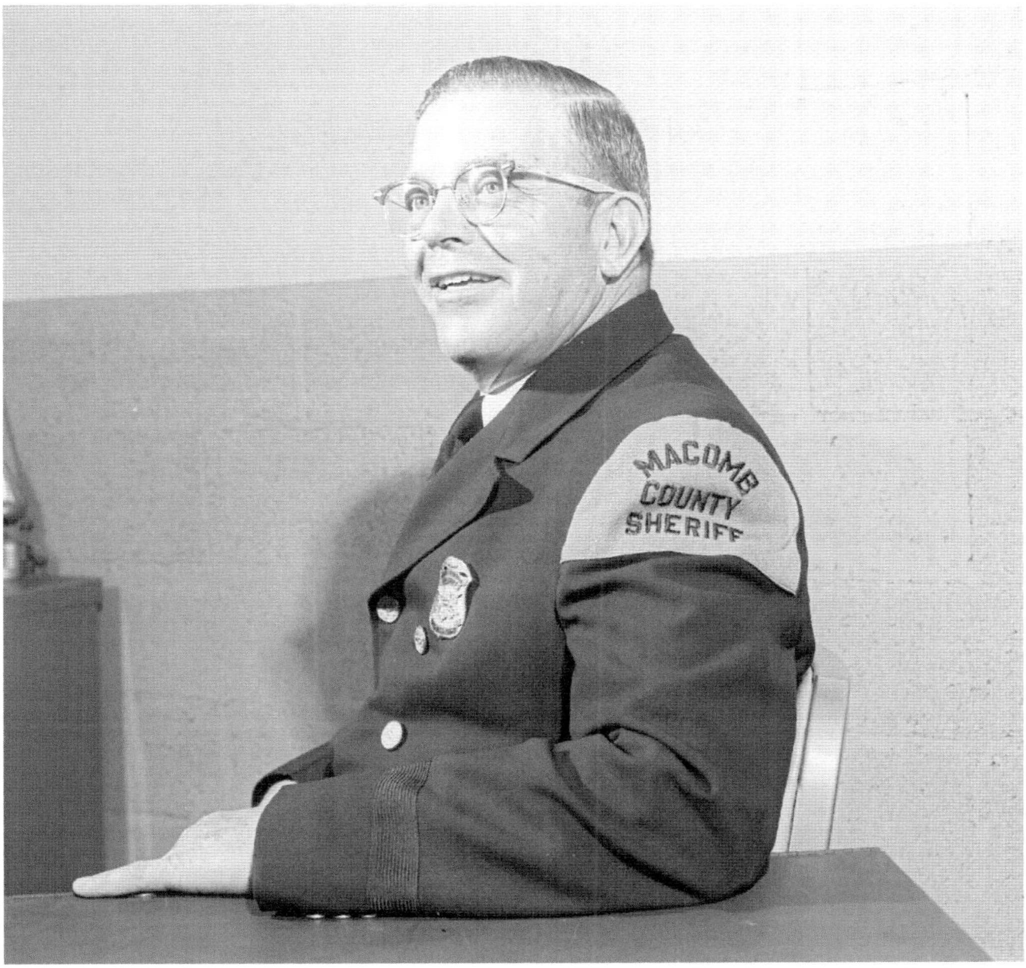

Harley Bertrum Ensign
When he died just weeks after his 1960 election to an eighth term as Macomb County sheriff, Ensign was eulogized by the local newspaper as "a blunt, outspoken man whose personal courage matched his powerful physique." Ensign began his long law enforcement career in 1923 as a motorcycle patrolman, and witnessed his department's growth from seven men to a complement of 97 full-time officers. His lasting contributions to the community included his personal crusade to see that the crumbling, nineteenth-century jail in Mount Clemens was replaced with a modern, state-of-the-art facility, and his establishment of the first sheriff's marine patrol in the state of Michigan, a life-saving service in a county that serves as a recreational boating center. (Courtesy of the *Macomb Daily*.)

Clayton Edwin Dubay

Dubay spent 35 years with the Mount Clemens Fire Department, the last 17 of them as fire chief. Born in Mount Clemens in 1902, Dubay joined the fire department in 1929 and was elevated to chief in 1946, serving longer as chief than any man in department history. During his tenure, the fire department was equipped with two-way radios for the first time, a fire prevention bureau was established, and a training center was created and equipped. Below, Dubay (left) is shown here in 1951, demonstrating the use of a new fire call box to local businessman Lawrence Oehmke. (Courtesy of the *Macomb Daily*.)

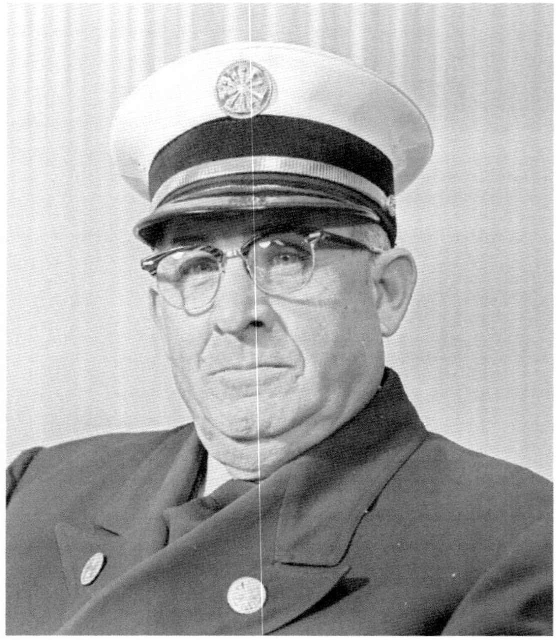

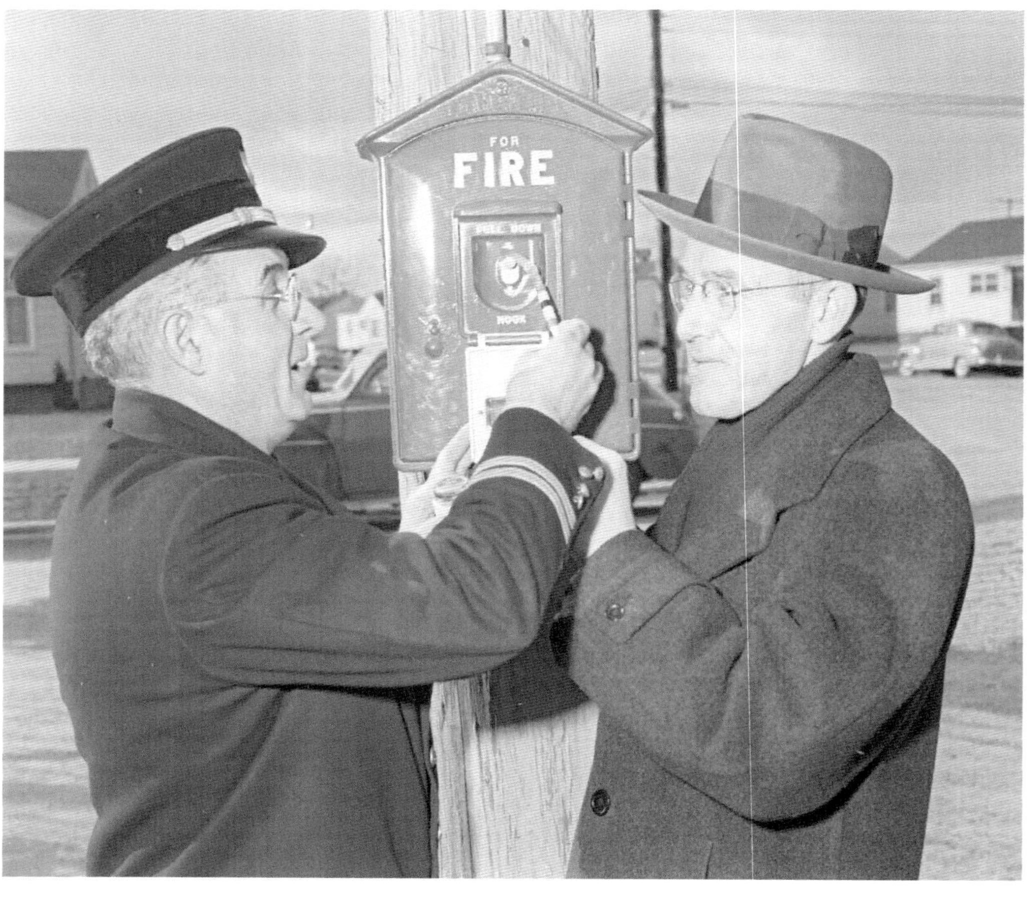

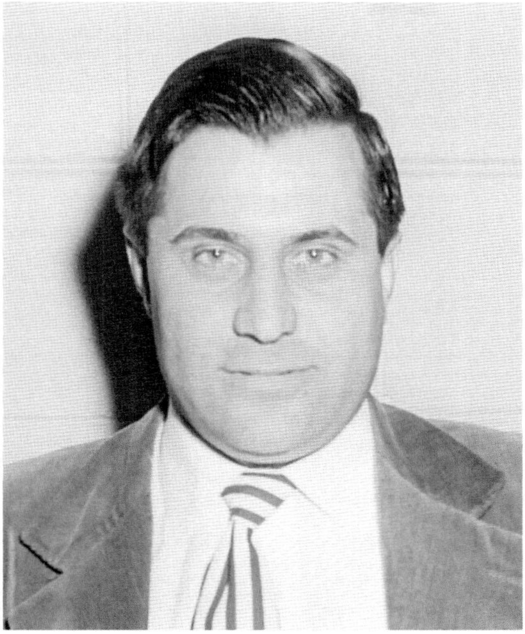

Edwin E. Whedon

When Whedon came to Mount Clemens to fill the position of city engineer in 1955, the town was on the verge of a major urban renewal project that encompassed fully one third of its total area. Two years later, Whedon was appointed city manager and found himself administering the largest modernization and redevelopment initiative in the city's history. During his 26-year tenure as manager, Mount Clemens built a new city municipal center, completed a nationally recognized urban renewal program in which the city itself served as developer of a new subdivision, and saw the replacement of the Macomb-Crocker Bridge. Whedon is seen below with fire chief Clayton E. Dubay, as he hands the chief the keys to his new emergency vehicle in 1959. (Courtesy of the *Macomb Daily*.)

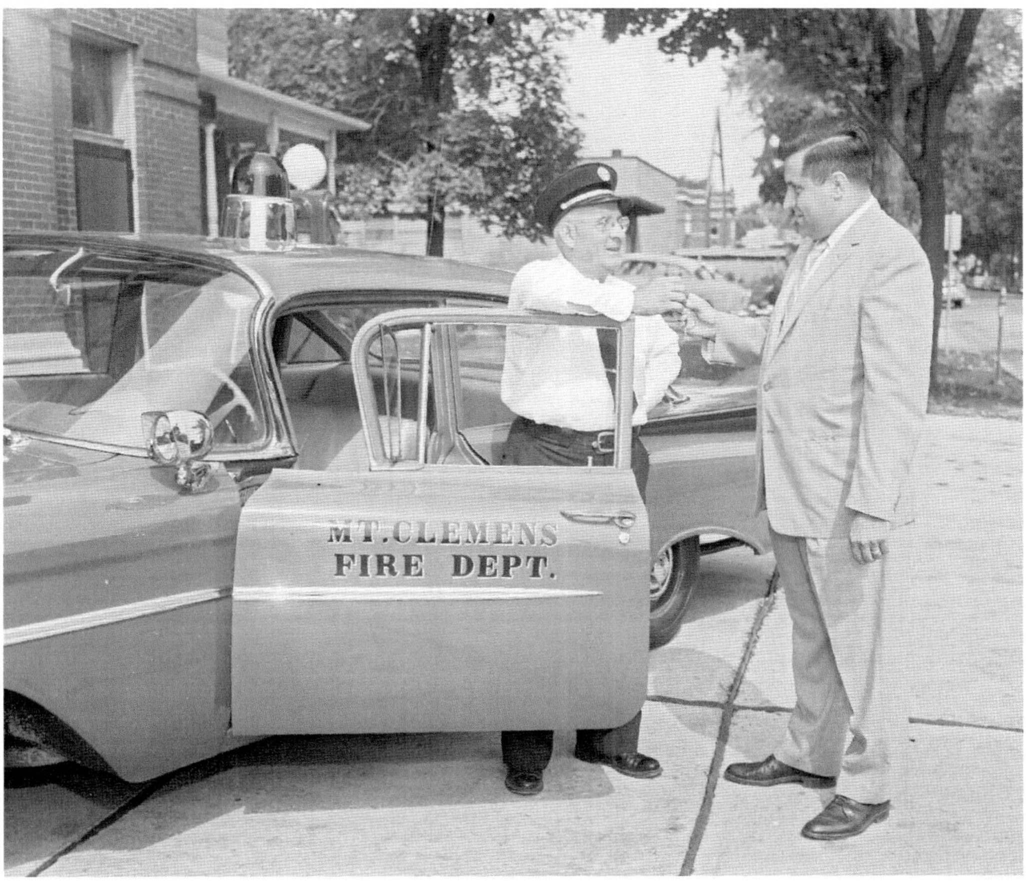

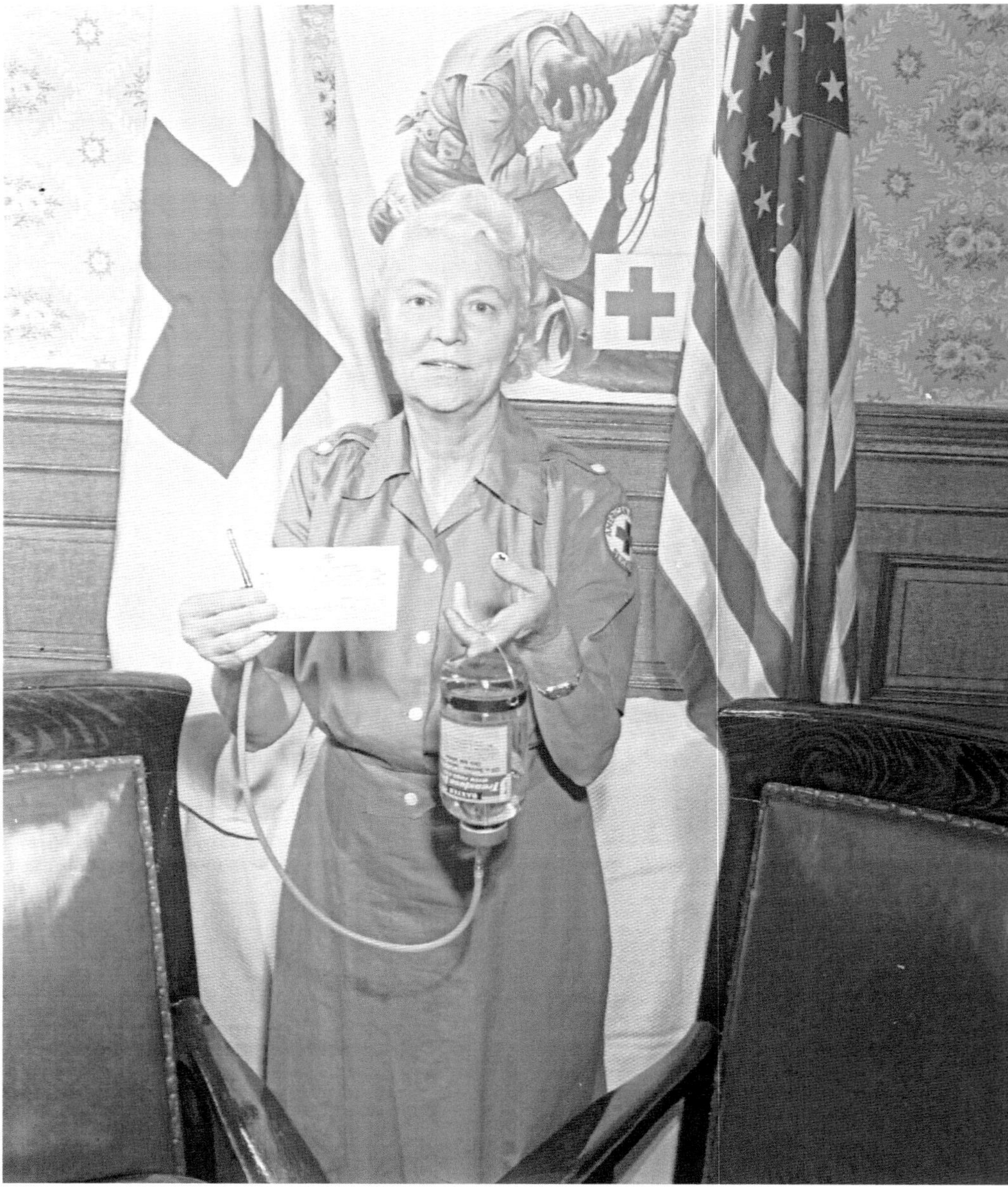

Jennie Clawson Fenton

Remembered as a gentle, soft-spoken woman who generously lent her time to community organizations such as the Girl Scouts, Macomb County Humane Society (founded by her husband, Walter), and Woman's National Farm and Garden Association, Fenton was best known in Mount Clemens for her leading role with the local American Red Cross chapter, which she served for 44 years. During World War II, Fenton organized the blood plasma program, and she chaired the local blood bank for many years after that. She was credited with hundreds of hours per year spent in planning bloodmobile schedules and helping with blood drives, and was named Woman of the Year in 1949 by the Mount Clemens Chamber of Commerce for her many patriotic and civic activities. (Courtesy of the *Macomb Daily*.)

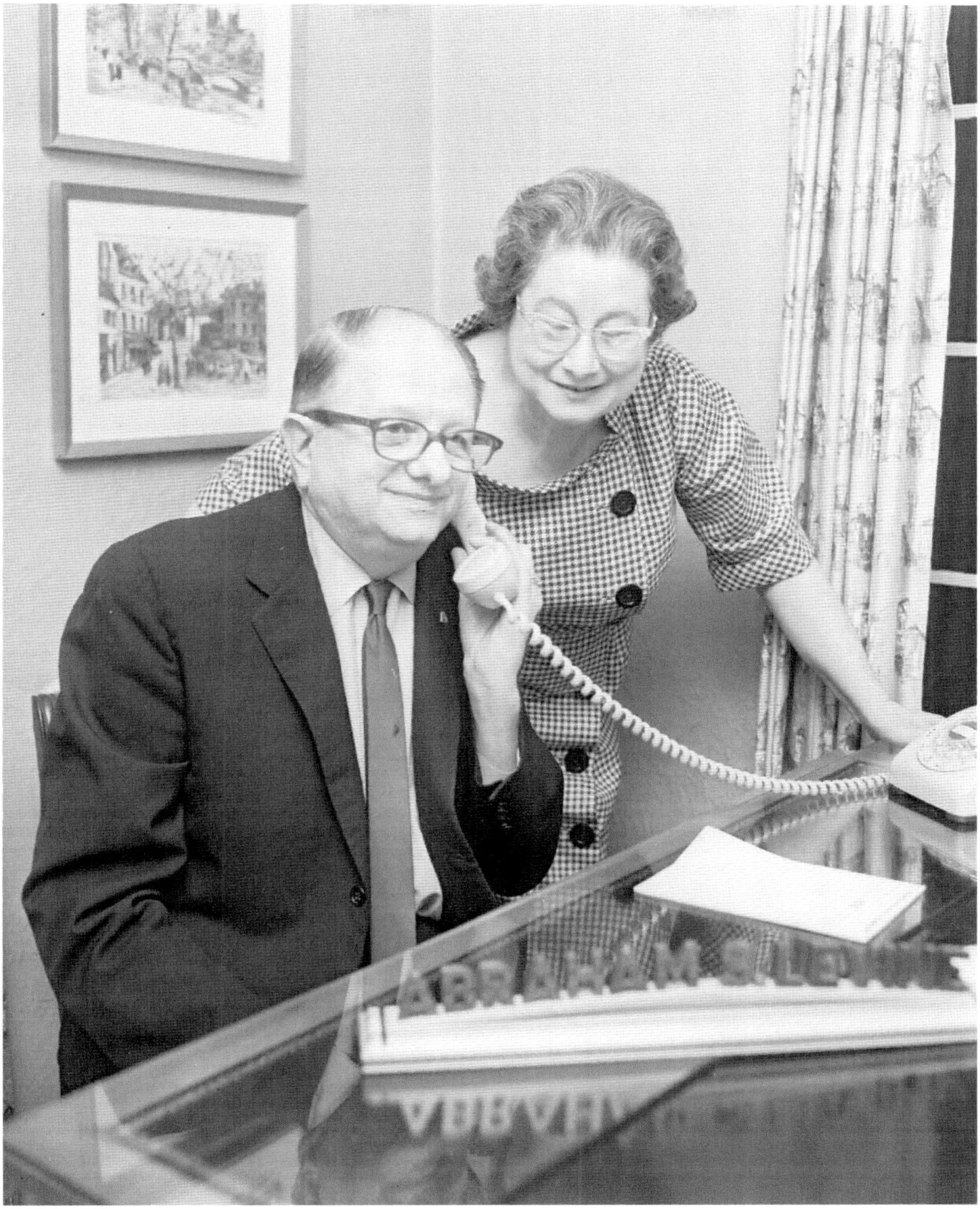

Abraham S. Levine

Shown here with his wife, Lillian, at his side in 1963, Levine receives news of his election to a second term as mayor of Mount Clemens. In 1965, when the city was debating how to develop some prime urban renewal property located downtown on the riverfront, it fell to Levine to break a 3-3 city commission deadlock and cast the fateful vote to bring the new Macomb County Court Building to the site. A Lithuanian immigrant who had lived in Mount Clemens since arriving in 1906 with his parents at the age of three, Levine was the longest-serving mayor in Mount Clemens history, overseeing city government during a turbulent 12-year period from 1961 to 1973. (Courtesy of the *Macomb Daily.*)

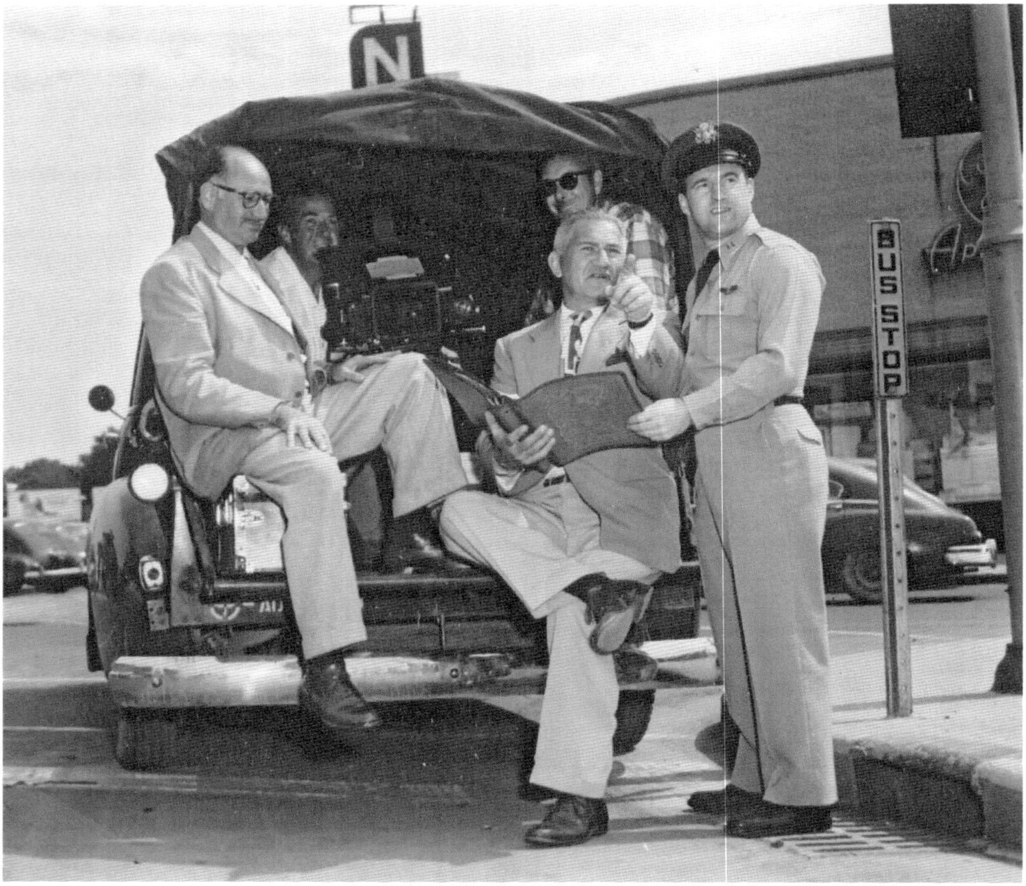

Military-Community Relations Committee

In 1950, a series of newspaper articles written by Desmond A. Arnsby informed the Mount Clemens citizenry of the plight of lonely airmen stationed at nearby Selfridge Air Force Base, and mayor Albert A. Wagner responded by appointing a Military-Community Relations Committee to provide hospitality to service personnel. The committee succeeded so well at integrating military personnel into the life of the community that in 1951 the United States Air Force sought to document the achievement as an example for others to follow. The air force commissioned a movie short entitled *The Mount Clemens Story* to demonstrate the ways in which the Bath City provided recreational, religious, and social facilities for the men and women from Selfridge Air Force Base. Filmed by Hollywood director Derwin Abrams and narrated by Desmond A. Arnsby, the movie was shot on the streets of Mount Clemens and featured many local residents. *The Mount Clemens Story* premiered at the Jewel Theater on August 13, 1951, to great fanfare and a host of Air Force dignitaries; it was afterward released nationwide as a theatrical trailer. The Military-Community Relations Committee evolved into the Selfridge Base Community Council, an organization that is active today in supporting the military service members and their families who are attached to Selfridge Air National Guard Base.

Shown below right at their inaugural meeting, the original members of the Military-Community Relations Committee are, from left to right (front row) Brig. Gen. Harry A. Johnson, Betty Blundo, and Col. James R. Gunn Jr.; (second row) Howard Harrison and Albert A. Wagner. Above, director Derwin Abrams (seated at center) confers with an unidentified airman and members of the movie crew while filming a scene for *The Mount Clemens Story* on the downtown streets. Above right, Air Force dignitaries arrive at the Jewel Theater for the film's world premiere. (Courtesy of the *Macomb Daily*.)

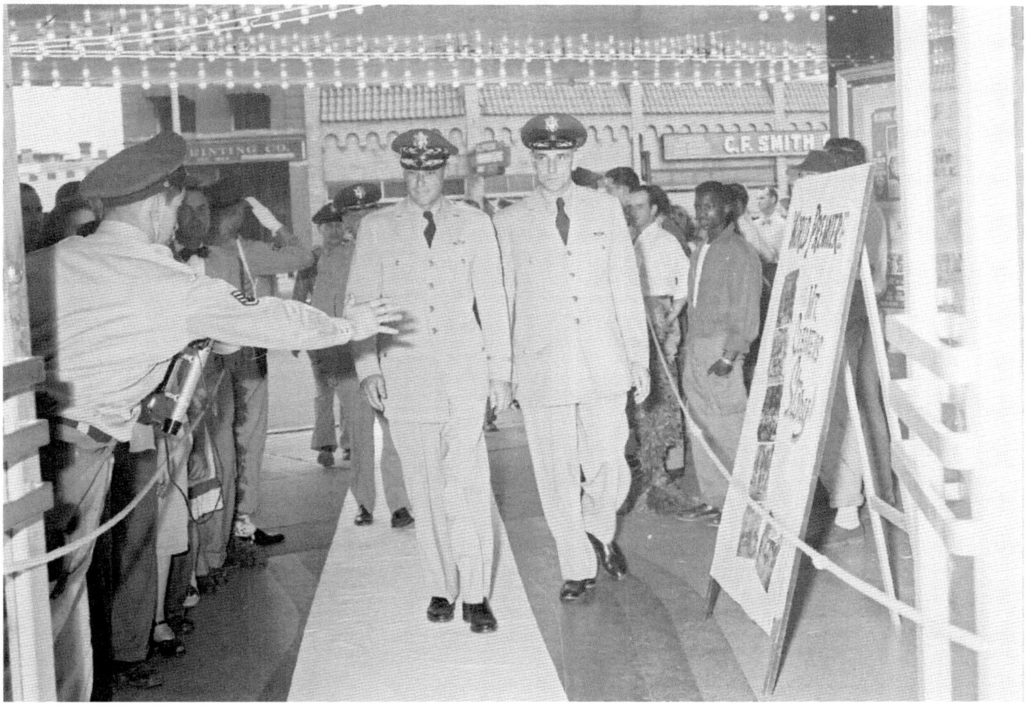
C.F. SMITH

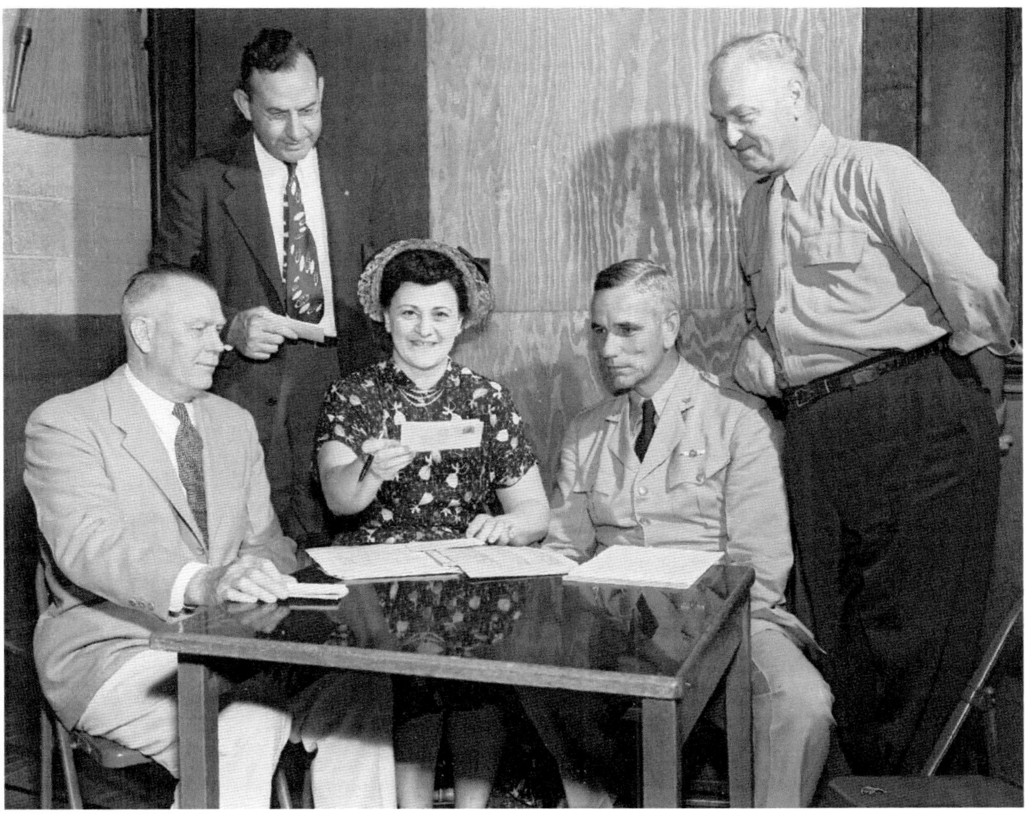

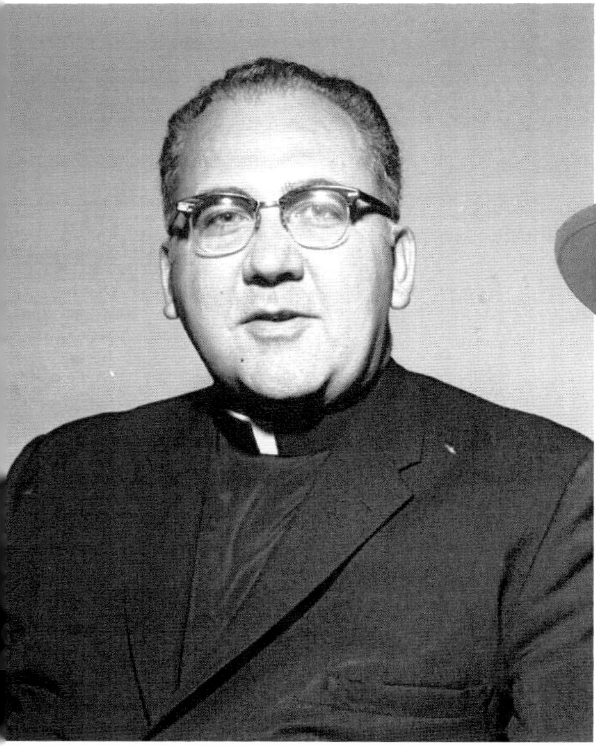

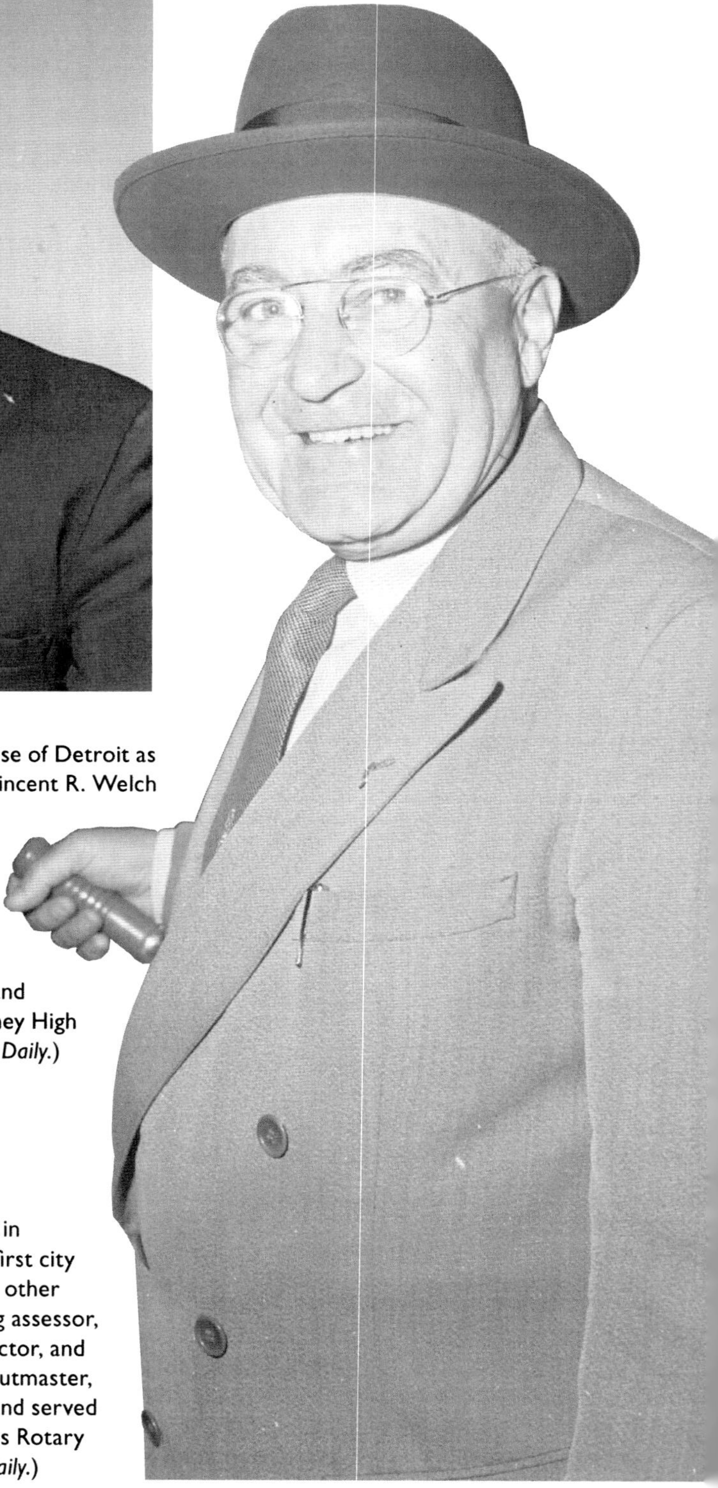

Vincent R. Welch
Known throughout the Archdiocese of Detroit as the "Bishop of the Ballpark," Fr. Vincent R. Welch was a fixture at Tiger Stadium where he watched his beloved Detroit Tigers play baseball and served as chaplain for the Old Time Baseball Players Association. Ordained in 1956, he came to Mount Clemens in 1970 and helped to establish Cardinal Mooney High School. (Courtesy of the *Macomb Daily.*)

Harold "Bugs" Lindsey
When Mount Clemens adopted commission-manager government in 1954, Lindsey became the town's first city manager. Lindsey also held several other posts in city government, including assessor, civil defense director, welfare director, and mayor. He was also active as a scoutmaster, as a director of the local YMCA, and served as president of the Mount Clemens Rotary Club. (Courtesy of the *Macomb Daily.*)

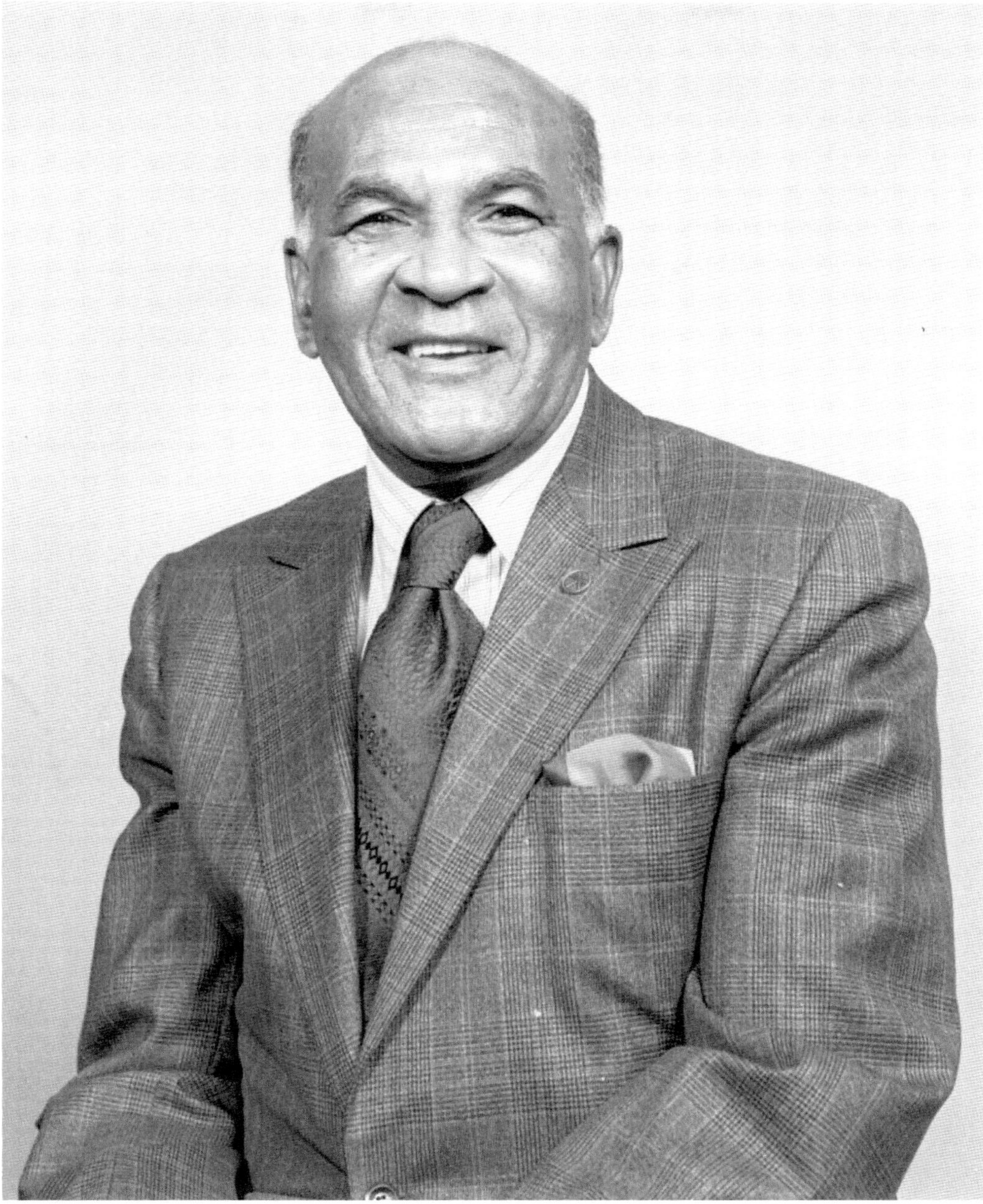

Ivan J. Harris

Jamaican-born Ivan J. Harris came to Mount Clemens in 1920 and worked in the bathhouse operated by his uncle, Henry Lightbourne. For 18 years after that, he was a linotype operator for the *Mount Clemens Daily Leader*, and then he moved on to a long career as a supervisor for Chrysler Corporation, but Ivan Harris is best remembered for his generous community service. A man of steadfast personal dignity and integrity, Harris built bridges among his fellow citizens during an era when racial strife and prejudice were strong. He served as president of St. Peter's parish and was also active in Big Brothers, Catholic Social Services, the NAACP, and the Mount Clemens Community Relations Commission, among many other organizations. (Courtesy of the *Macomb Daily*.)

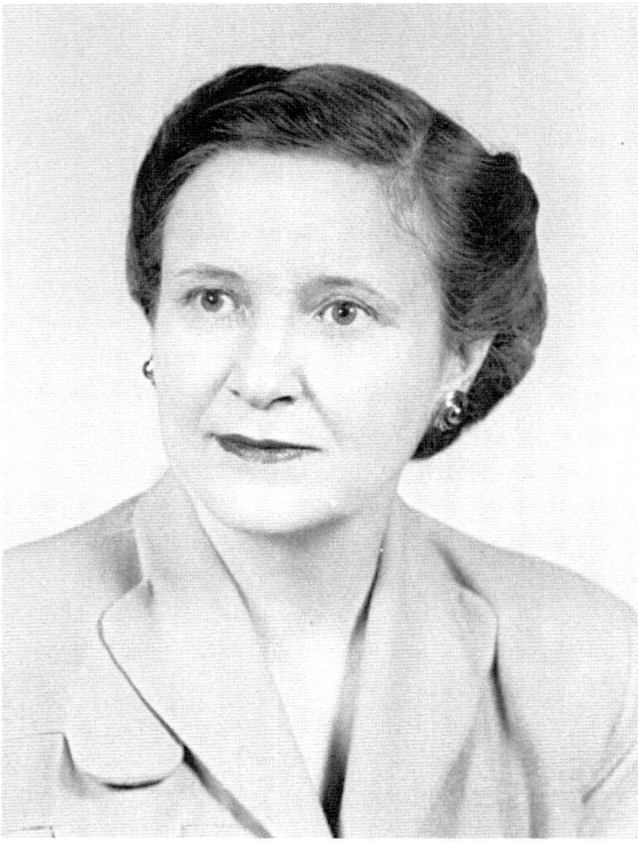

Gretchen M. Thompson

As the supervisor of elementary education for Mount Clemens Community Schools and a member of the Mount Clemens Board of Education, Thompson enriched the lives of many students entrusted to her care over the years. She left the community a bricks-and-mortar legacy, however, when she and two other women led a drive to establish an art center in the former Carnegie library building in 1969. Known today as the Anton Art Center, the institution Thompson helped to found has been bringing fine arts to the community for over 40 years. (Courtesy of the *Macomb Daily*.)

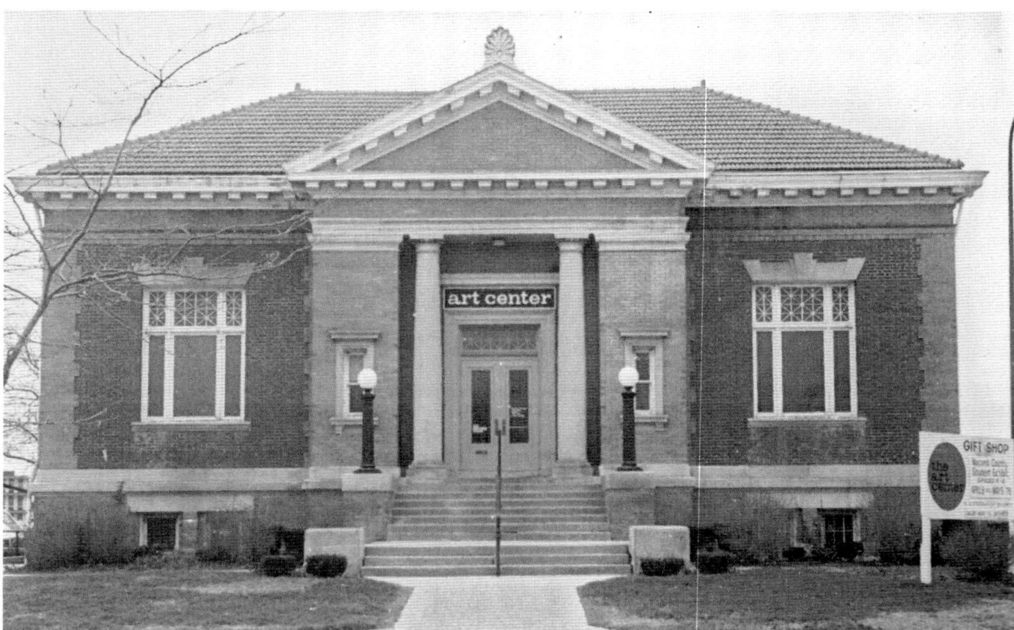

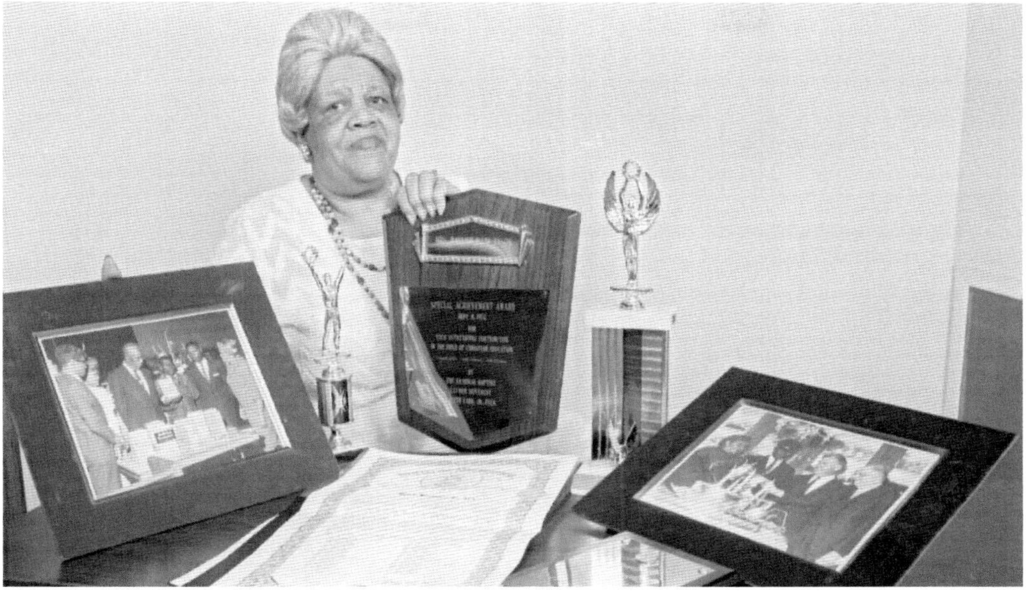

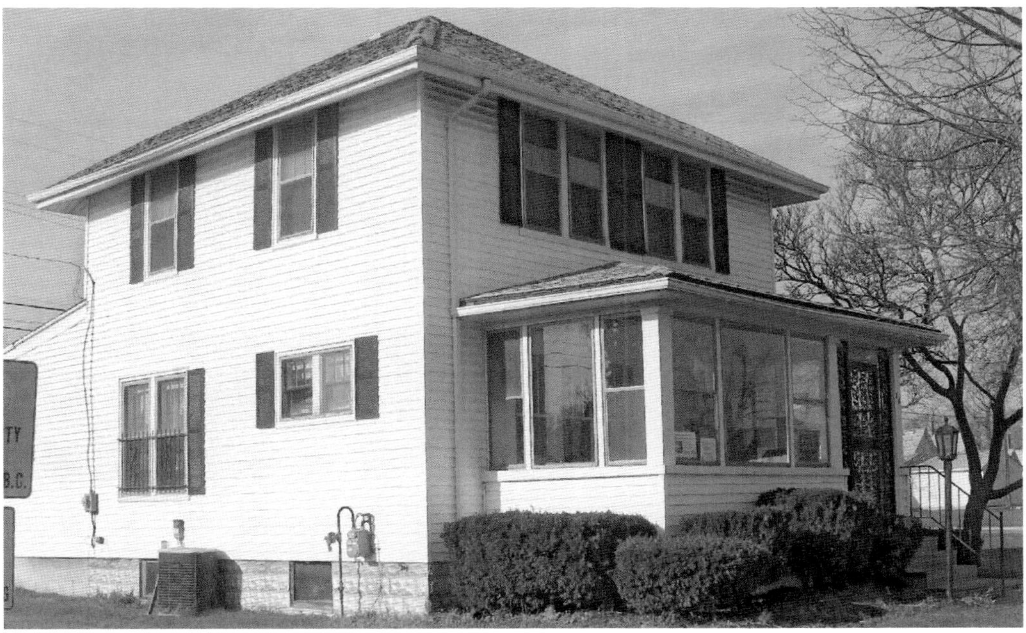

Pauline Wade-Tyson

Until the day that she died in 1992 at the age of 88, Wade-Tyson was a steadfast community volunteer who always found time for a worthy cause. In addition to being deeply involved in her church, Wade-Tyson worked with the Salvation Army, St. Joseph Mercy Hospital hospice, NAACP, United Negro College Fund, March of Dimes, and many other organizations, and was presented with the United Foundation Heart of Gold Award in 1985. Shown above is Wade-Tyson's former home, where everyone, regardless of race, creed, or color, was welcomed as a friend during her lifetime. Fittingly, the house is now part of the campus of Greater Morning Star Missionary Baptist Church and serves as the congregation's community outreach center. (Courtesy of the *Macomb Daily*; photograph by Deborah J. Larsen.)

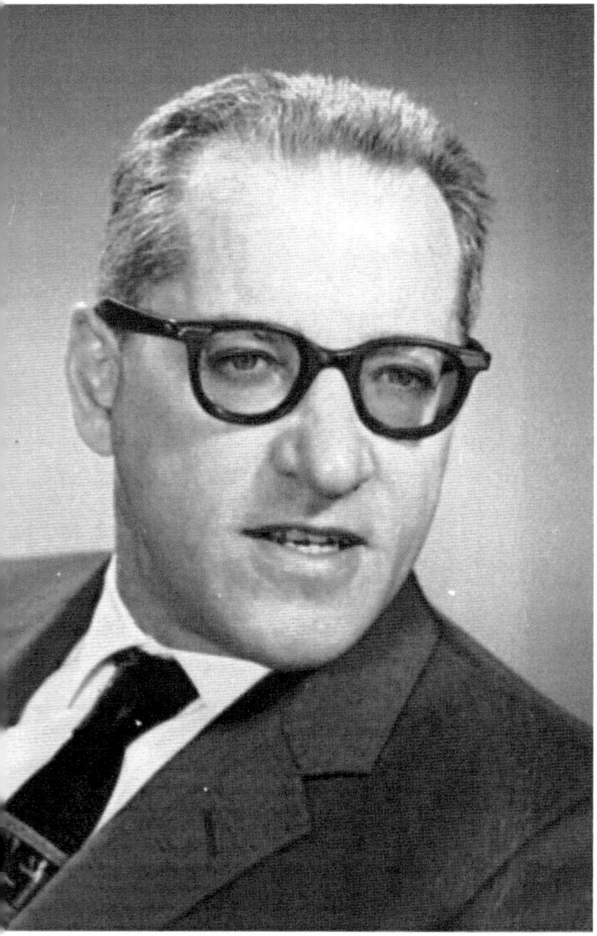

Alex D. Walker
Industry brought Walker to Mount Clemens in 1937 when he served as president of the Cadillac Manufacturing Company, but he is best remembered for his pivotal role in public service. Walker served 29 years on the Mount Clemens Board of Education, sat on the City of Mount Clemens Charter Commission, and directed a successful building campaign for the Macomb YMCA. (Courtesy of the *Macomb Daily*.)

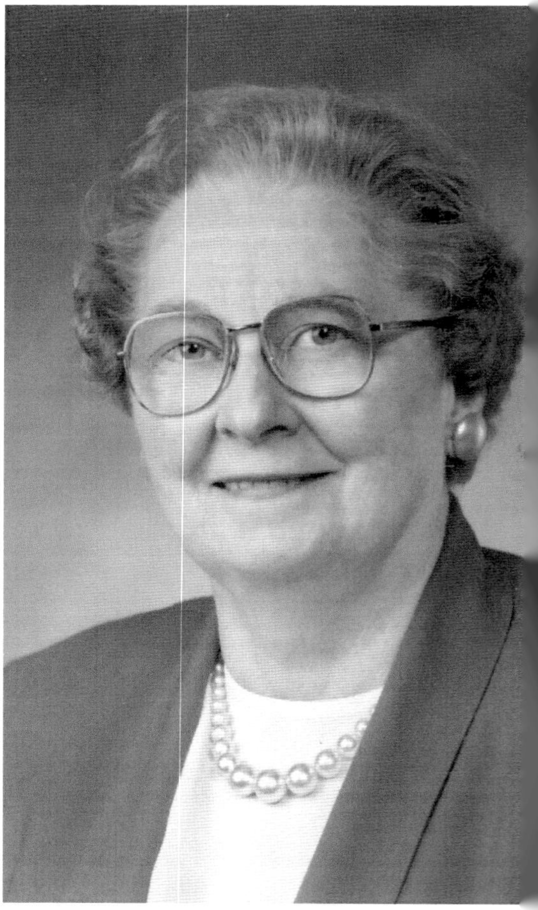

Betty Lou Morris
When Morris arrived in Mount Clemens in 1959, it took her all of one week to become involved in civic affairs by attending a League of Women Voters meeting. Her lengthy resume of community service has since included two terms on the Mount Clemens Board of Education and nearly two decades as a trustee of Mount Clemens Public Library. (Courtesy of Mount Clemens Public Library.)

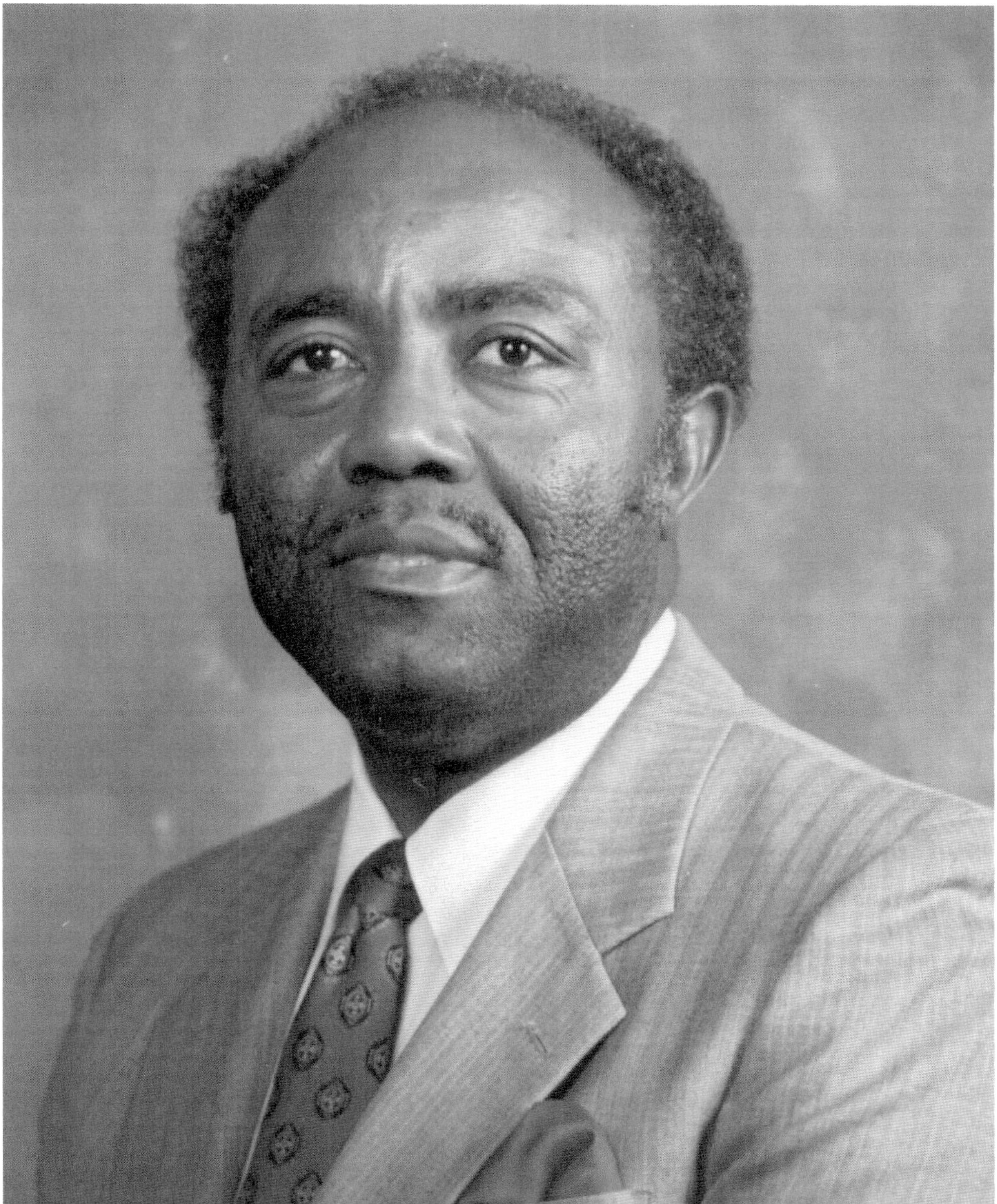

Bobby L. Hill Sr.

In 1991, Hill became the first African American to win a seat on the Macomb County Board of Commissioners, a position in which he served with distinction for 15 years. His long record of public service included more than a decade as a member of the Mount Clemens City Commission, and 20 years as a staff member of the Mount Clemens Community School District, where he held the position of director of vocational and adult education. Hill was also instrumental in establishing a community bank in Mount Clemens in 1996, and served on the board of directors of Community Central Bank from 1996 to 2007. (Courtesy of City of Mount Clemens.)

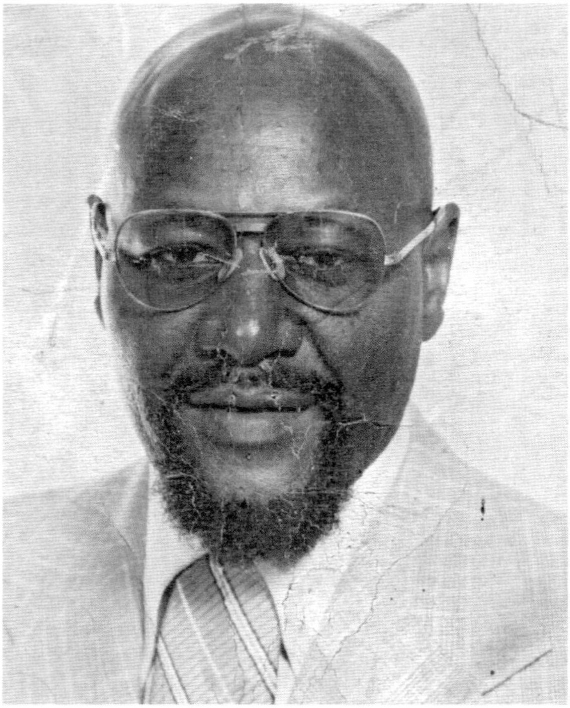

John C. Lee
Mount Clemens Board of Education member and former Macomb NAACP president John C. Lee was remembered by all who knew him as an outspoken leader whose honesty and fierce integrity earned the respect of everyone he encountered. During his 10 years of service on the school board, he was an advocate for curriculum improvement and equitable treatment of students. (Courtesy of Mrs. John C. Lee.)

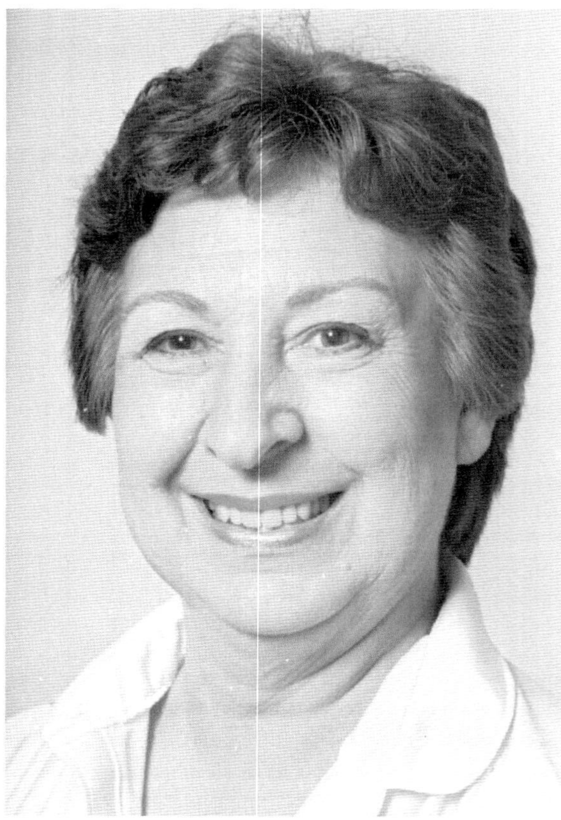

Jeanne T. Russo Nelson
A former child actor in local radio programs who developed an early interest in politics, Nelson surprised Mount Clemens residents in 1985 when she unseated a popular incumbent mayor with a slim 25-vote margin. During her single term in office, Nelson focused on redeveloping aging retail and commercial properties to strengthen the downtown district. (Courtesy of the *Macomb Daily*.)

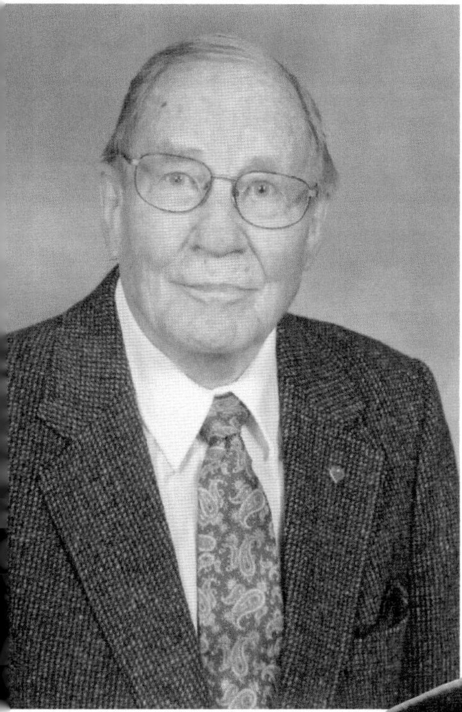

Paul John Sonnenberg
Lifelong Mount Clemens resident Paul Sonnenberg was an enthusiastic booster of his hometown and was dedicated to preserving its history. Sonnenberg was a longtime member of the Macomb County Historical Society, serving as its president and a trustee of the society's endowment fund, and he donated countless hours of his time to the care and preservation of the Crocker House Museum. (Courtesy of Mount Clemens Public Library.)

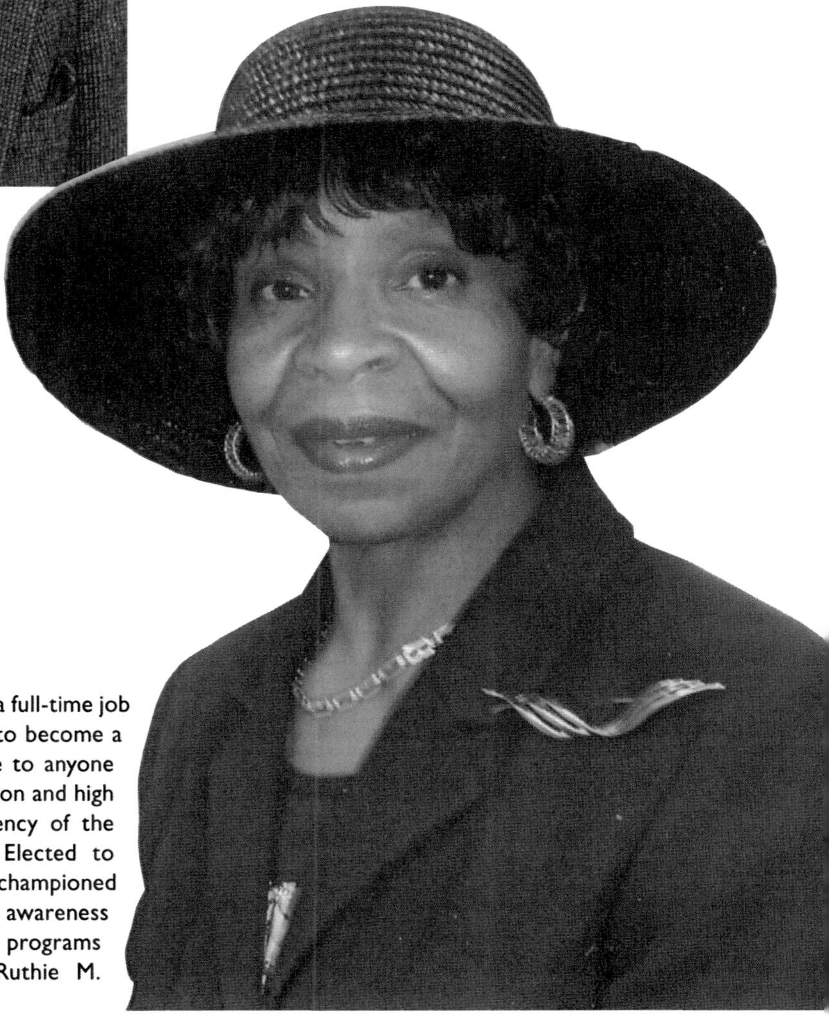

Ruthie M. Stevenson
Stevenson balanced a family, a full-time job at Ford, and college classes to become a nurse, so it was no surprise to anyone that she brought determination and high expectations to the presidency of the Macomb County NAACP. Elected to the post in 2000, Stevenson championed voter registration, public awareness of civil rights issues, and programs for youth. (Courtesy of Ruthie M. Stevenson.)

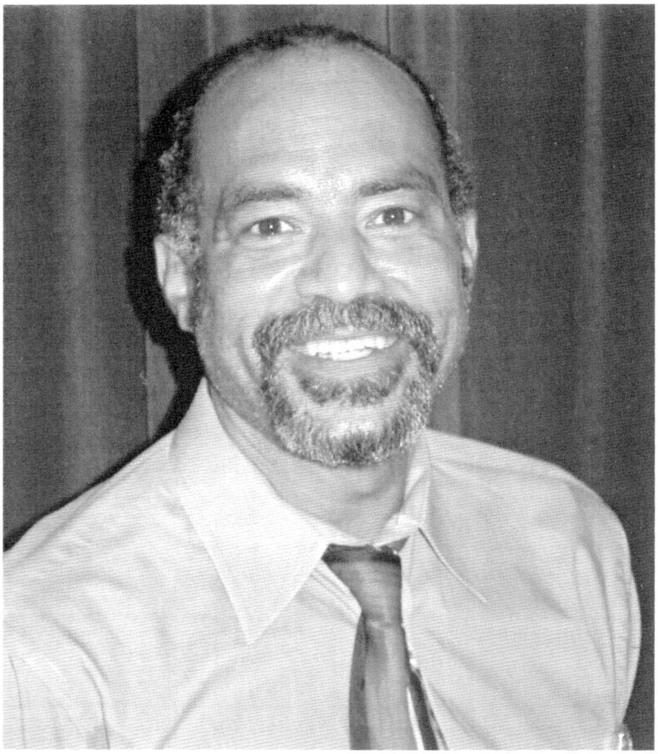

Earl C. Rickman

In 1984, Rickman became the youngest person ever elected to the Mount Clemens Board of Education. Rickman, a Mount Clemens native, has held a seat on the school board for the past quarter century, and also serves as executive director of the Mount Clemens Housing Commission. He served as president of the National School Boards Association in 2010. (Courtesy of Mount Clemens Community Schools.)

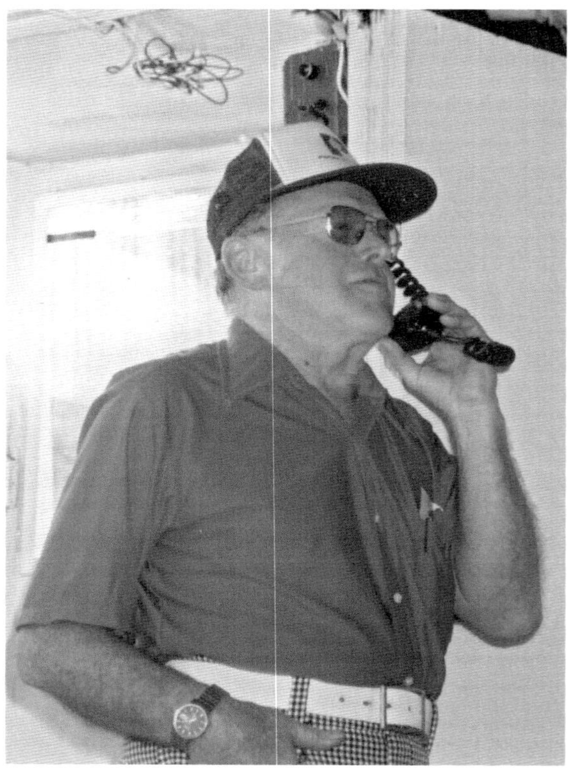

Norman O. Lorway

A resolution passed by the Mount Clemens City Commission in 1994 named Lorway the "unofficial historian" of Mount Clemens. A retired printer and lifelong resident of the area, Lorway founded the Bath City Collectors club and was a familiar sight on the Clinton River cruise boats, captivating passengers with stories of local history. (Courtesy of Deanna Black.)

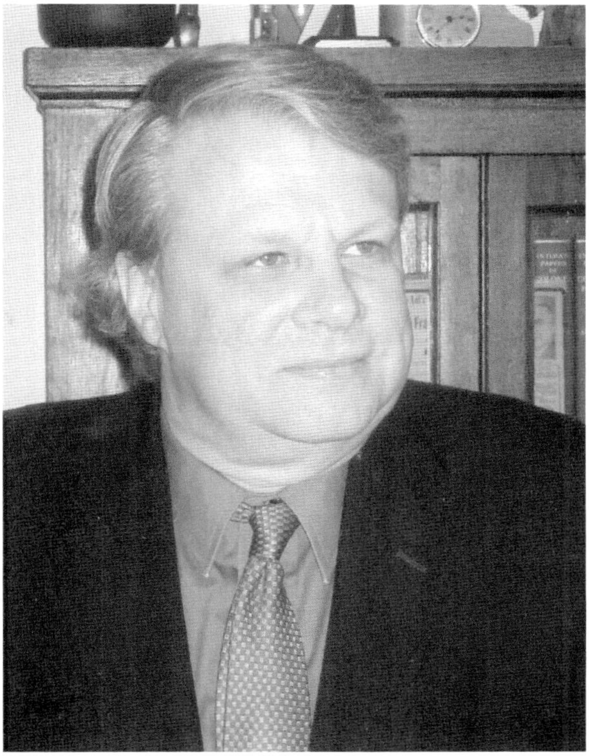

Mark Brewer
A graduate of Mount Clemens High School, Brewer earned degrees from Harvard College and Stanford University Law School before embarking on a distinguished career in politics and government. Active in the Michigan Democratic Party for over 30 years, Brewer has served as the state party chairperson since 1995 and has chaired the Michigan delegations at the last four Democratic National Conventions. (Courtesy of Mark Brewer.)

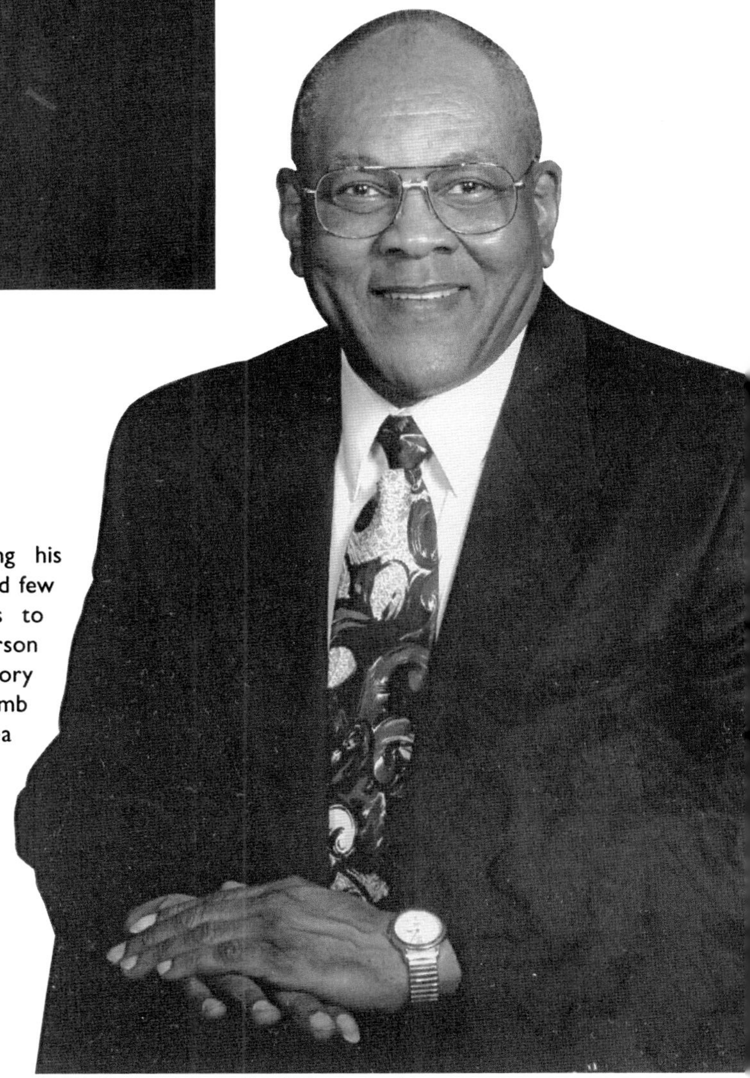

John M. Emerson Sr.
When Emerson began researching his family history in the 1980s, he found few local resources available. Curious to learn more about his heritage, Emerson began to collect records on the history of African Americans in Macomb County, and donated them to area public libraries. He also created the first collective history of African American churches in the county. (Courtesy of John M. Emerson Sr.)

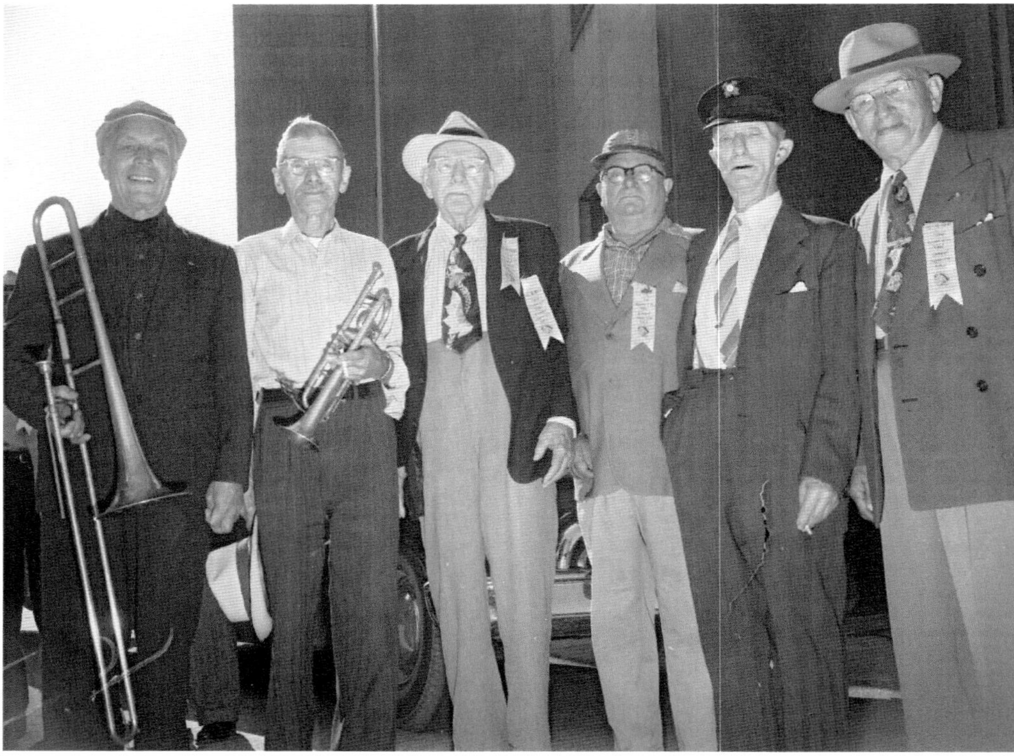

The Old Crowd

In 1880, three Mount Clemens business leaders invited men who were longtime residents of the area to attend a social reunion of what they dubbed the "Old Crowd." On the appointed day, a river steamer carried the assembly to the mouth of the Clinton River, where revelers enjoyed a meal followed by fishing, swimming, card games, cigars, and excursions on the lake. Women were not invited. To this day, the Old Crowd continues to gather each August for a parade from the courthouse, followed by an afternoon filled with traditional social events. A president is elected each year to serve for one day, and by-laws govern membership, which has included many sets of grandfathers, fathers, and sons. Shown here are Old Crowd members gathering for their annual parade in the 1950s. (Courtesy of the *Macomb Daily*.)

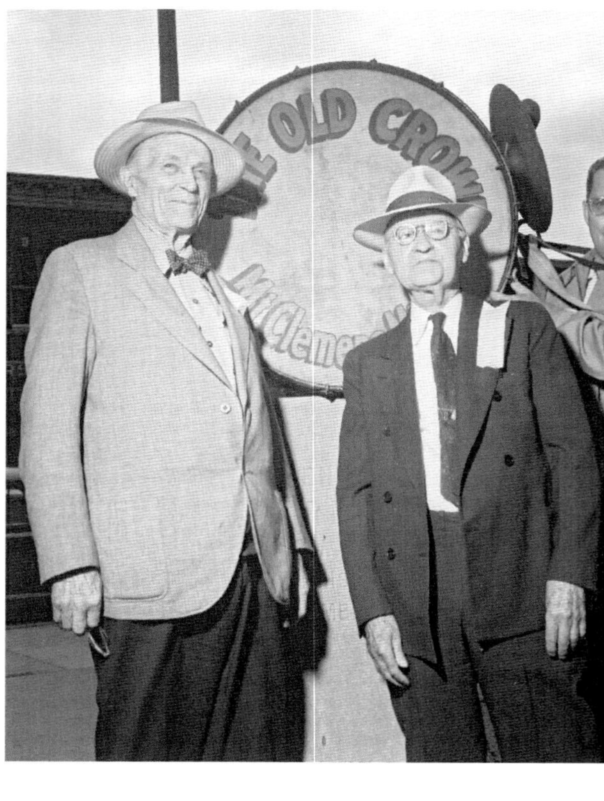

CHAPTER THREE

Business Leaders and Professionals

As happened in most developing towns, citizens with entrepreneurial spirit and critical skill sets fueled the economic engine that drove Mount Clemens forward during the mineral bath era and beyond. The healing waters were exploited for the benefit of the community by hotel and bathhouse operators, physicians, merchants, builders, and developers. Growth was managed and good order maintained by those who served in public office as aldermen and commissioners, judges, and magistrates, or city managers and mayors.

Mount Clemens attracted physicians of all medical philosophies and training to her public and private hospitals, and thus was the center of medical care for the entire county of Macomb. As the county seat of justice, the town also boasted some highly respected legal minds, including Michigan Supreme Court justices Franz C. Kuhn and Neil E. Reid, among others who served with distinction.

Numerous Mount Clemens business leaders also made their marks in city, county, or state government. Several local families, including the Nunneleys, Westendorfs, Crockers, Ullrichs, and Roskopps, saw more than one of their members—and in some cases, multiple generations—serving terms in elected or appointed public office. Here are the stories of those who led in business and in government, who stepped to the front of the line and showed the way for others to follow, and whose contributions, though in some cases made as long as a century or more ago, are still paying dividends for the Mount Clemens of today.

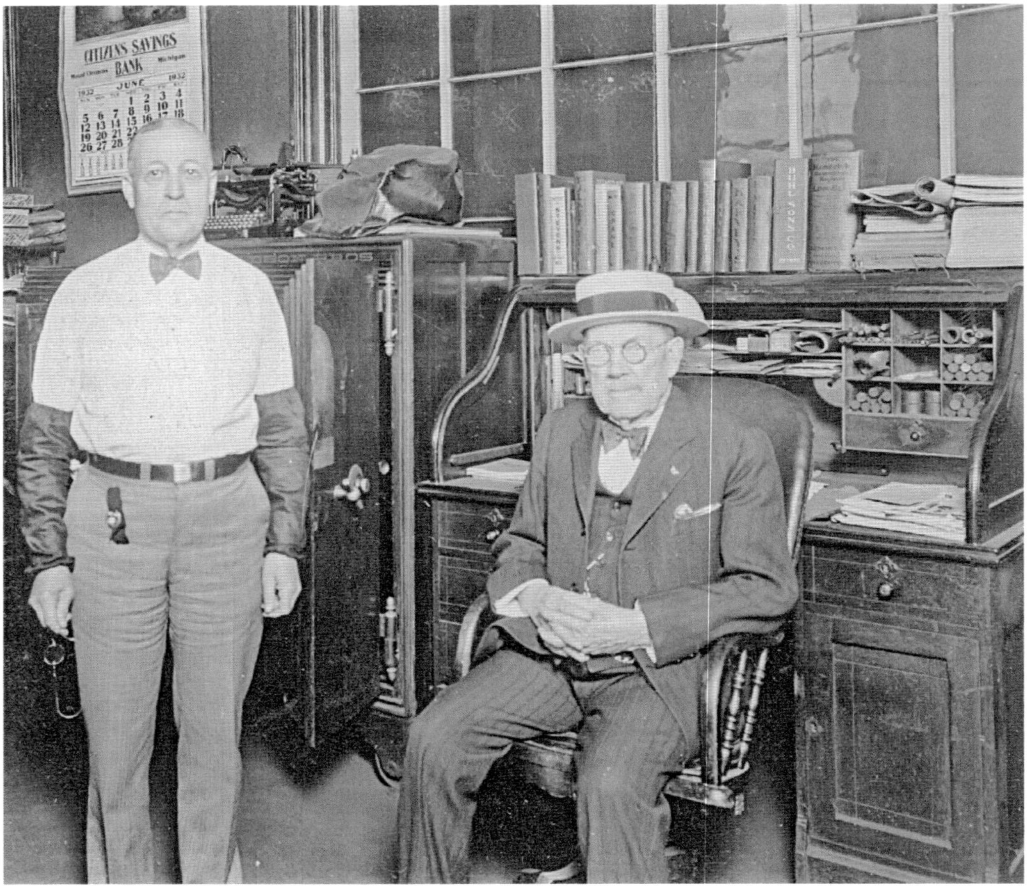

Andrew True Donaldson

Few characters in the annals of Mount Clemens history wore more hats than Donaldson. Born in Ireland in 1843, he came to the Bath City with his parents the following year. He and his brother, William, learned the blacksmith trade at their father's feet and worked together on the crews laying the Grand Trunk Railway tracks through Mount Clemens before the Civil War. A family story passed down through the generations reports that Donaldson eventually became an acquaintance of Thomas Alva Edison, who was a newsboy on the Grand Trunk train out of Port Huron, and purchased a newspaper from him each day at the Mount Clemens depot.

Donaldson and his brother entered business together in 1862; by 1875, the Donaldson Brothers Foundry that they subsequently established was one of Mount Clemens's principal industries. In a three-story brick building that employed as many as 125 men at a time, Donaldson Brothers manufactured wagons, sleighs, carriages, and farm implements and shipped their products all over North America. Donaldson also lent his business acumen to other local enterprises, and was involved in the establishment of the Mount Clemens Pottery, the Mount Clemens Sugar Factory, and the Citizens Savings Bank. When asked to serve as receiver of the failing Mount Clemens Brewing Company in 1904, Donaldson is said to have turned the company's fortunes around through the simple act of boarding up the brewery's free tap room. He also lent his considerable expertise to local government, serving 30 years on the school board and four years as mayor. The school board showed its appreciation for his years of dedication to public education by naming Donaldson Elementary School in his honor in 1903. Donaldson is shown here seated in the office of the Donaldson foundry, with his nephew, Arthur Leonard Donaldson, standing next to him. (Courtesy of Macomb County Historical Society.)

Paul J. Ullrich

Seen (right) with his bicycle while his parents and sister look on from their buggies, Ullrich grew up in Mount Clemens as a member of a family prominent in business and civic affairs. Ullrich was a financier and president of the Ullrich Savings Bank, shown below, as well as a director of the Detroit Fidelity & Surety Trust Company. In civic affairs, Ullrich served two terms as mayor of Mount Clemens, and was one of three members of the Ullrich family to hold that office. (Courtesy of Macomb County Historical Society and Mount Clemens Public Library.)

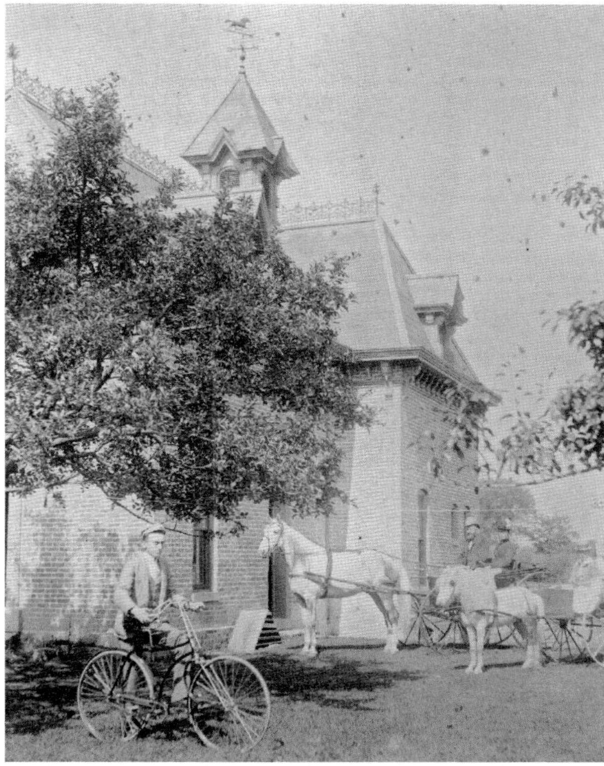

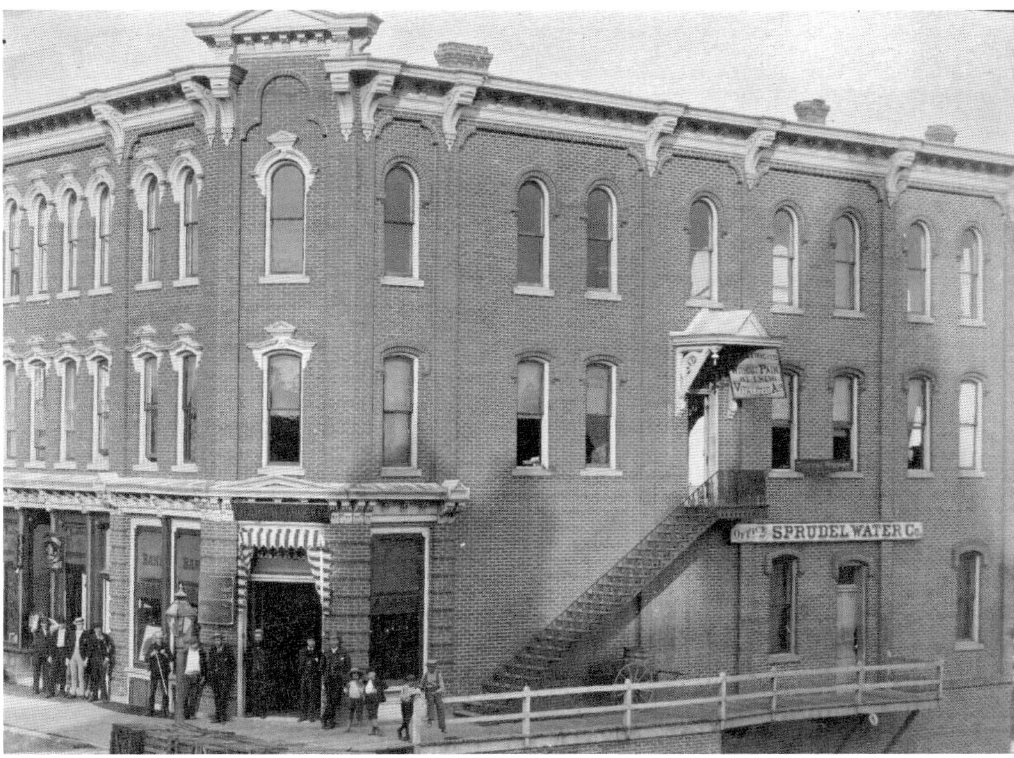

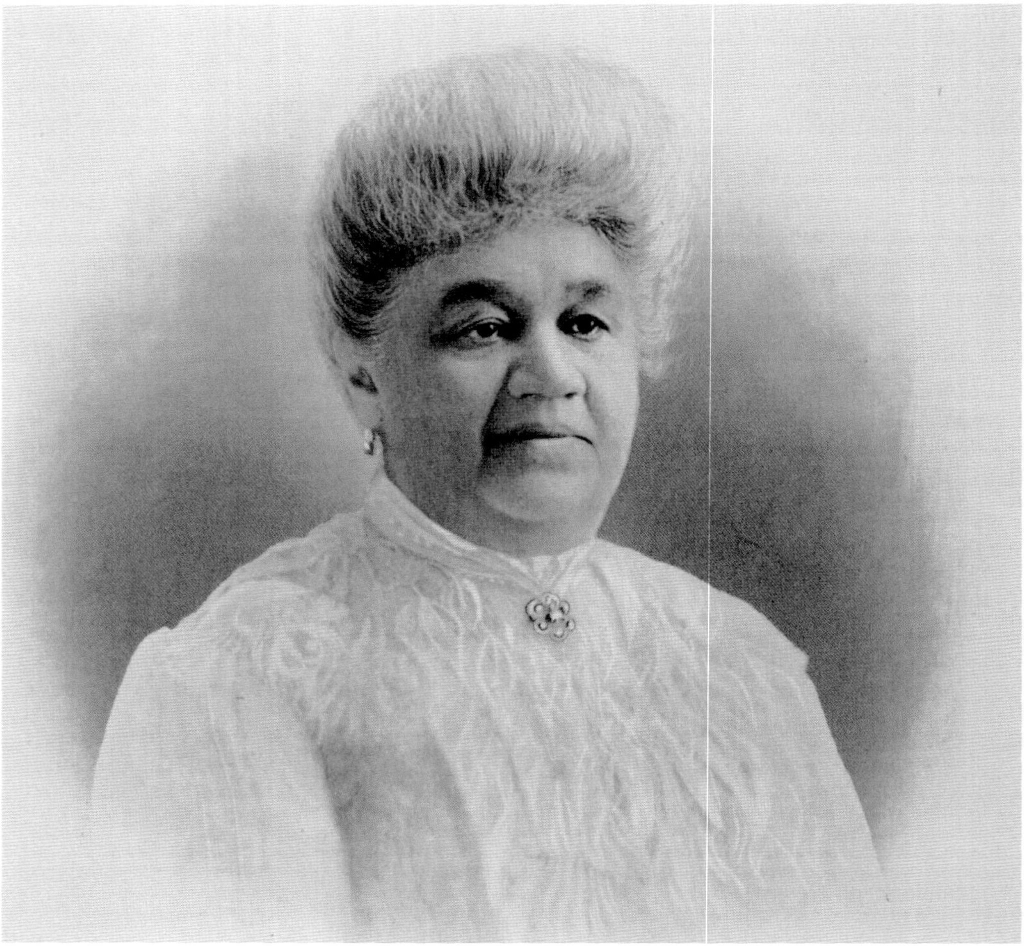

Margaretha Schmidt Kieffer
Kieffer came to Mount Clemens as a visitor to the healing mineral baths but was destined to stay and become the town's most powerful woman business leader of her day. She was born in Germany in 1836 and emigrated with her parents to the United States, where the family settled in Buffalo, New York. In Buffalo she met and married hardware merchant John Kieffer, and the couple traveled to Mount Clemens to take the baths in 1885. The city and its prospects as a health resort impressed the Kieffers so profoundly that they decided to invest in a small hotel called the Central Park. Envisioning a luxurious house that would appeal to the most prosperous of visitors, the Kieffers expanded the building and grounds and added a bathhouse and a formal garden along the riverfront. By 1897, the 200-room Park Hotel, as they renamed it, was the best-known and most exclusive accommodation in Mount Clemens, and Margaretha Kieffer was recognized as the driving force behind its success. Celebrities of the day, looking for privacy and posh surroundings, routinely chose the Park when they came to the Bath City to "take the cure." Among Kieffer's guests there were Helena Rubinstein, Jerome Kern, William Jennings Bryan, Alice Roosevelt Longworth, and George M. Cohan. After the death of her husband in 1900, Kieffer continued to operate the property, which profited from her business acumen and vision. When she died in 1911, the local newspaper commented that "it was her unflagging industry, her largeness of view, her unconquerable faith in Mount Clemens, her sagacity, her courage, that contributed so decisively to the largest business success that Mount Clemens has ever known, to a success that has carried our renown to the corners of the earth." (Courtesy of Mount Clemens Public Library.)

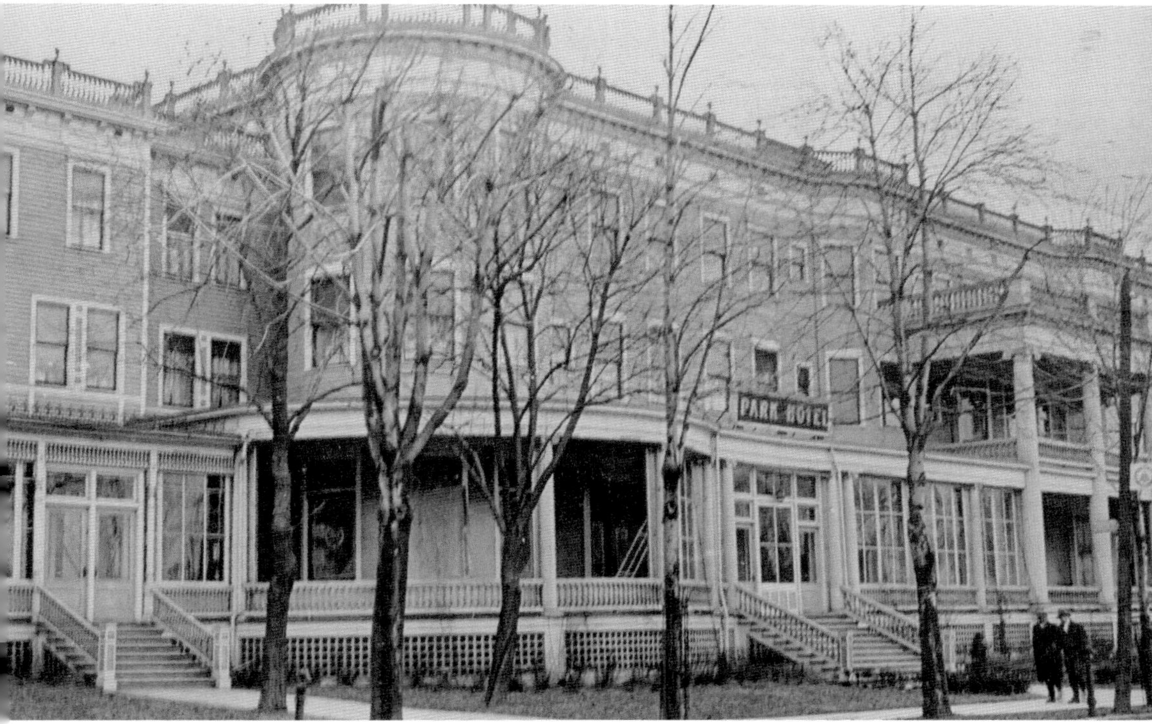
PARK HOTEL

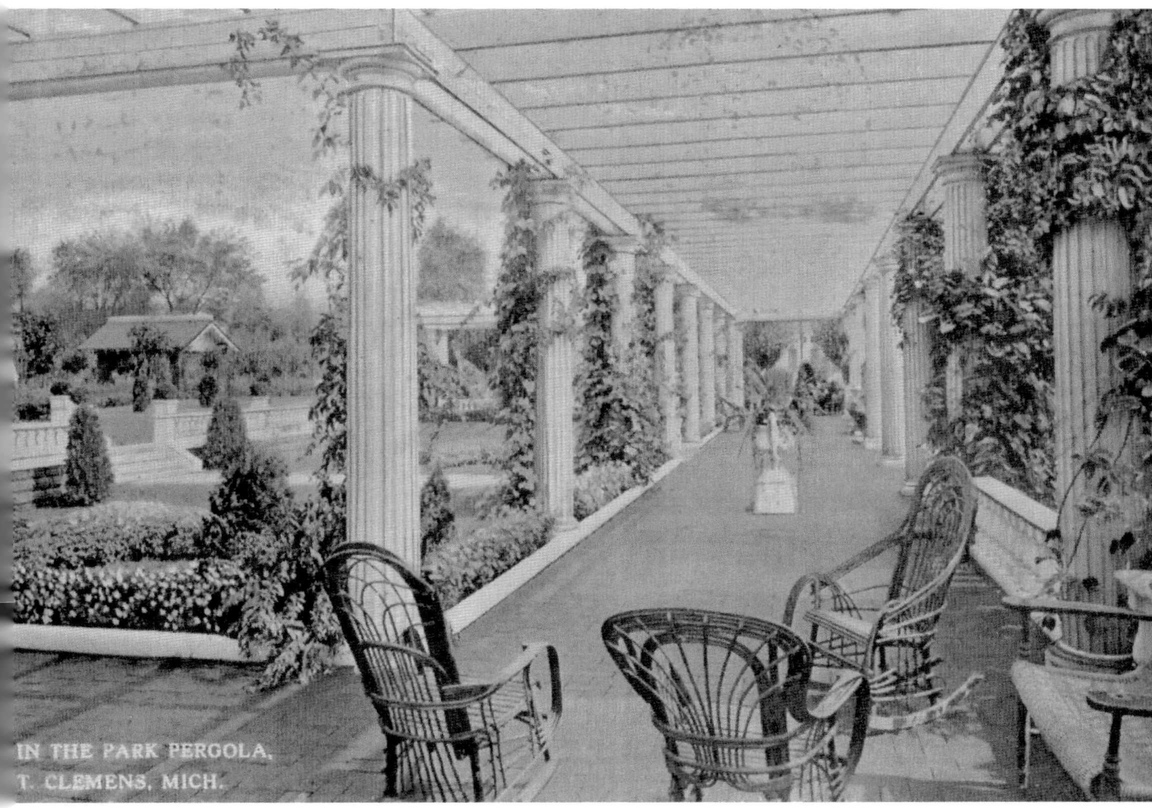
IN THE PARK PERGOLA,
T. CLEMENS, MICH.

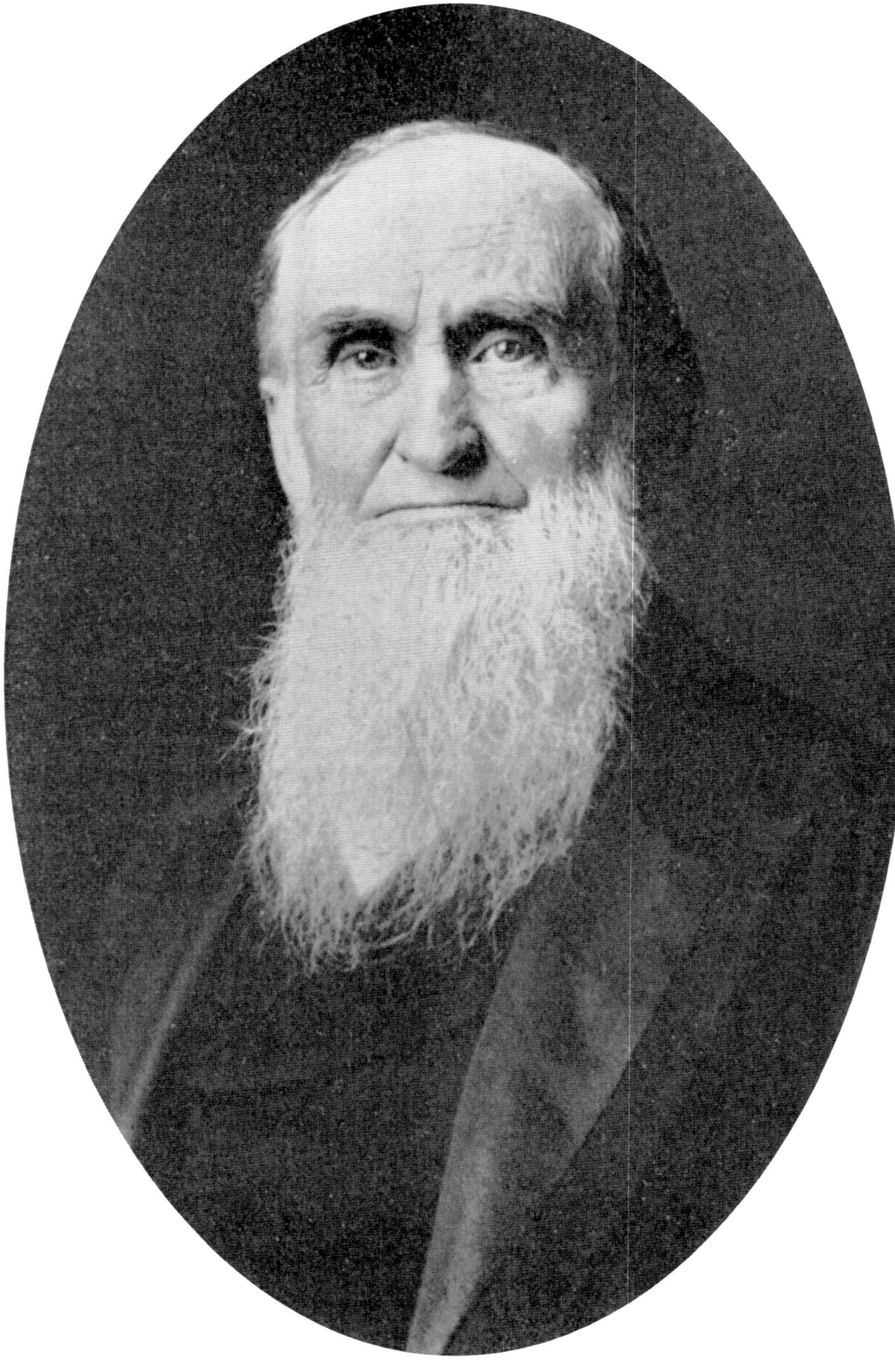

Abner Hayward (LEFT)
It was Hayward who claimed to have launched the mineral bath industry in Mount Clemens by being the first physician to use the water therapeutically. Trained as a homeopath, Hayward first came to Mount Clemens in 1871 and soon began prescribing mineral water baths for his patients with rheumatism and related ailments. So successful were the treatments that a public bathhouse was opened in 1873 and the town's mineral bath industry was born. Hayward's medical practice in the Bath City spanned nearly three decades, and he was considered to be the family physician not only of his patients in Mount Clemens, but also of many people from other parts of the country who traveled to Mount Clemens to seek his professional counsel and prescription for the healing baths. (Courtesy of Mount Clemens Public Library.)

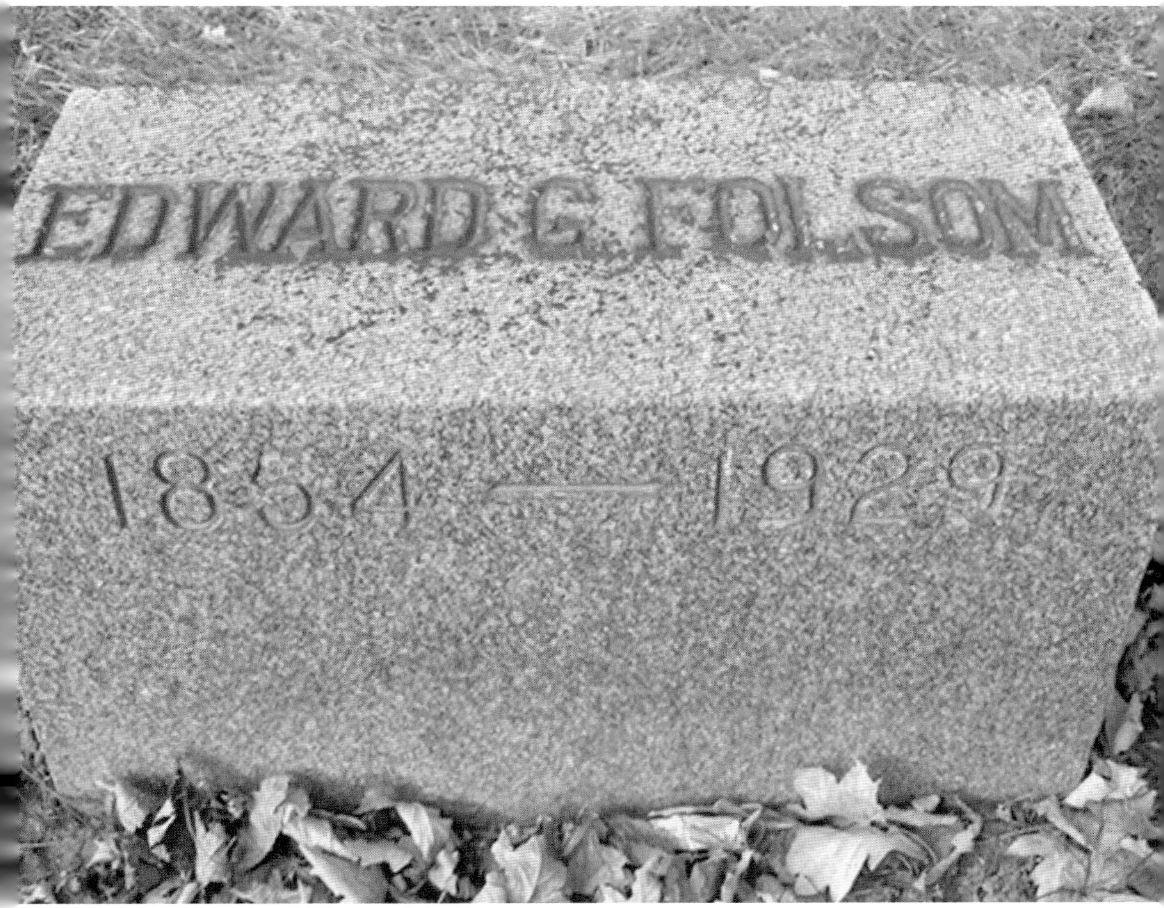

Edward Graham Folsom
Folsom spent more time on his public practice of medicine than he did on his private practice, and was known for his generosity to those less fortunate than himself. He settled in Mount Clemens in 1884 and served 34 years as city health officer and three years as county coroner. Folsom treated the indigent citizens of Mount Clemens without regard for remuneration and was described by his peers as "one of the greatest benefactors of the city." Mount Clemens was understandably grief-stricken in 1929, when tragedy struck and Folsom was run over and killed by his own automobile as he attempted to extricate it from a snow bank in his driveway. (Courtesy of Macomb County Historical Society.)

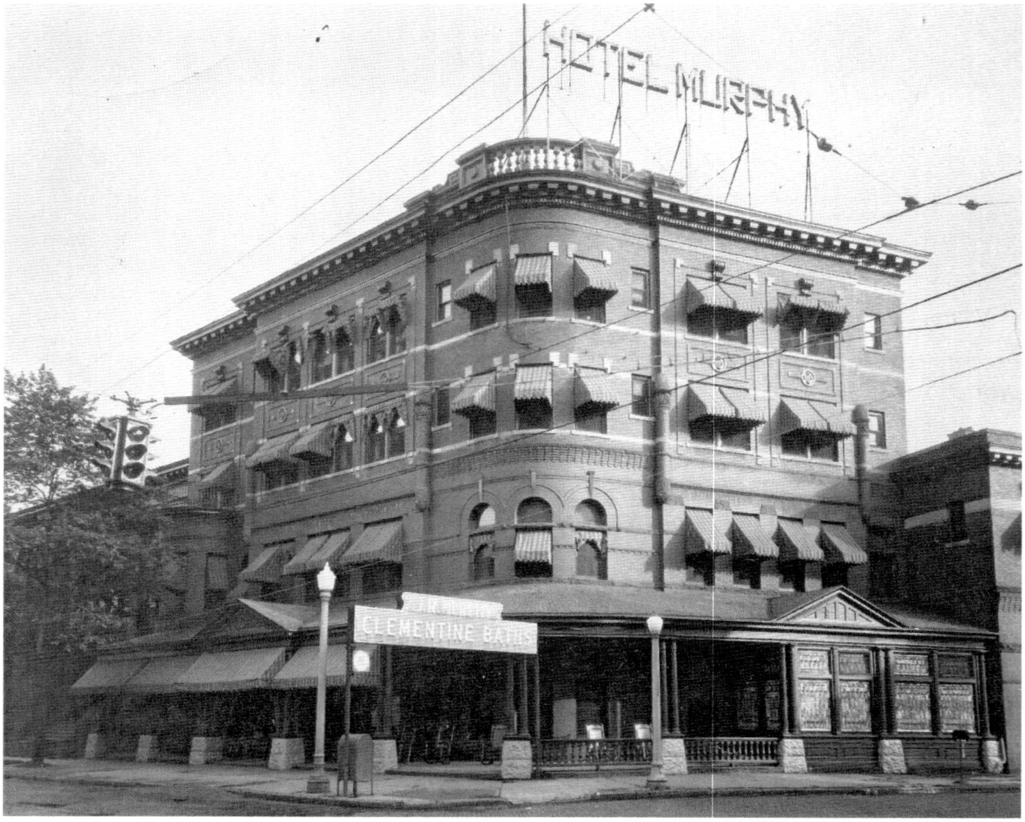
HOTEL MURPHY
CLEMENTINE BATHS

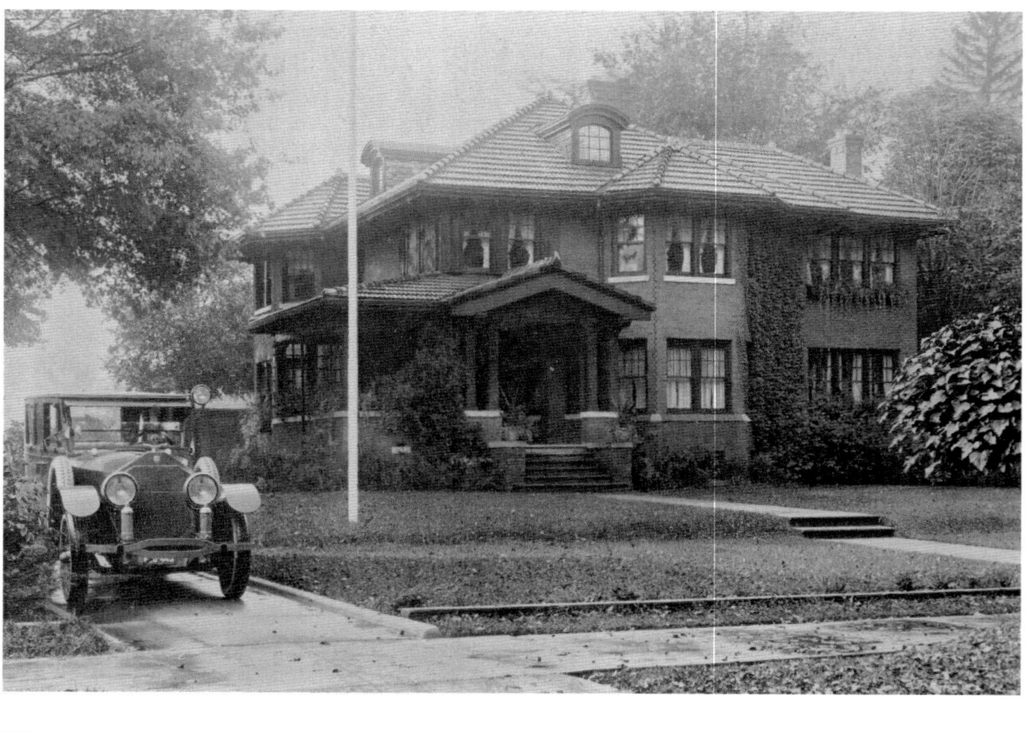

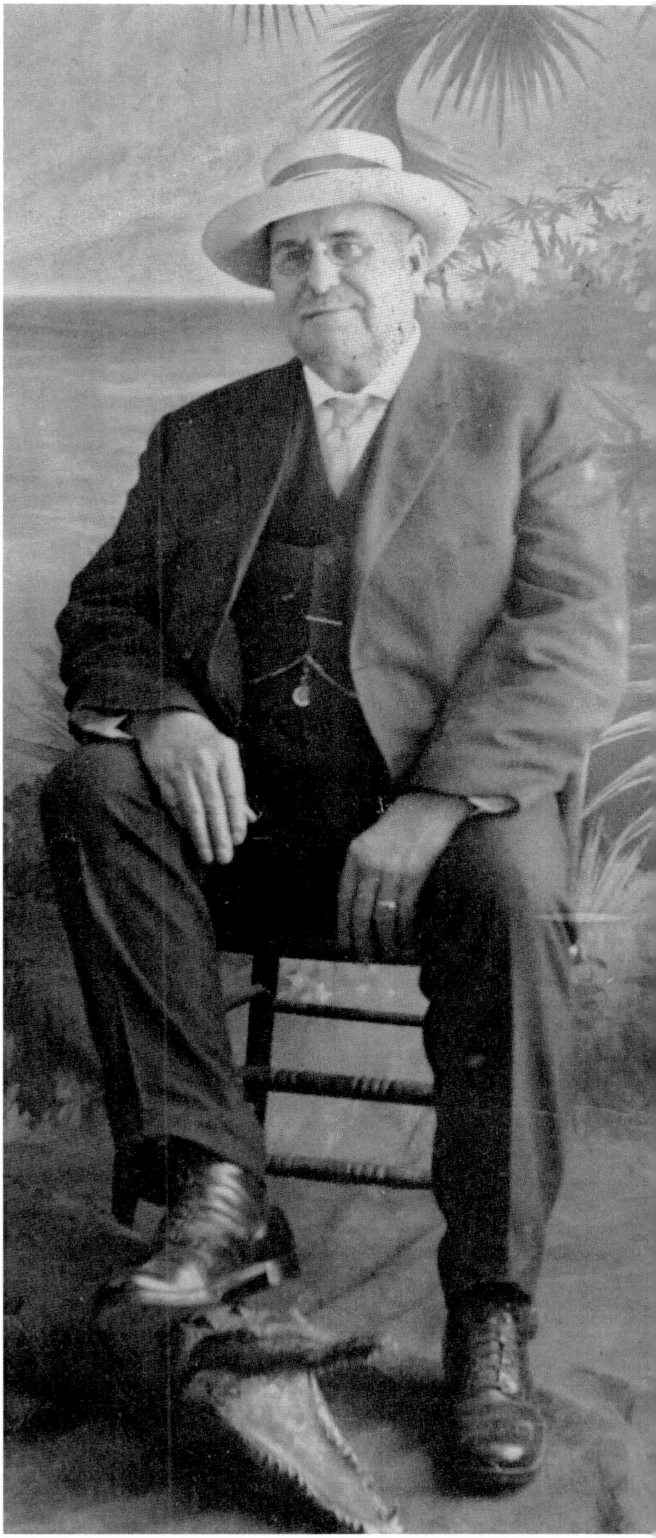

John Robinson Murphy

Murphy was chief of police in Allegheny, Pennsylvania, when he first began visiting Mount Clemens to rest and take the baths. He was the definition of a self-made man; born of humble origins, he left school at the age of 12 and began working on his father's truck farm. A succession of jobs with increasing responsibility led to his appointment as a constable, and later as chief of police. He became a prominent political figure in his native state and was elected to the Pennsylvania legislature, where he served two terms as the Republican representative of the first district. After frequent visits to Mount Clemens, Murphy decided in 1904 to make the Bath City his permanent home. Recognizing value in the mineral baths that had drawn him to Mount Clemens, he purchased the Clementine Bath House (above left), which he greatly improved and expanded. He took an interest in the business and civic affairs of his new home and quickly became a respected leader among its citizens. In a tribute to Murphy, the local newspaper editor said: "Chief Murphy is our idea of a high grade citizen. His horizon is broad; his sympathies generous and unselfish; his head level and sane; his heart strings responsive to the misfortunes of his fellow men." In 1911, the widowed Murphy married the Clementine's manager, Nellie D. Metler, and immediately commissioned plans for a new residence from local architect Theophilus Van Damme. The couple's impressive home on Cass Avenue (below left) was finished in 1912, but John R. Murphy had little time to enjoy it. The portly man, who was often noted for his resemblance to Pres. William Howard Taft, succumbed in 1917 after a two-year illness. Back in his home state, the Pennsylvania legislature adjourned out of respect for his memory. His widow, who continued to manage the couple's business holdings on her own following Murphy's death, remodeled the old Eastman Hotel and christened it the John R. Murphy Hotel in honor of her late husband. (Courtesy of Mount Clemens Public Library.)

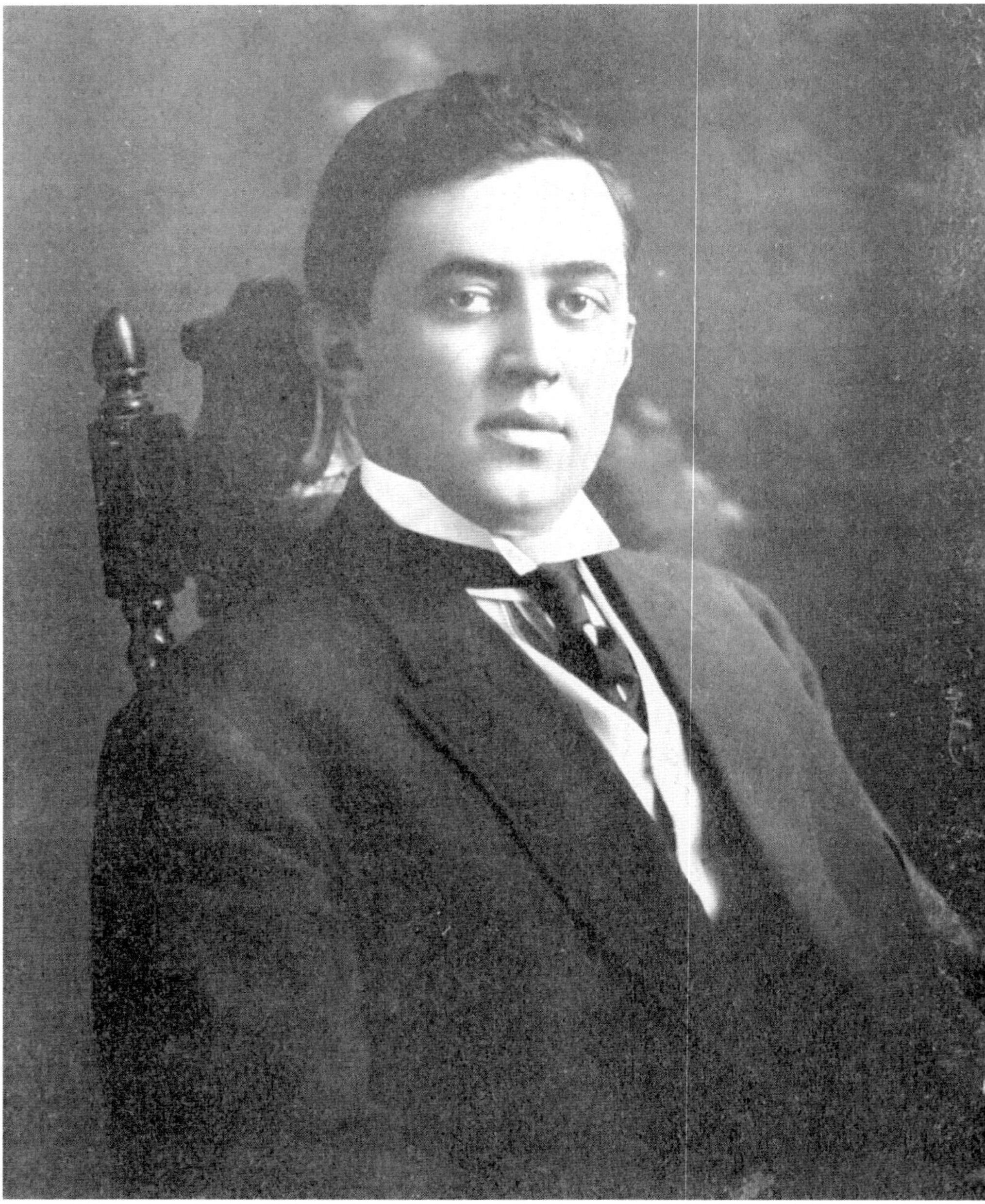

Franz Christian Kuhn

When he received his law degree from the University of Michigan in 1894, Kuhn was already deeply involved in Republican Party politics. He organized the National League of College Republican Clubs on campus, and after opening a law office in Detroit was nominated—at age 22—for circuit court commissioner by Macomb County Republicans. He went on to serve as county prosecuting attorney and probate judge, and began a rapid rise in state politics. Kuhn became attorney general of Michigan in 1910 and in 1912 was appointed to the Michigan Supreme Court. He was named chief justice of the state's high court in 1917 and served until 1919, when he resigned to take a position as president of the Michigan Bell Telephone Company. (Courtesy of Mount Clemens Public Library.)

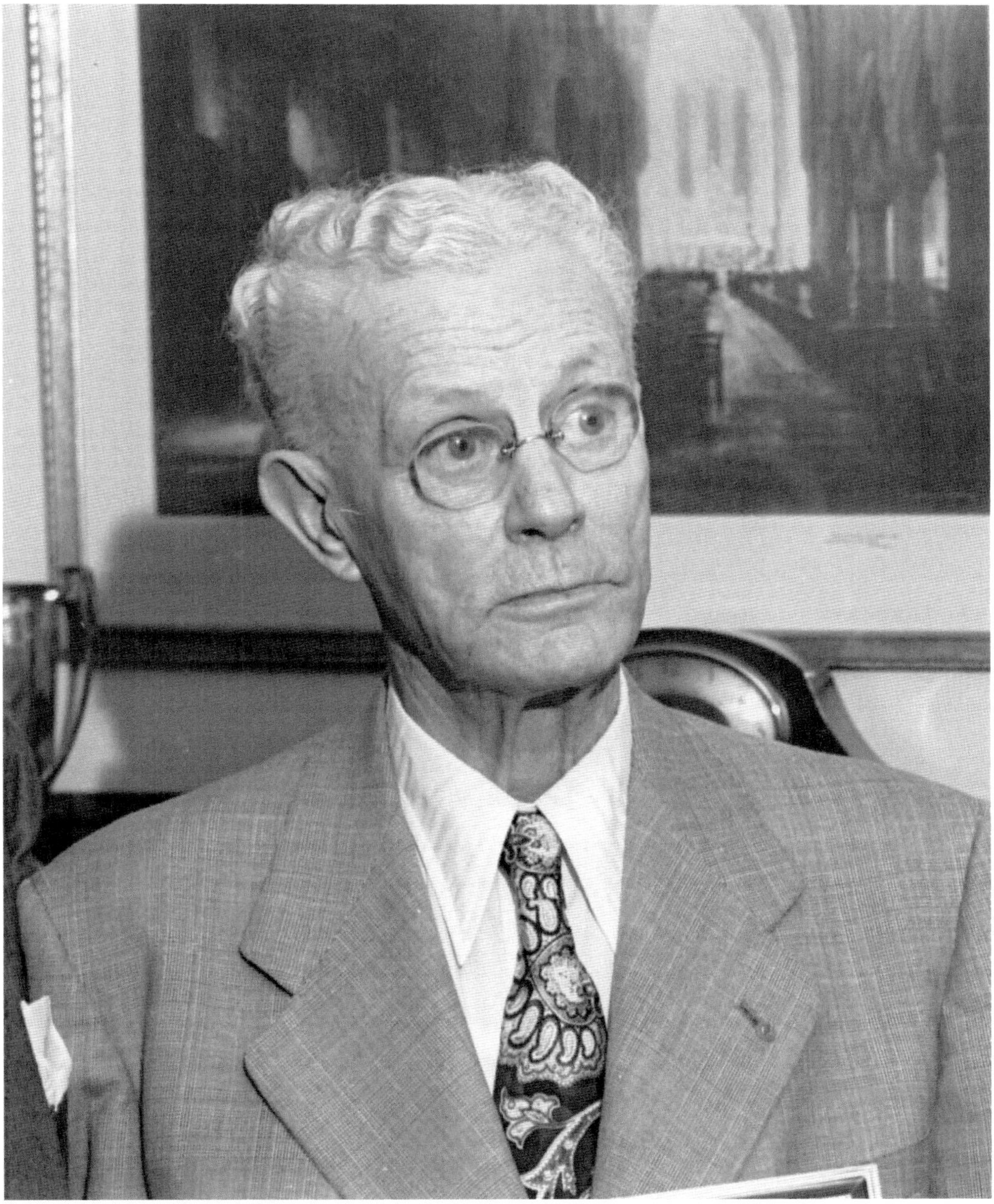

Walter Napoleon "Dad" Trombley

Born in Mount Clemens to one of Macomb County's pioneer families, Trombley was best known for his role in the community's entertainment industry. He was a partner in the Bijou Theater, which he ran with Robert G. Peltier for three decades and billed as "Bob and Dad's Bijou." In addition to the theater business, Trombley managed a semi-professional baseball team called the Mount Clemens Old Timers, and in 1909, when the automobile industry was in its infancy, he invested in a car called the Alpena Flyer, which was produced for only four years. Trombley was also one of a small contingent of Mount Clemens men to serve in the Spanish-American War. (Courtesy of the *Macomb Daily*.)

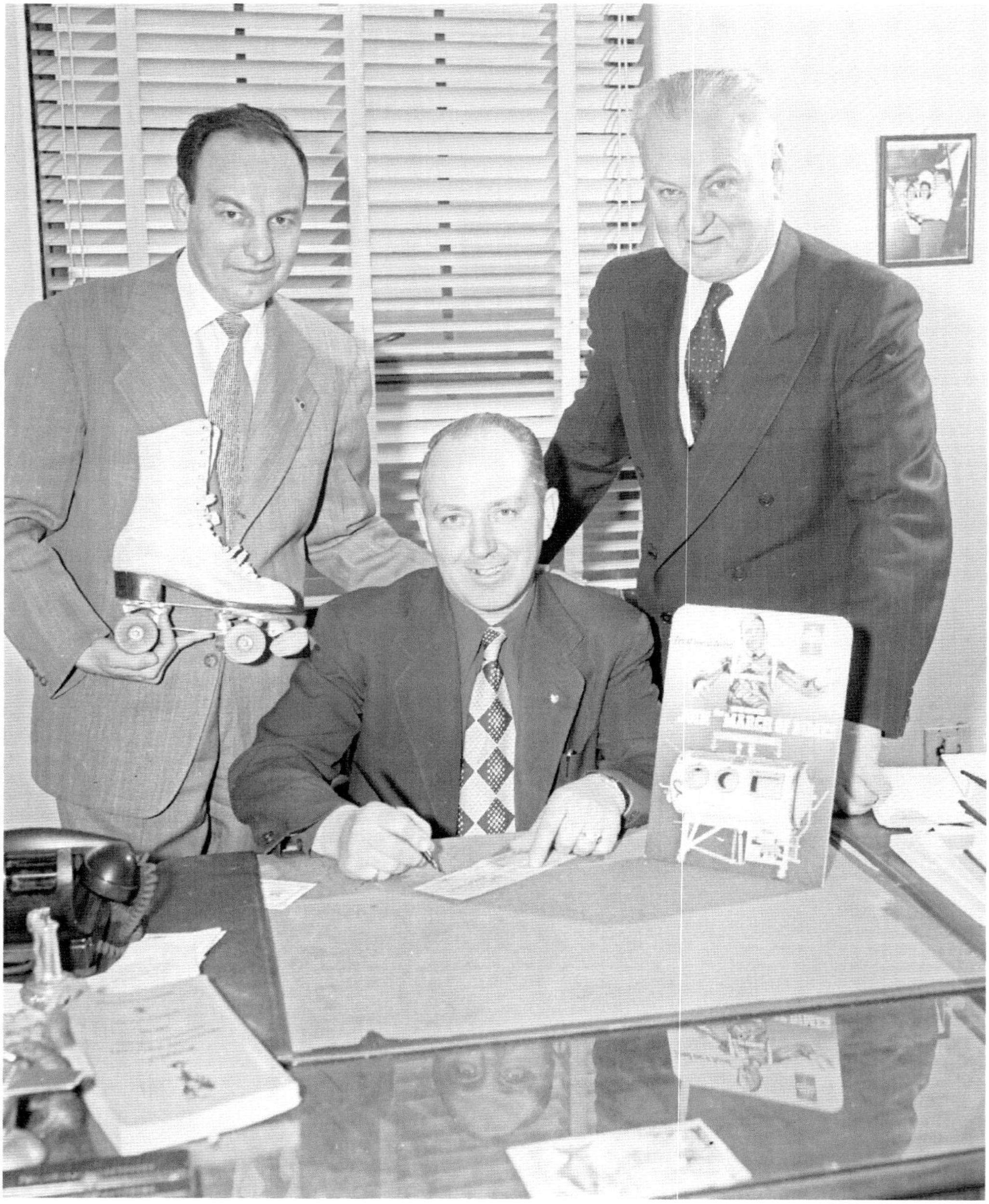

Albert Alexius Wagner

Baseball brought Wagner to Mount Clemens in 1906, when he came from his native Indiana as a player with the Southern Michigan League. But when he met and married a local woman in 1911, he made the Bath City his permanent home. Wagner entered politics in 1934 when he was elected to a term in the Michigan legislature; 10 years later, he was elected mayor of Mount Clemens and served three terms before moving on to a decade-long career as Macomb County clerk. In private life, Wagner was a charter member of the Macomb March of Dimes and a member of the Old Crowd. He is shown here (right) with Earl J. Dunn (center) and John Matthews, working on a March of Dimes fundraiser. (Courtesy of the *Macomb Daily*.)

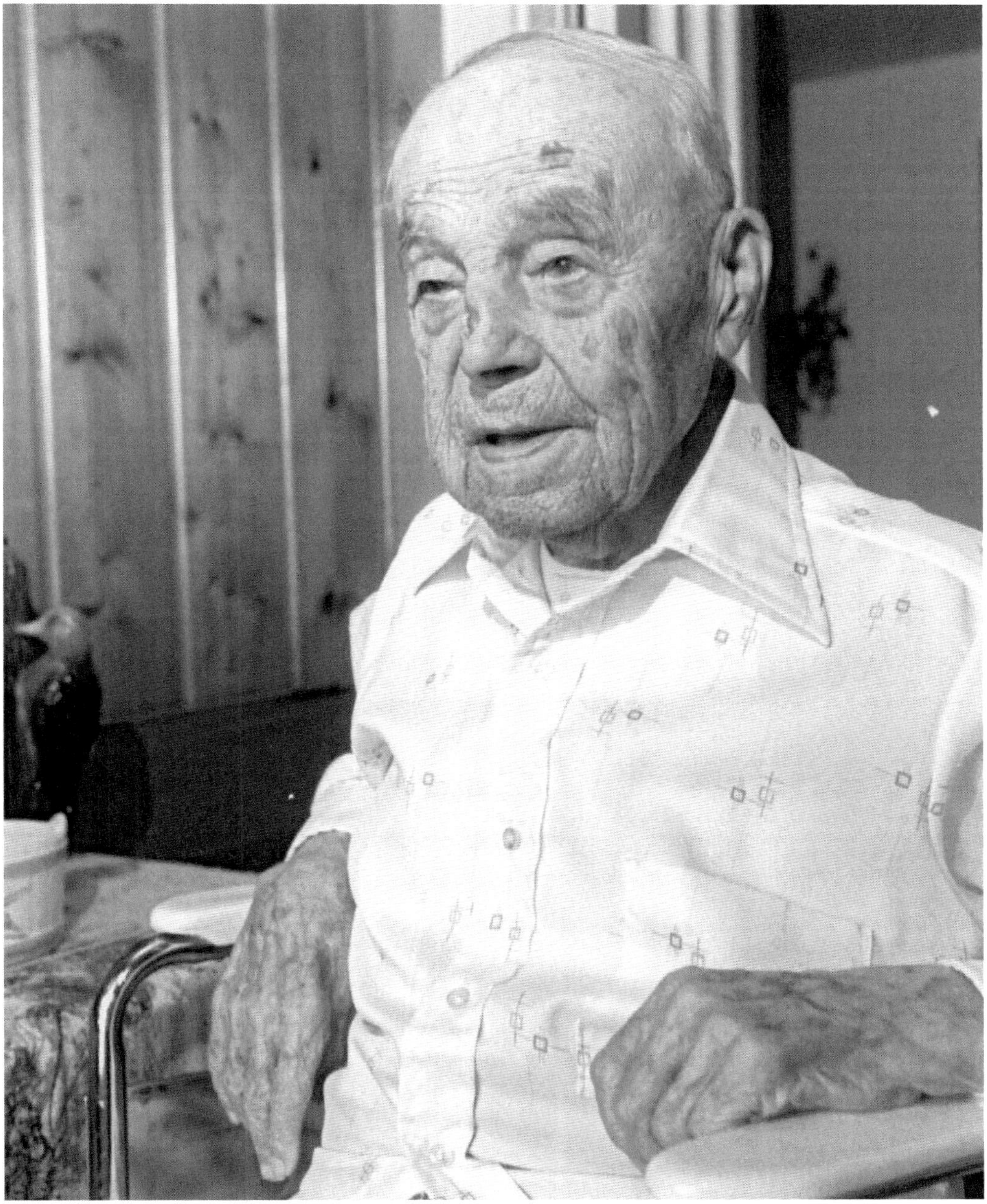

Joseph Emile St. Pierre
Although he grew up in Canada speaking both French and English, St. Pierre was very proud that his birthday was on the Fourth of July. Nicknamed "Sam" as a youth in Canada, St. Pierre kept the name when he came to Mount Clemens in 1927 and opened a cigar shop on Walnut Street. Sam's Cigar Store was one of several small cigar makers in Mount Clemens, and part of a larger cigar industry that flourished in the Detroit area in the late nineteenth and early twentieth centuries. St. Pierre retired from business in 1940, as the cigar industry was fading away in the area, but he remained in the Mount Clemens community and lived to celebrate his 100th birthday in 1983. (Courtesy of the *Macomb Daily*.)

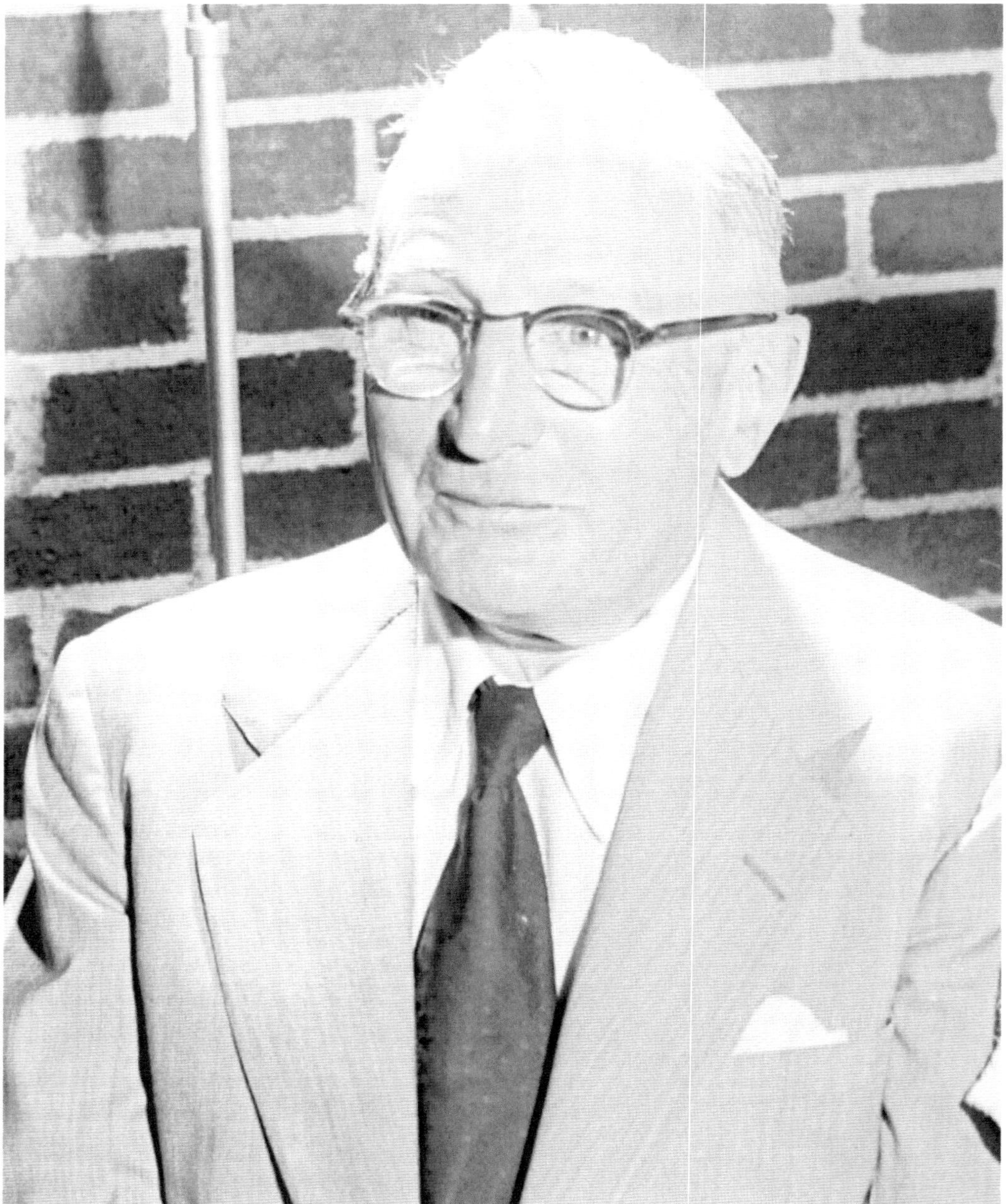

Bert Verne Nunneley

After graduation from the University of Michigan School of Law in 1903, Nunneley founded the Mount Clemens law firm that still bears his name today. In the 1940s, he was a principal participant in a landmark legal case when he represented the Mount Clemens Pottery Company in a class action lawsuit in which pottery employees alleged that they were not being paid in accordance with the Fair Labor Standards Act. So significant was the case that the United States Supreme Court heard it in 1946 and Nunneley represented the pottery company before the high court. The decision in what was popularly known as the "portal to portal pay case" became a milestone in American labor law history. (Courtesy of Mount Clemens Public Library.)

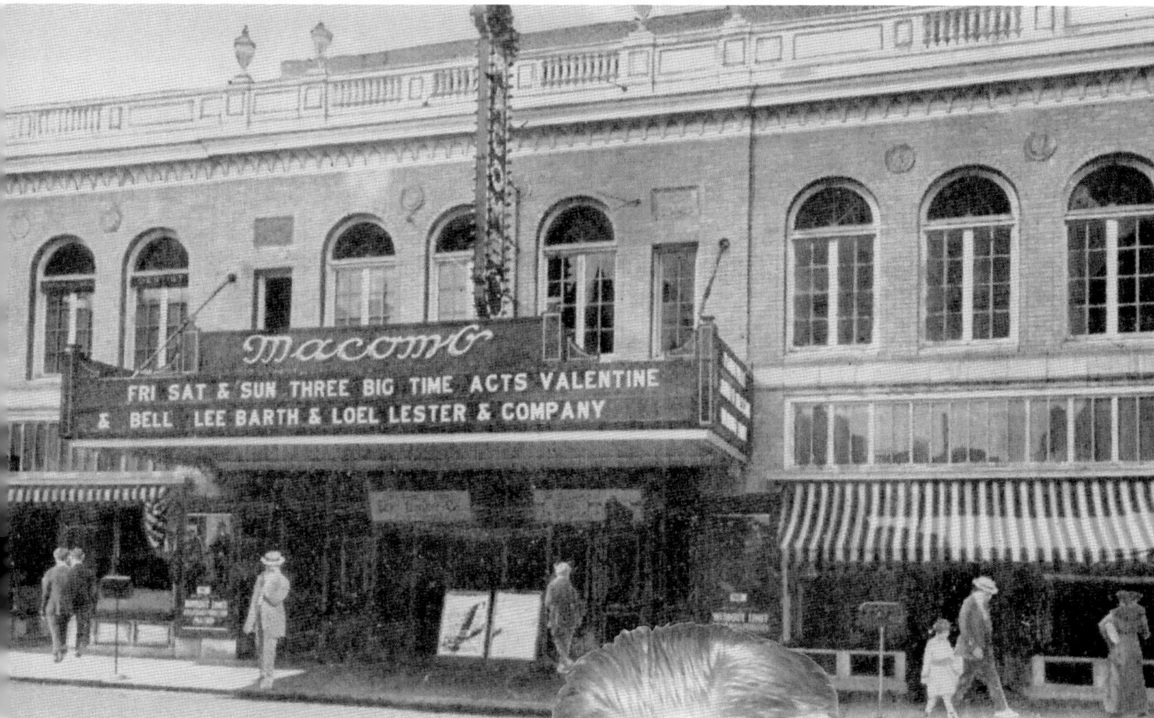

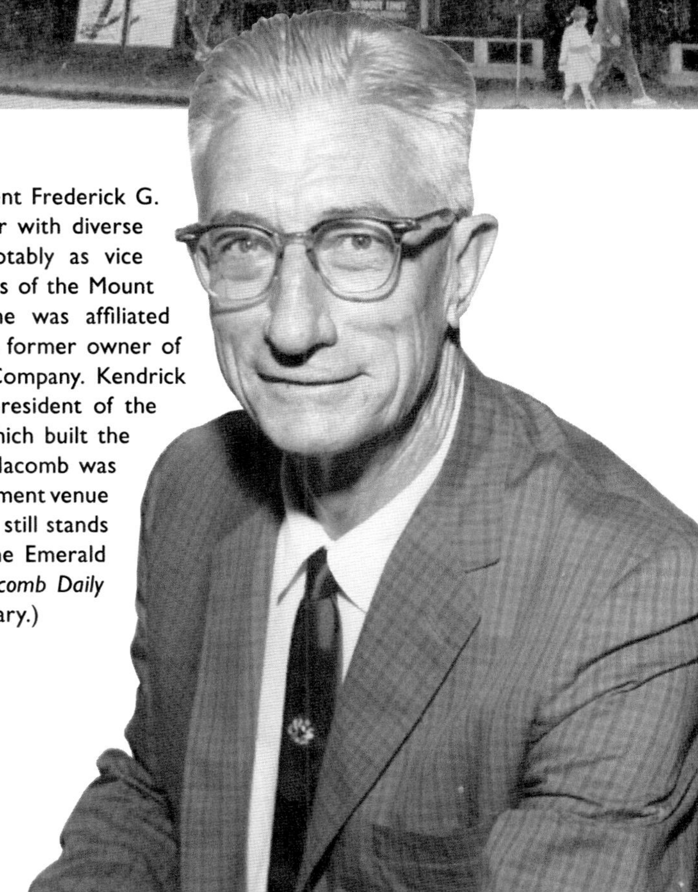

Frederick G. Kendrick

Lifelong Mount Clemens resident Frederick G. Kendrick was a business leader with diverse interests. He served most notably as vice president and director emeritus of the Mount Clemens Bank, with which he was affiliated for 34 years, and was also the former owner of the Kendrick & Ullrich Coal Company. Kendrick also succeeded his father as president of the Macomb Theater Company, which built the grand Macomb Theater. The Macomb was the Bath City's largest entertainment venue in its time; the historic building still stands today and is now known as the Emerald Theatre. (Courtesy of the *Macomb Daily* and Mount Clemens Public Library.)

Alan George Straight Sr.

In 1906, Straight came to Mount Clemens to work as a linotype operator and reporter for the *Daily Leader* newspaper. He left the newspaper for a career in public service when he became police chief of Mount Clemens in 1916 and attracted the notice of state and federal officials in 1919 when he presided over the sensational Stanley Brown murder investigation. From Mount Clemens, he went on to a distinguished career with the US Secret Service during which he was involved in the Lindbergh kidnapping investigation and served on the protection detail for Pres. Warren G. Harding. Tragically, Straight died of a self-inflicted gunshot wound at the height of his law enforcement career. He is shown here at far right, with other members of the *Leader* staff. (Courtesy of Macomb County Historical Society.)

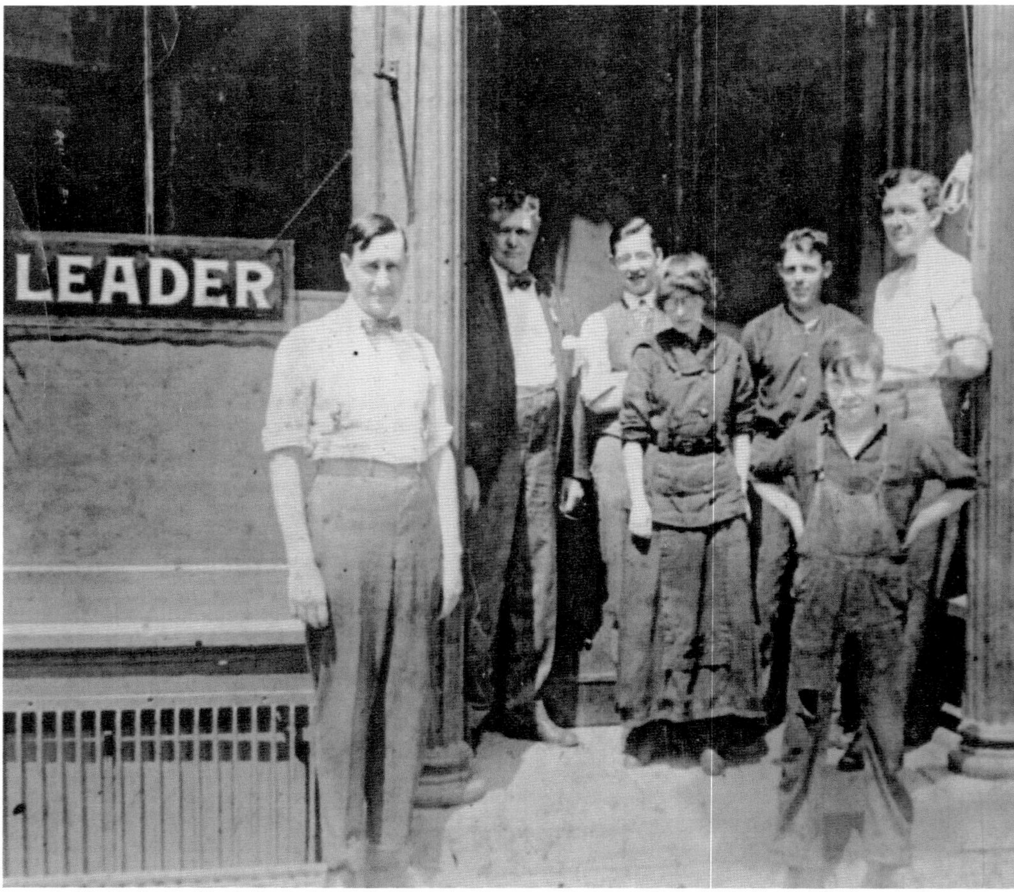

Merritt Langford Green (RIGHT)

The jewelry firm of M.L. Green and Son was founded in Mount Clemens in 1907 and was a fixture in the downtown business district for generations. Merritt Langford Green, a watchmaker born in Hespeler, Ontario, in 1859, operated the business until his sons Harold and Stuart were ready to carry on the family enterprise. A third generation was represented in the company when grandson Donald W. Green joined the firm after his grandfather's retirement. Patriarch and founder Merritt L. Green is shown here in his shop in 1952 with son Stuart Green, grandson Donald W. Green, and great-grandson Gregory Green. (Courtesy of the *Macomb Daily*.)

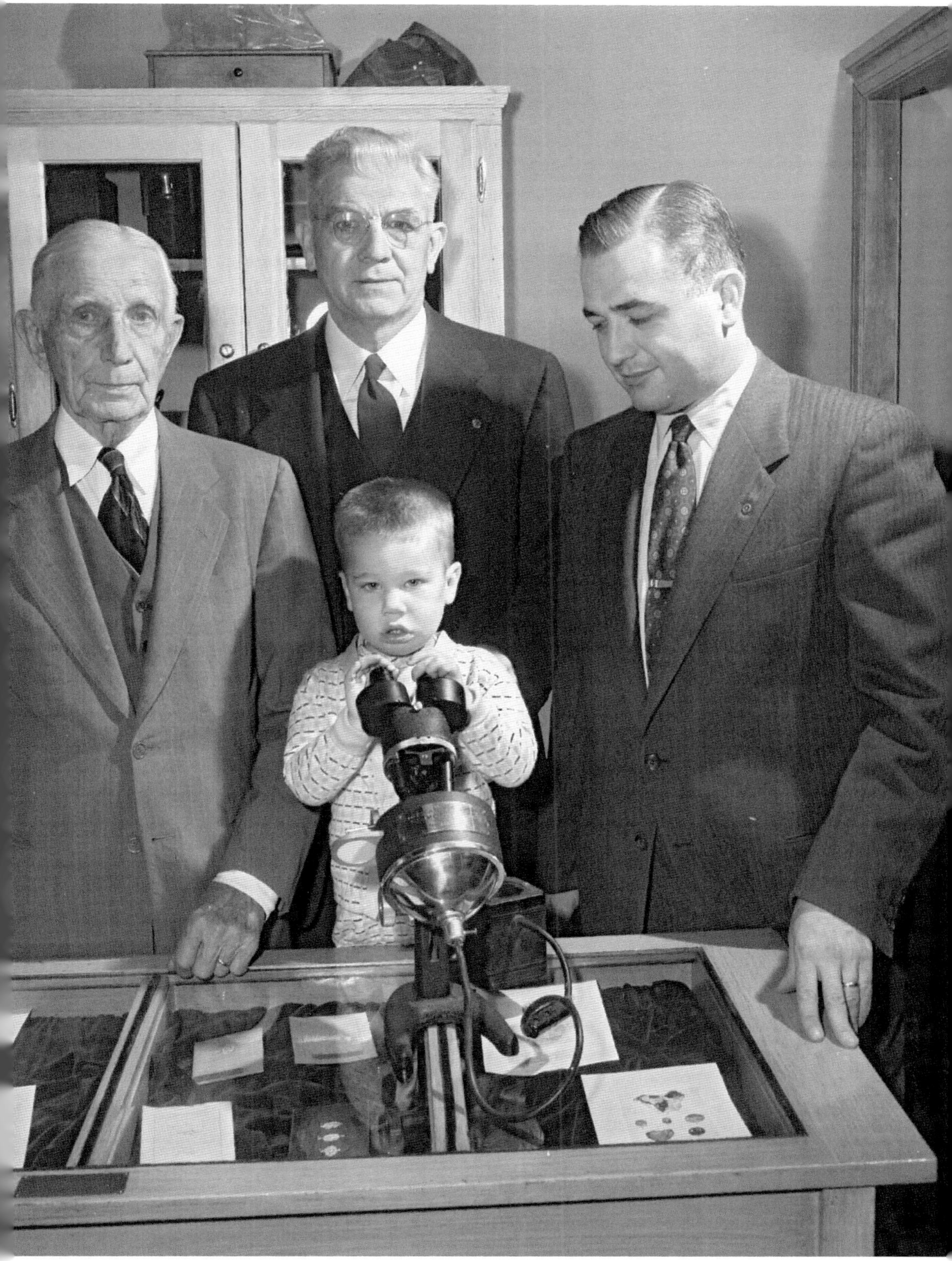

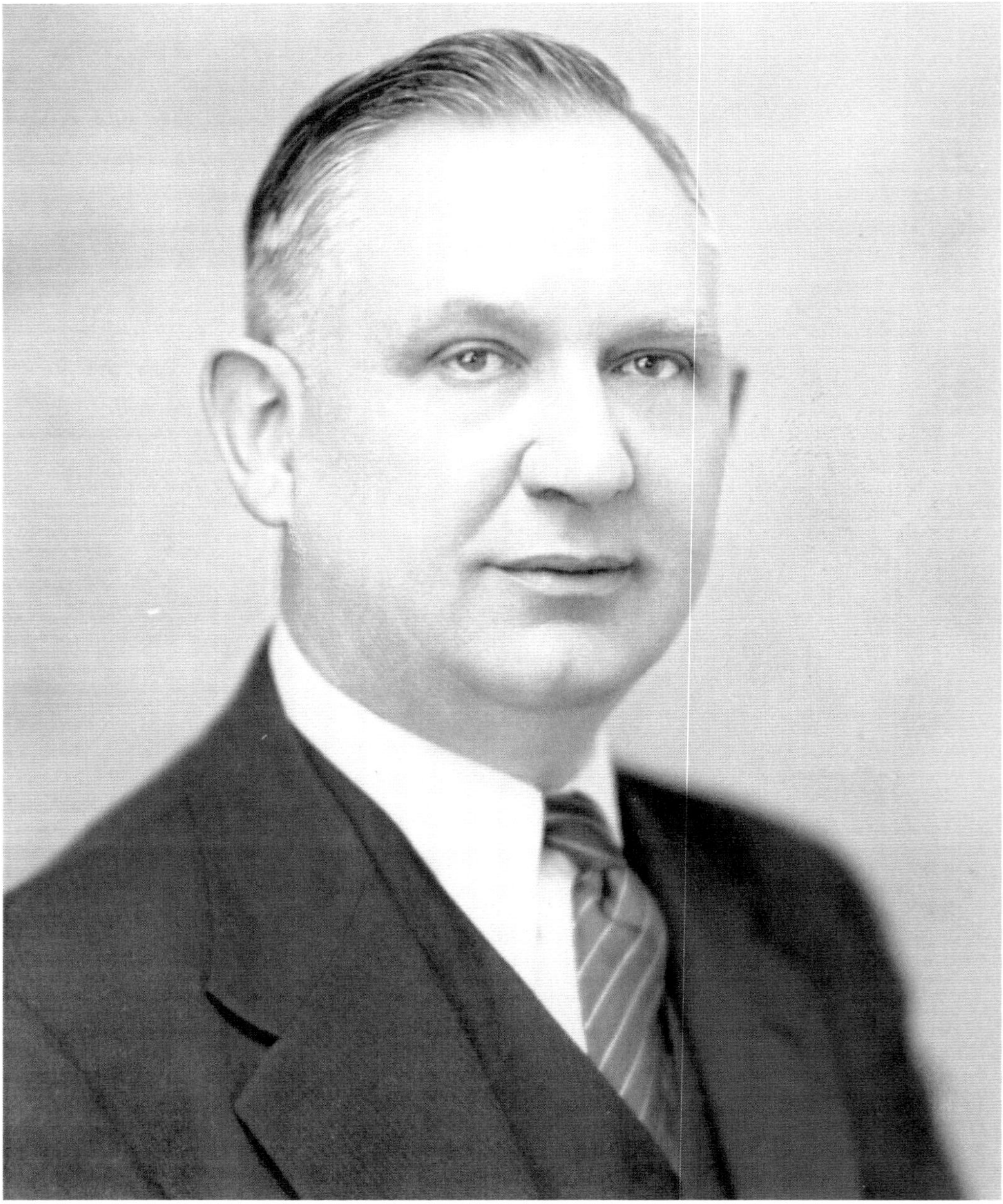

Donald Robert Westendorf

Born in Mount Clemens in 1888, Westendorf was the son of former Mount Clemens mayor and businessman John H. Westendorf, and followed in his father's footsteps in business and civic affairs. Westendorf graduated from Ferris State University as a pharmacist in 1910 and purchased his father's Weather Flag Drug Store, which he operated for over 40 years. He served the city as mayor during the Great Depression and World War II and was re-elected four times. Westendorf's greatest legacy as mayor was his advocacy for desperately needed flood relief measures that eventually led to the construction of the Clinton River Spillway in the 1950s. (Courtesy of Macomb County Historical Society.)

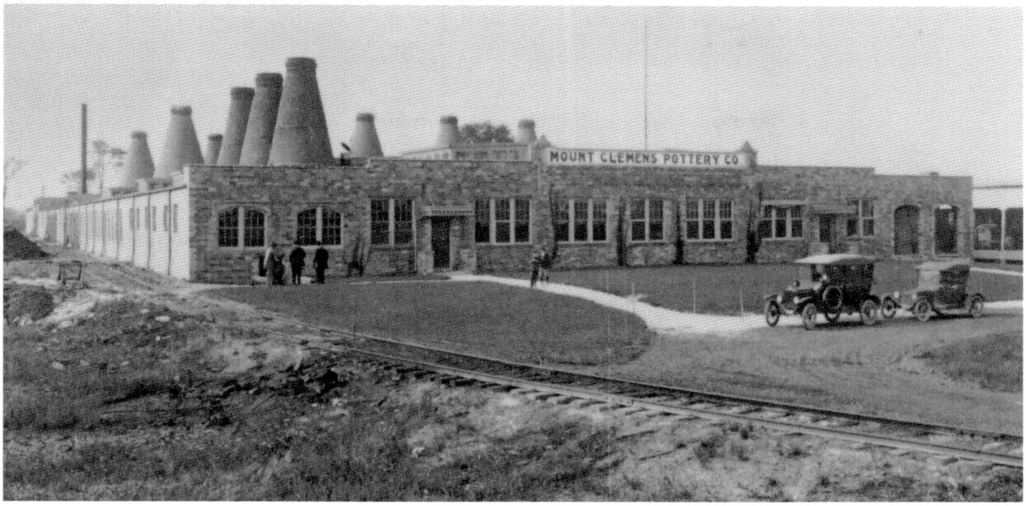

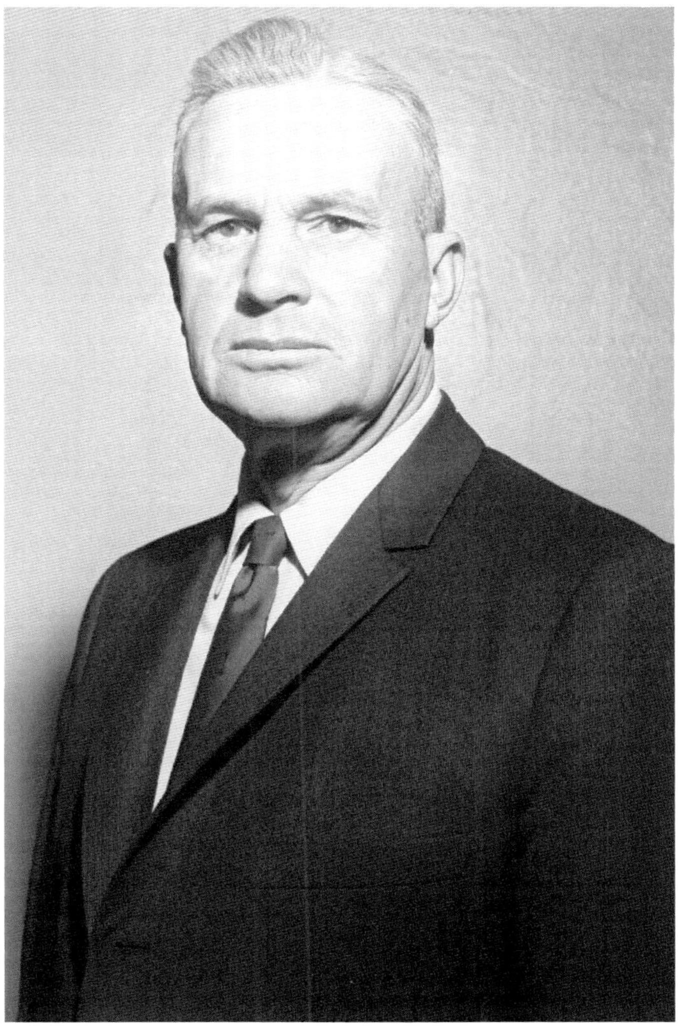

Charles Edward Doll Jr. Doll spent his entire professional career at the Mount Clemens Pottery Company and eventually rose to the position of general manager of the plant his father had come to Mount Clemens to build in 1914. While his father had learned the pottery trade through on-the-job experience, Doll earned a degree in ceramics engineering before joining his father in the factory and putting it on a modernization course that kept it competitive while other pottery plants were failing. At one point under Doll's management, the Mount Clemens Pottery Company was the largest semi-vitreous dinnerware producer in North America. (Courtesy of the *Macomb Daily* and Mount Clemens Public Library.)

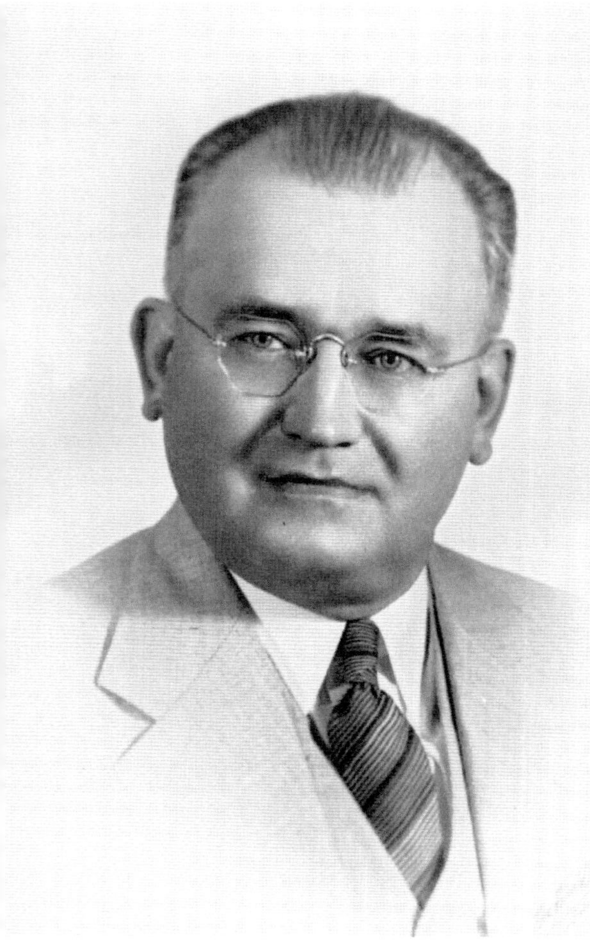

Austin William Heine

City commissioner and prominent physician Austin William Heine made his greatest contributions to his hometown quietly, and without fanfare. Heine provided cots in the rear of his office and money for meals to youths who were having trouble at home and might have otherwise lived on the streets. He was remembered as having never turned away a youngster in need. (Courtesy of Mount Clemens Public Library.)

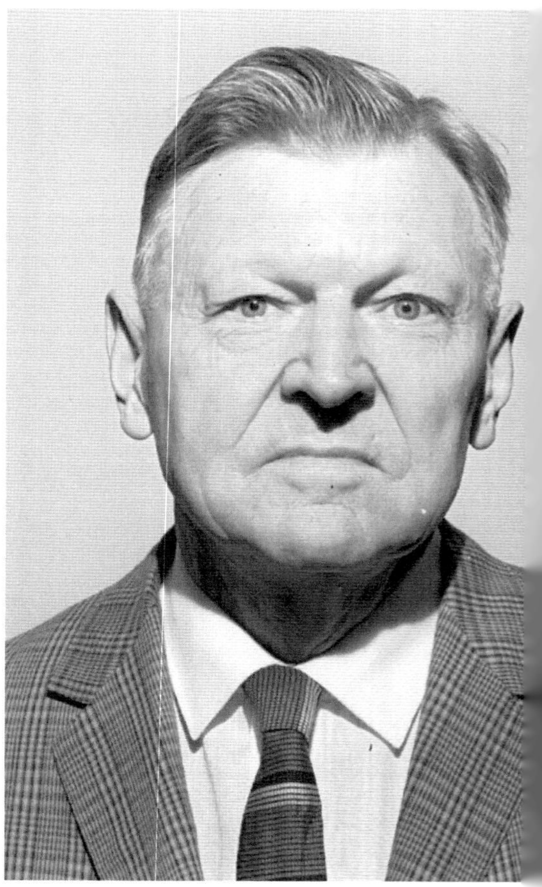

John Frank Breitmeyer Sr.

Besides its mineral baths, Mount Clemens was known nationwide for its floral industry, and Breitmeyer was a leader in the business. The lifelong Mount Clemens resident joined his father and brothers in the Breitmeyer Floral Company, which was established in 1900, and operated it until it was sold in the early 1990s. (Courtesy of the *Macomb Daily*.)

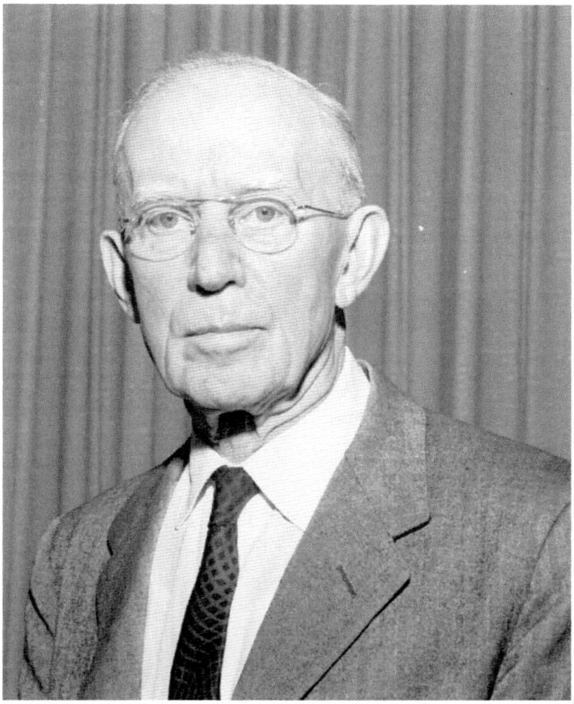

Duncan Burton Hubbard

At the time of his death in 1971, Hubbard was Michigan's oldest mortician and was president of the funeral home that had borne his family name since 1875. He was the first person of his profession in the state to serve simultaneously as a county coroner, and was elected to one term as mayor of Mount Clemens in 1912. (Courtesy of the *Macomb Daily.*)

Samuel Malbin

Malbin came to Mount Clemens in 1914 and joined his father and brothers in the family furniture business in 1923. Elected president of the Mount Clemens Board of Education, Mount Clemens Board of Commerce, and the local Rotary Club, the prominent businessman was also a member of the board of directors of St. Joseph Mercy Hospital and the local Salvation Army. (Courtesy of the *Macomb Daily.*)

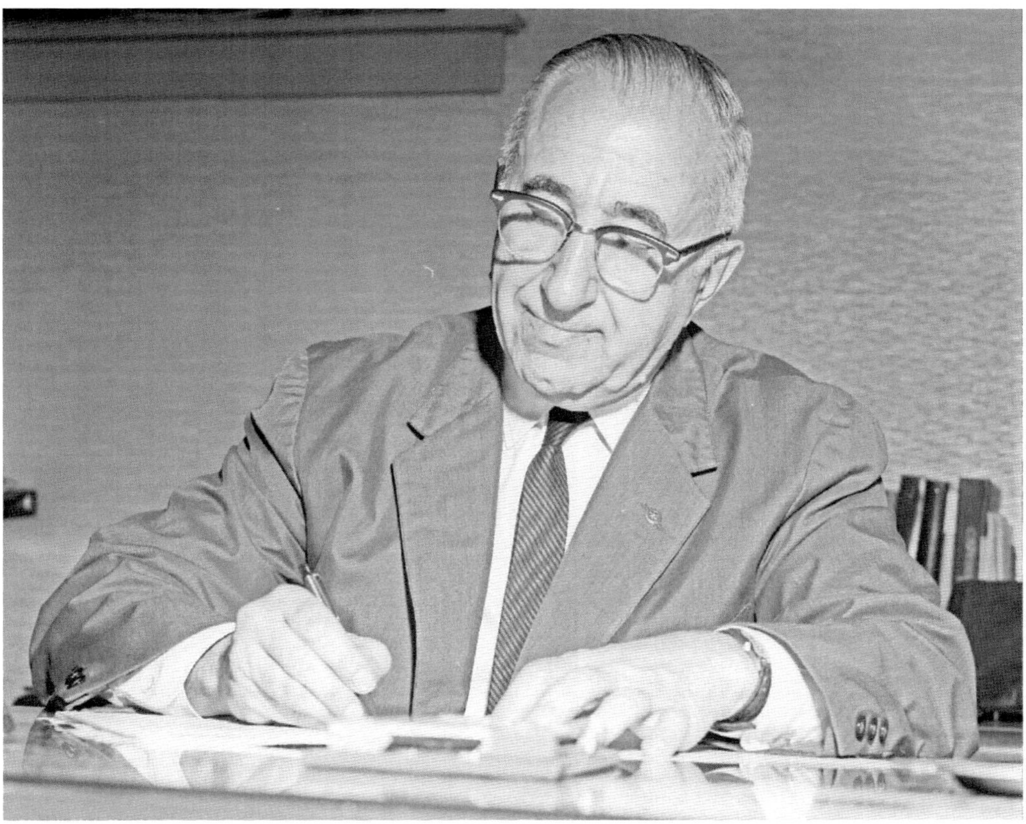

George William Priehs

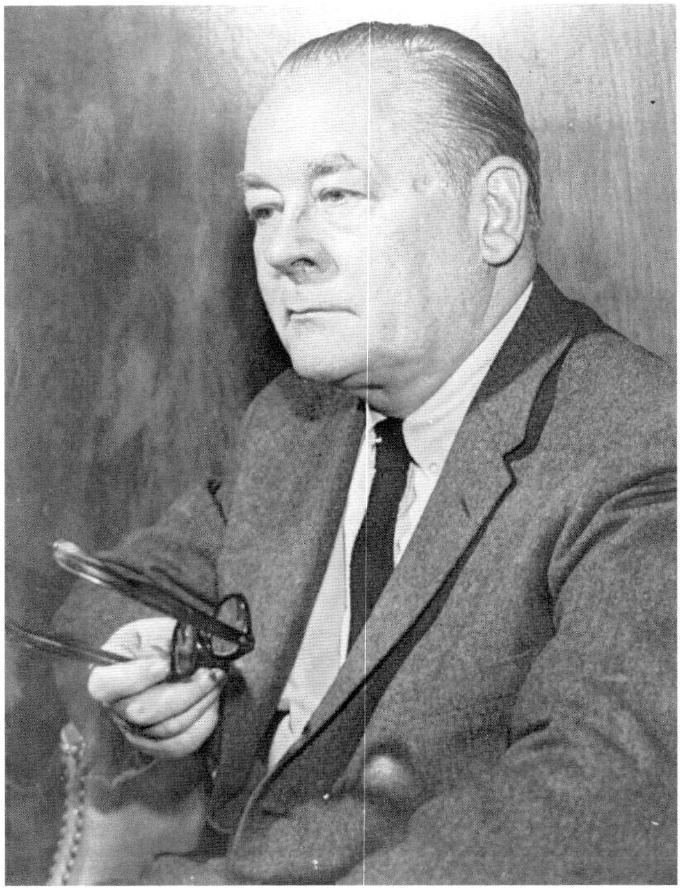

Although he spent much of his adult life running the department store that his family had founded, flamboyant Mount Clemens native George William Priehs had a passion for literature and theater. After parts in high school drama productions ignited his interest in the stage, Priehs went on to the University of Michigan, where he defied tradition when he was named to the prestigious Comedy Club while still a freshman. Moving on to New York to try his luck on Broadway, Priehs worked at Macy's Department Store and as a newspaper reporter to make ends meet. He returned to Mount Clemens in 1932 to run Priehs Department Store after the death of his father, and continued to operate it—along with several other businesses—until the store closed in 1982. (Courtesy of the *Macomb Daily.*)

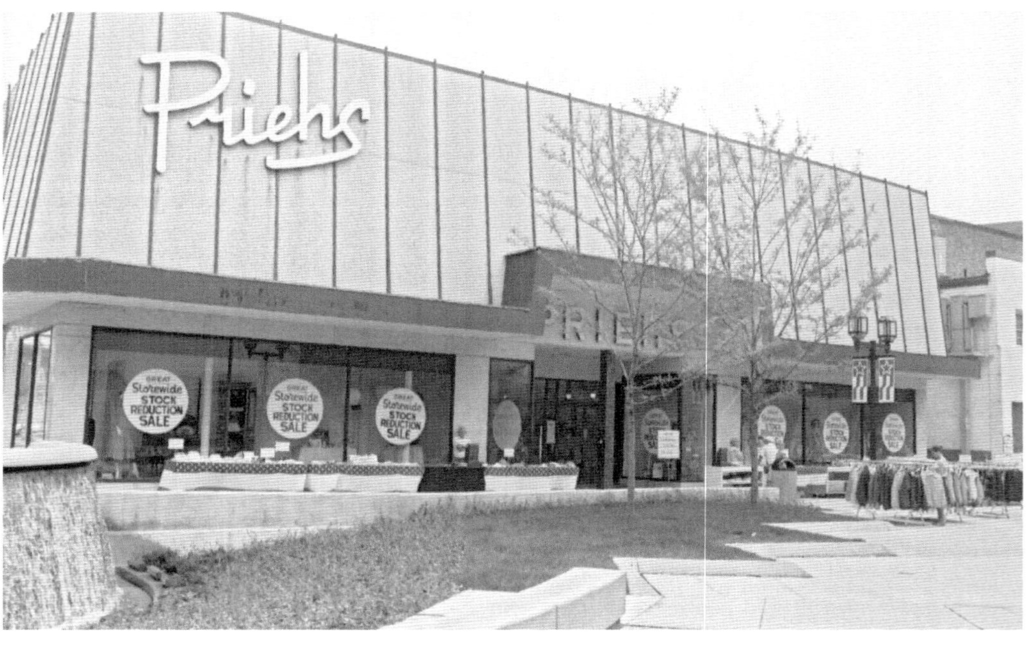

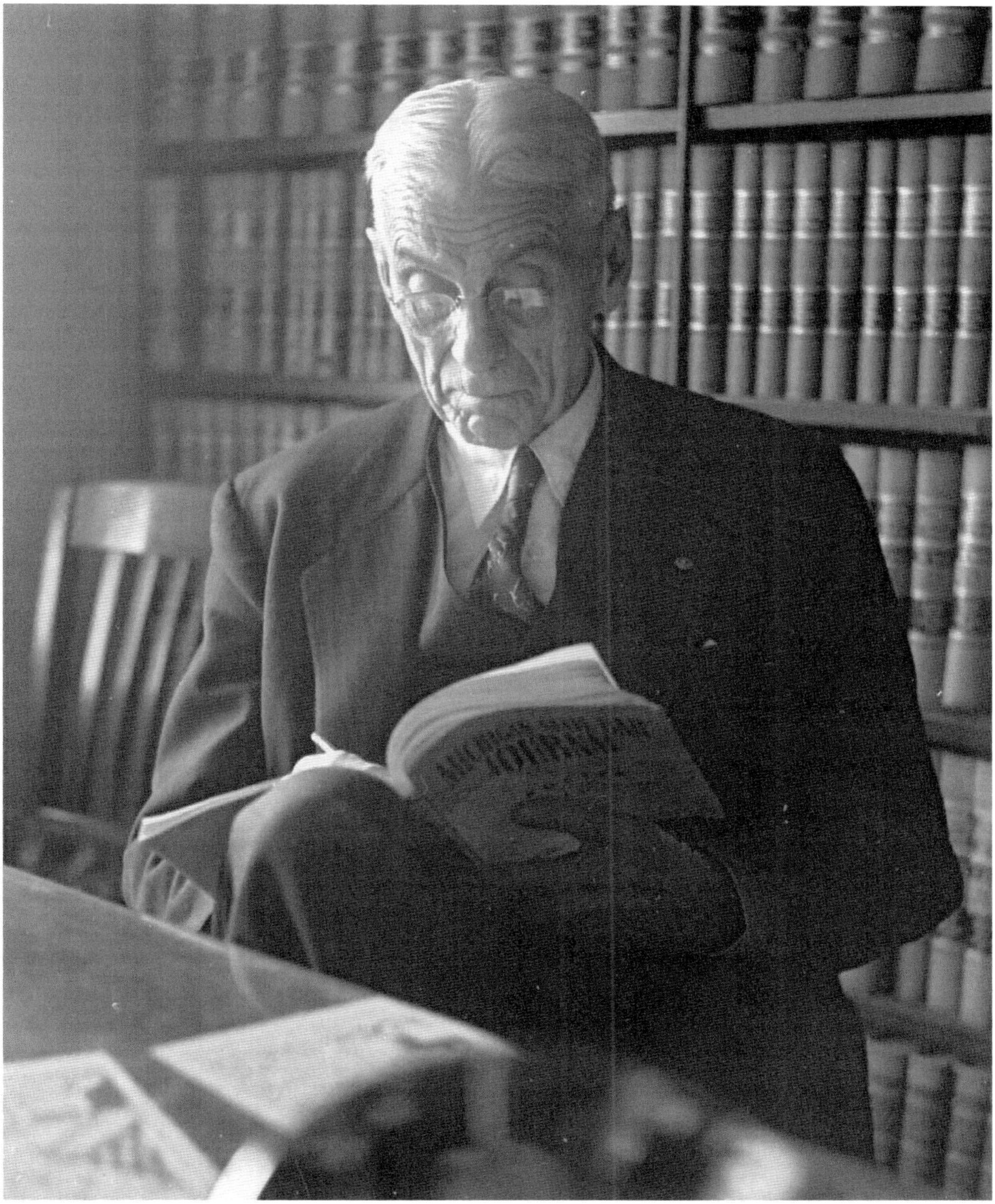

Neil Edwin Reid

The second distinguished jurist from Mount Clemens to sit on Michigan's high court, Reid was sworn in as a justice of the Michigan Supreme Court in 1944. He won election by using a penny postcard campaign to rally his supporters and unseated an incumbent justice, a feat never before accomplished in Michigan at that time. Reid was known as a scrupulously fair judge who rendered stiff sentences for violent offenders, but took pride in using probation as a corrective measure whenever possible in other cases. In private life, he was especially devoted to the Boy Scouts, often hosting campouts for local troops at his summer home on Drummond Island. Among all of his many accolades, Reid was especially proud to hold scouting's highest honor, the Silver Beaver Award. (Courtesy of the *Macomb Daily.*)

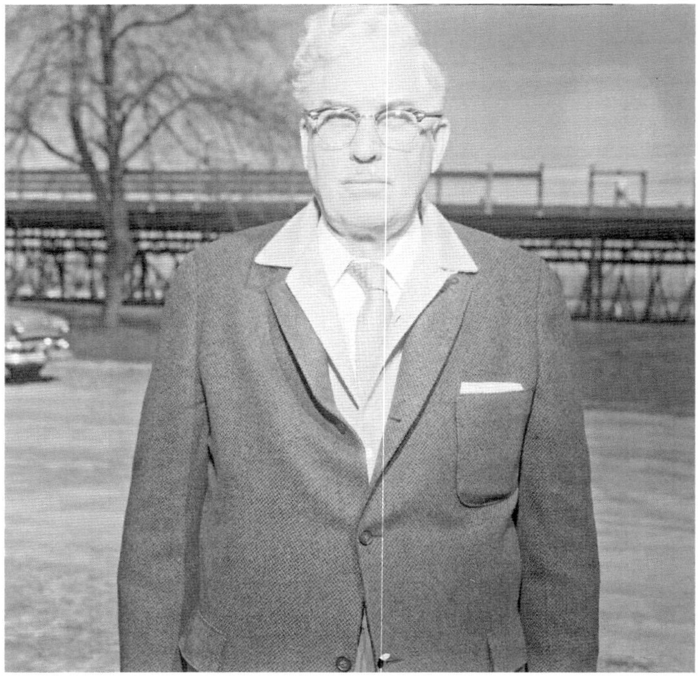

Clayton Thomas Stubbs
Stubbs earned his medical degree from Detroit College of Medicine in 1919 and had a practice in Highland Park, but he and his wife resided in Mount Clemens in her stately family home, known as Whitehall. Both Stubbs and his wife, Ruth, were nature and sports enthusiasts, and in 1951 they founded the Mount Clemens Race Track on property northeast of town that they had formerly acquired as a pheasant hunting preserve. The track featured MMSRA stock car races and was a popular entertainment venue in the area for 35 years. (Courtesy of the *Macomb Daily.*)

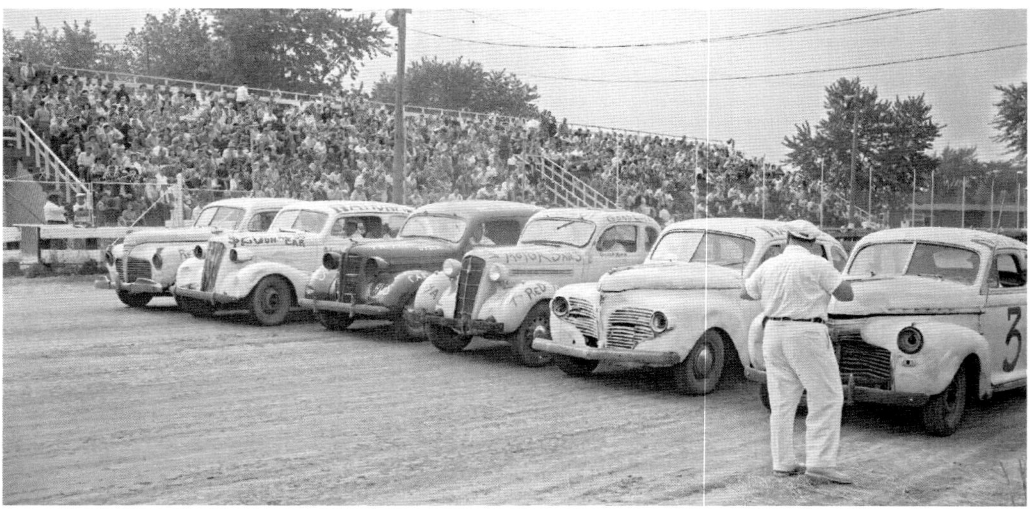

John Harold Nunneley (RIGHT)
In 1928, Mount Clemens High School and University of Michigan graduate John Harold Nunneley worked as a $15-a-week associate in his father's law firm, launching a distinguished career that would span nearly half a century. After several years in general practice, he was elected in 1942 to represent Macomb County on the board of the Huron-Clinton Metropolitan Authority, and twice served as chairman of the organization that developed a five-county park system. As a partner in the prestigious Detroit law firm of Miller, Canfield, Paddock and Stone, Nunneley became an expert in municipal financing and bond administration, and worked on notable state projects such as the Mackinac Bridge and the Detroit expressway system. When he retired in 1971, he was nationally recognized for his expertise in municipal funding. (Courtesy of John F. MacArthur.)

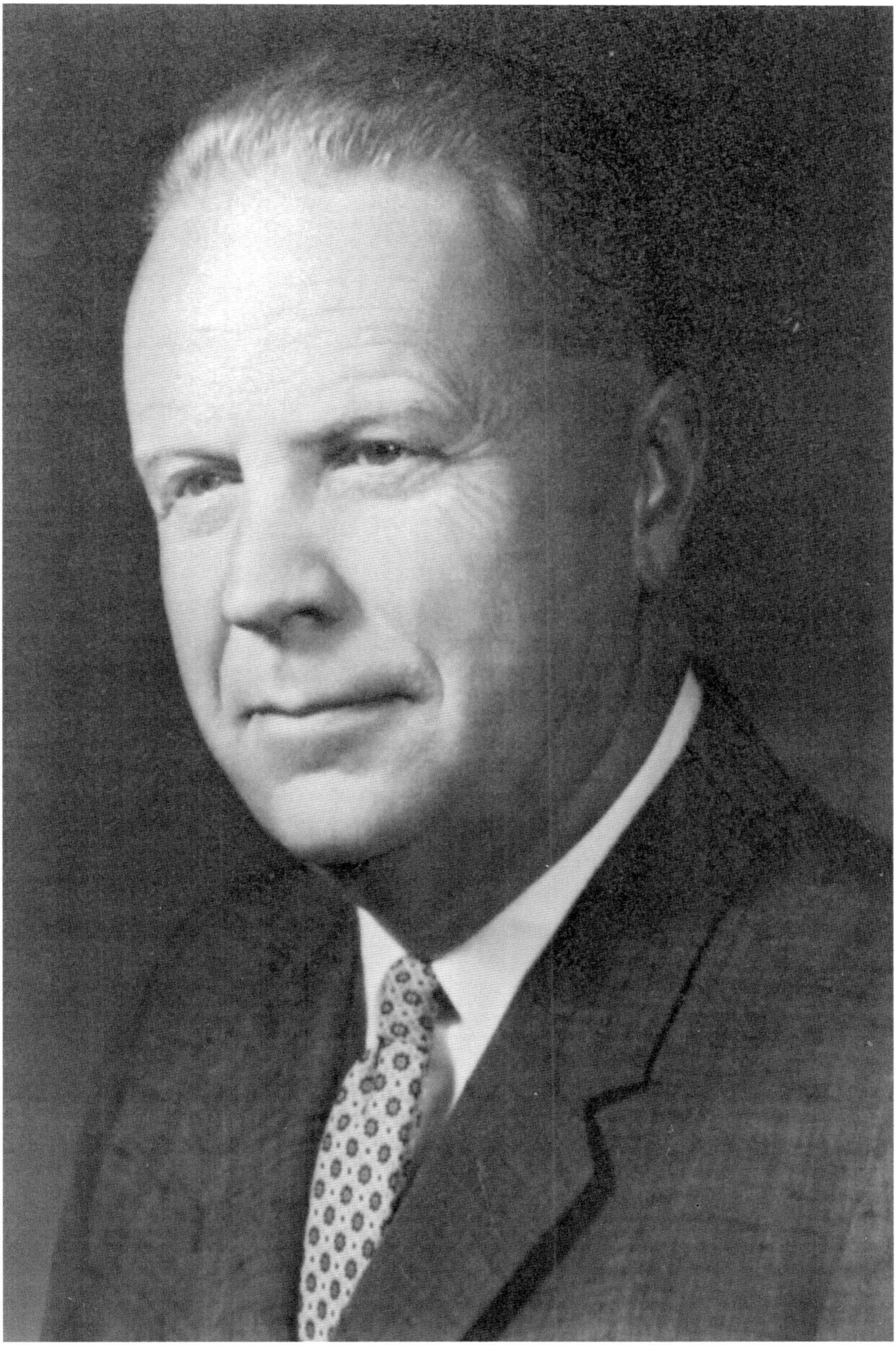

Campbell A. Ward

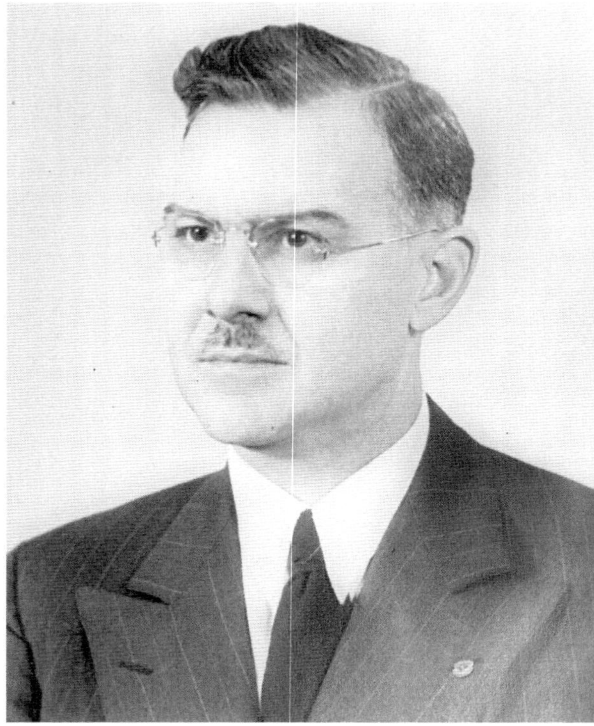

Osteopathic physician Campbell A. Ward established his medical practice in Mount Clemens in 1928, and in 1945 helped to found Mount Clemens General Hospital in this former apartment building. Ward served as chairman of the board, chief of staff, and chairman of the building committee of the hospital, which broke ground for a modern new facility on Harrington Road in 1955. He was also part of a committee that established an osteopathic school of medicine at Michigan State University in 1970. In his personal life, Ward was deeply committed to agencies that benefited children, and served as a board member of the Children Aid and Family Service of Mount Clemens and as chairman of the Macomb County Boy Scouts. (Courtesy of the *Macomb Daily*.)

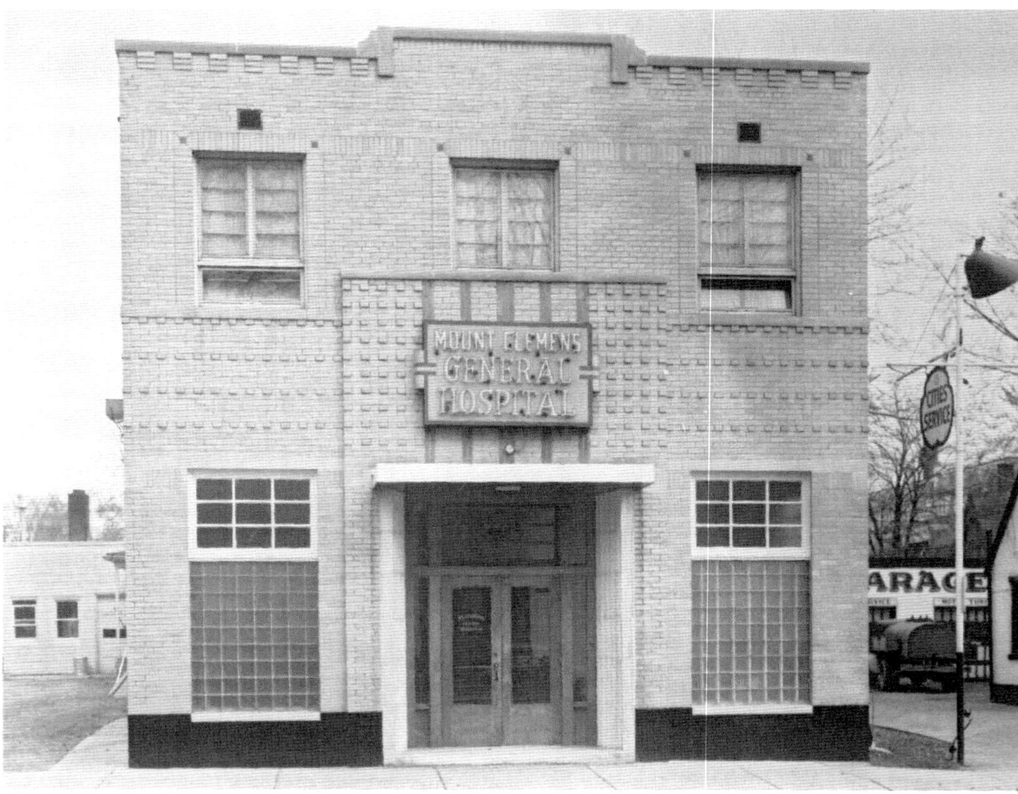

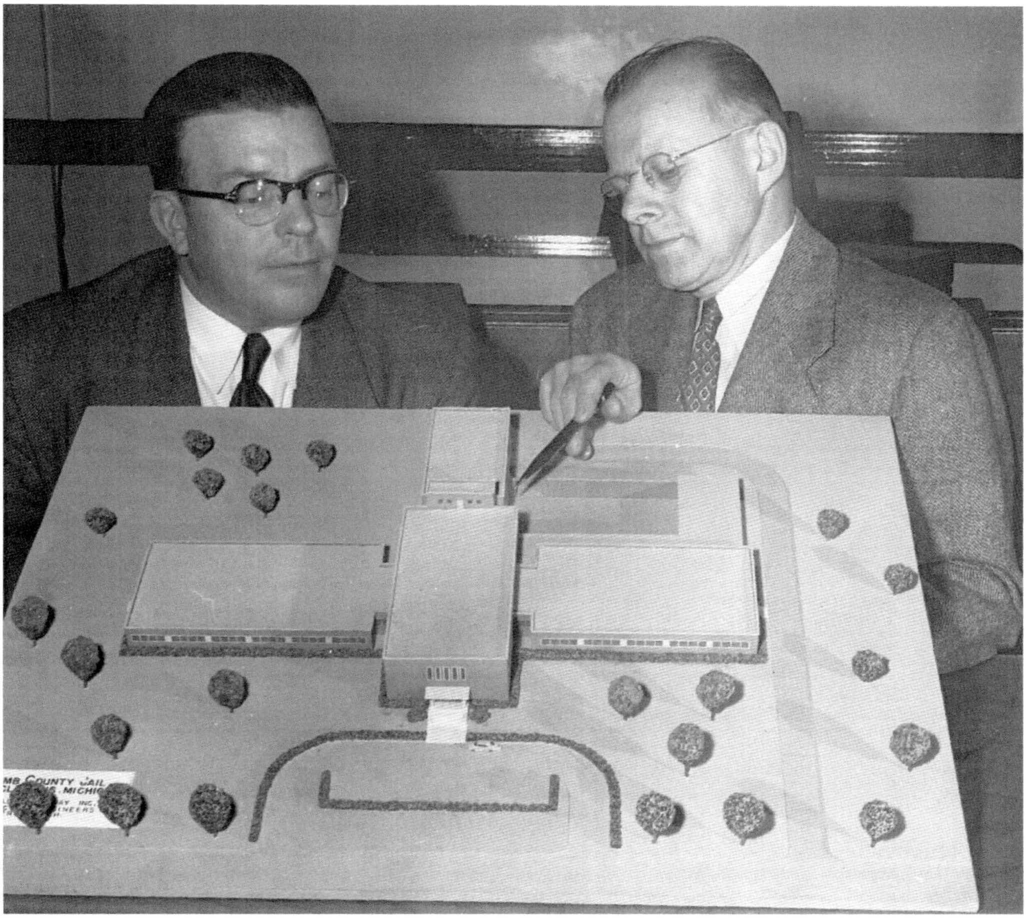

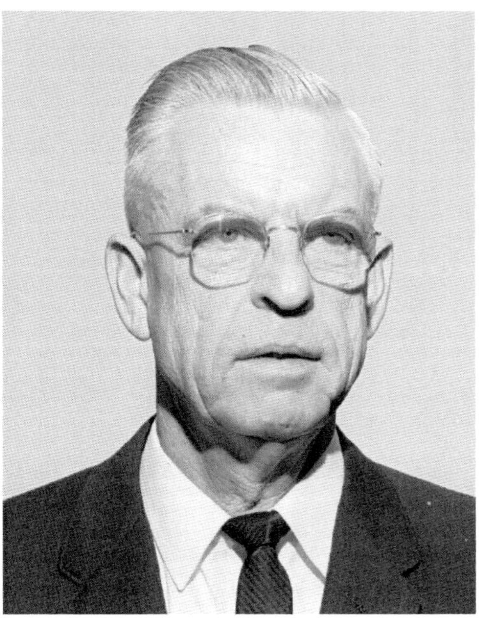

Sherwood J. Bennett

Long before the position of county executive was established, Bennett served as the de facto manager of Macomb County government during his many years as controller. He is shown here, at right, with Sheriff Harley Ensign, reviewing a model of the new county jail in 1951. (Courtesy of the *Macomb Daily.*)

Lawrence Frederic Schott

Mount Clemens native Lawrence Frederic Schott was a member of one of the community's pioneer families and was a longtime business leader in the Bath City. Schott was president of the Hubarth and Schott Lumber Company, which his father founded in 1892, and also served as president of the Mount Clemens Savings Bank for 20 years. (Courtesy of the *Macomb Daily.*)

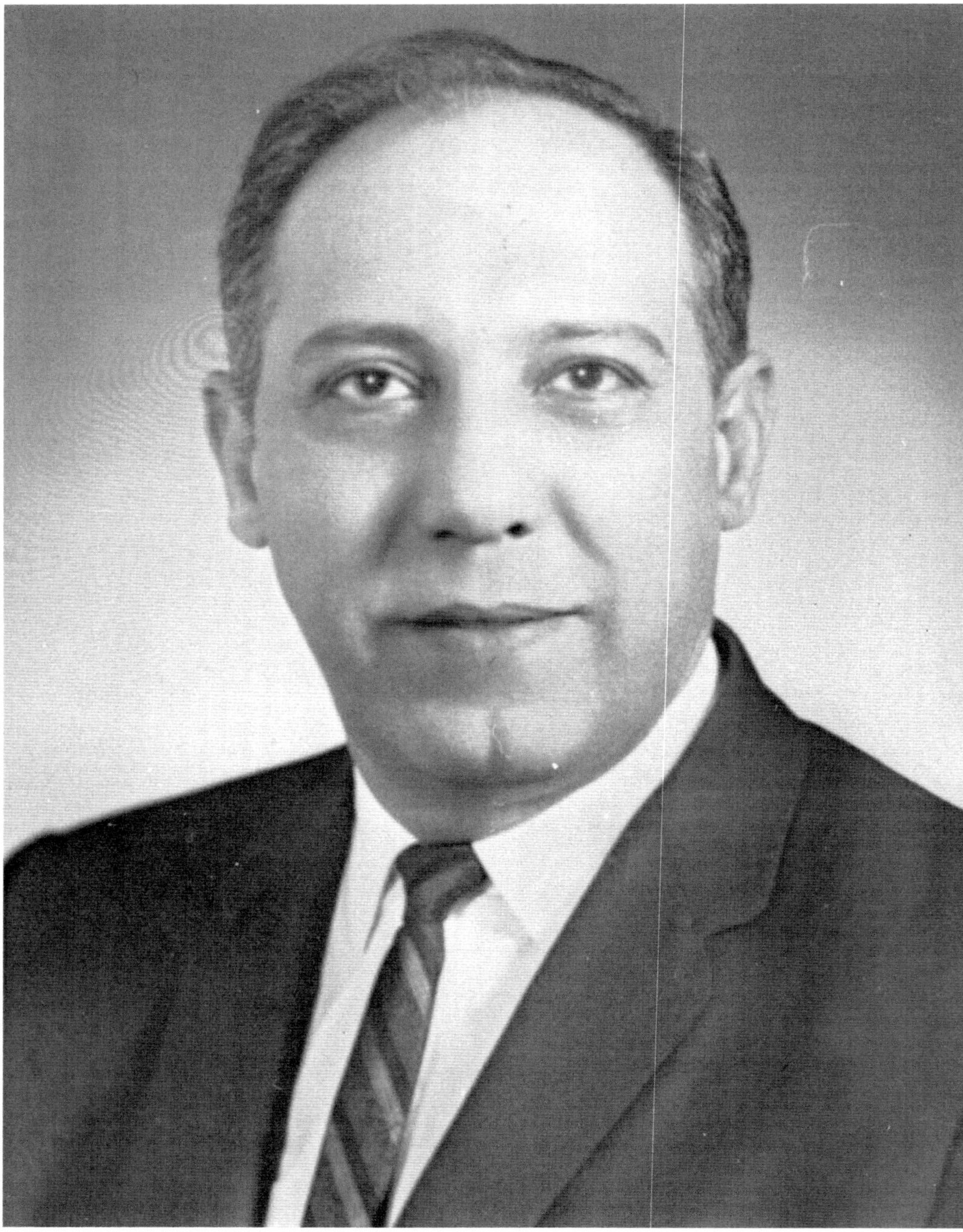

George Caram Steeh II

The first Democrat ever elected to the state house from his Macomb County district, Mount Clemens High School and University of Michigan graduate George Caram Steeh II served one term in the Michigan House of Representatives before being elected three times to the Michigan Senate. The US Navy veteran became a judge in Michigan's 41-B District Court in 1980, and upon retirement from the bench has served as an interim judge in Macomb County Circuit Court, and as a mediator. He is the father of federal district court judge George Caram Steeh III. (Courtesy of the *Macomb Daily*.)

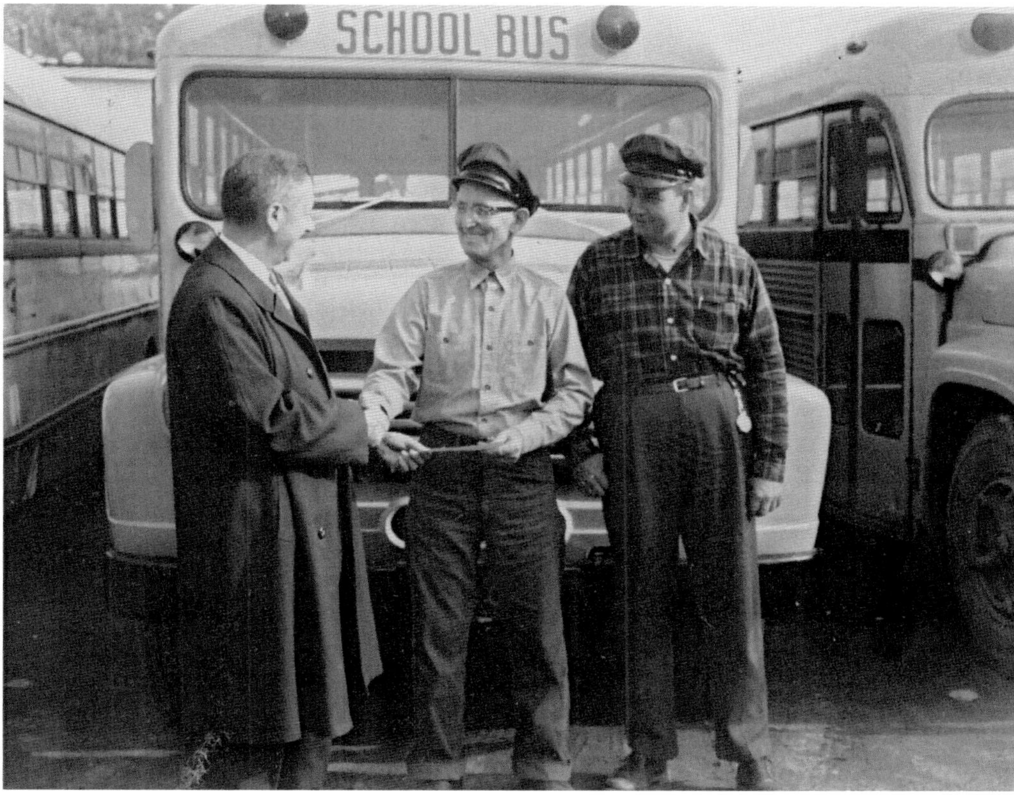

Angelo Fisher

Thousands of Mount Clemens school children rode to classes each day on buses operated by Angelo Fisher's Tower Bus Company. Fisher, a native of Greece, began his business career in Mount Clemens in 1935 when he opened a chain of hamburger stands called Fisher's Tower; he launched the Tower Taxi and Bus Service 10 years later. In addition to offering charter services, Tower Bus provided student transportation for Mount Clemens Community Schools for many years. Deeply involved in civic affairs, Fisher was a founder and first president of the Mount Clemens YMCA and was also a longtime member of the Mount Clemens Fire Department and the city's Zoning Board of Appeals. He is shown (above) at left, with bus drivers Arthur Conklin and Charles Sayers. (Courtesy of the *Macomb Daily*.)

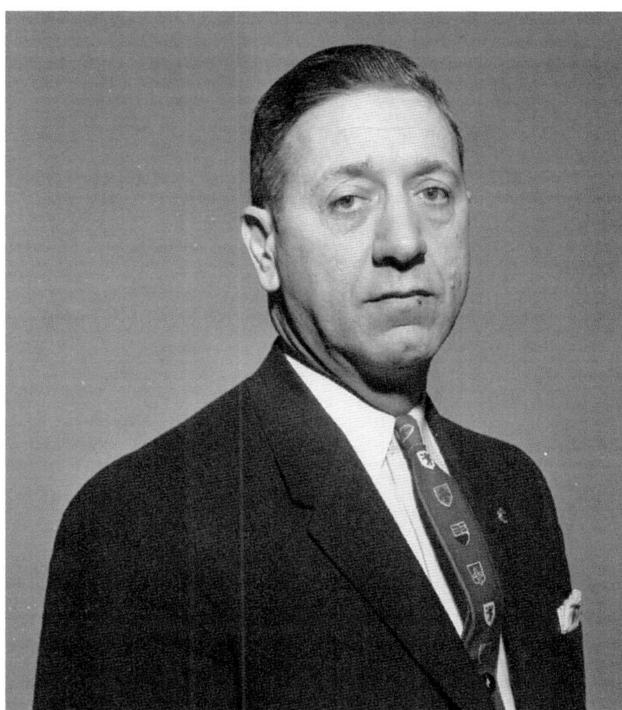

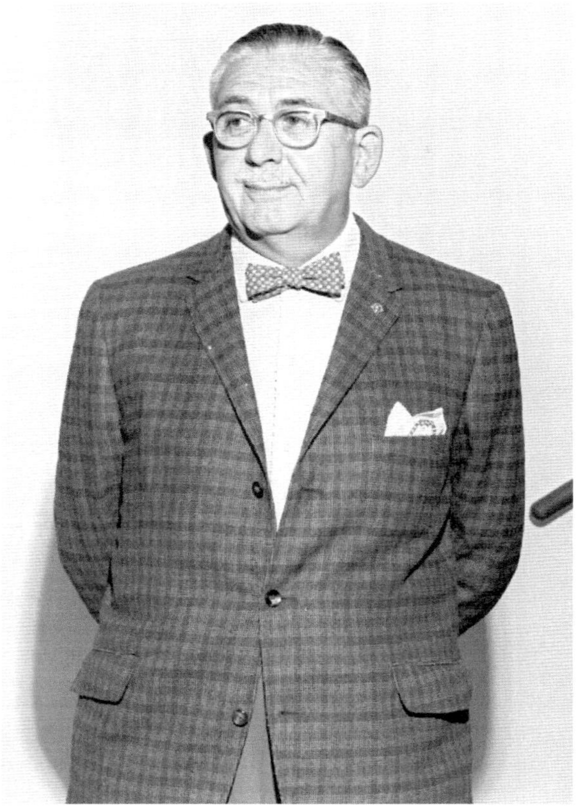

Joseph Nathan Scher

Known to his patients simply as "Doctor Joe," Scher spent his entire medical career in Mount Clemens as a general practitioner with a special interest in obstetrics and pediatrics. Dr. Scher was team physician for Mount Clemens High School's athletics program for 33 years, and he delivered more than 5,000 babies during his active practice. (Courtesy of the *Macomb Daily*.)

John George Roskopp

A member of a family with a tradition of public service, Roskopp earned his law degree from the University of Detroit Law School after serving in the Army during World War II. Appointed to the Macomb County Circuit Court bench in 1980, he is shown here (left) being sworn in to office by circuit judge George R. Deneweth. (Courtesy of the *Macomb Daily*.)

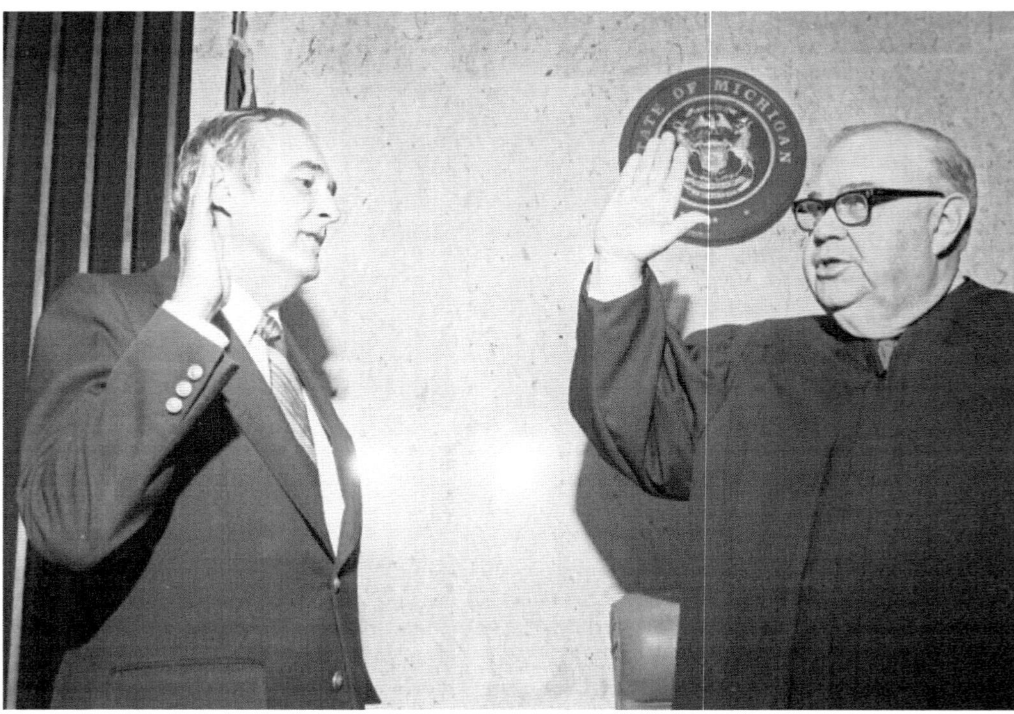

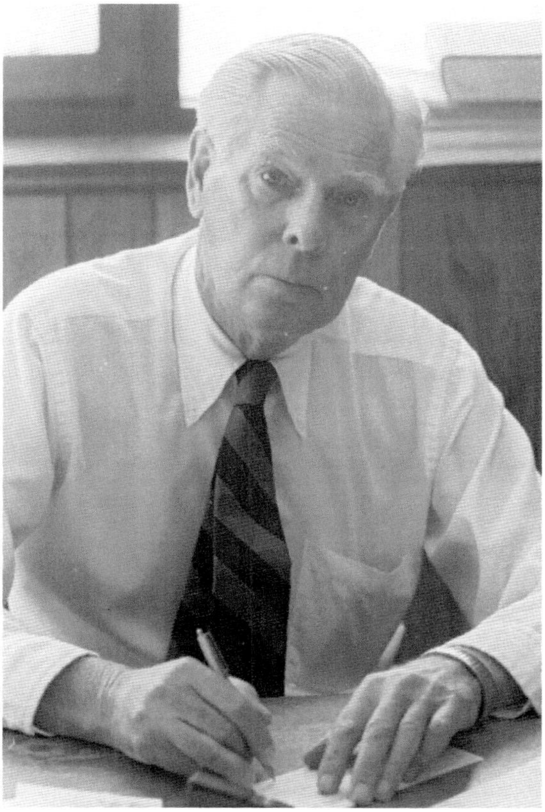

Frederic C. Weiss

After earning a degree from Dartmouth College in 1936, Weiss came to Mount Clemens to join his father in operating a rose greenhouse on the banks of the Clinton River. Under Weiss's management, Mount Clemens Rose Gardens grew to be the 12th largest rose-growing firm in the nation, shipping more than a million roses to florists around the Midwest. Weiss was actively involved in civic affairs and served on the board of Mount Clemens General Hospital. In private life, the former college swimming star enjoyed sailing and canoeing. He is shown below canoeing on the Clinton River with his son, Paul Weiss, in 1960. (Courtesy of the *Macomb Daily*.)

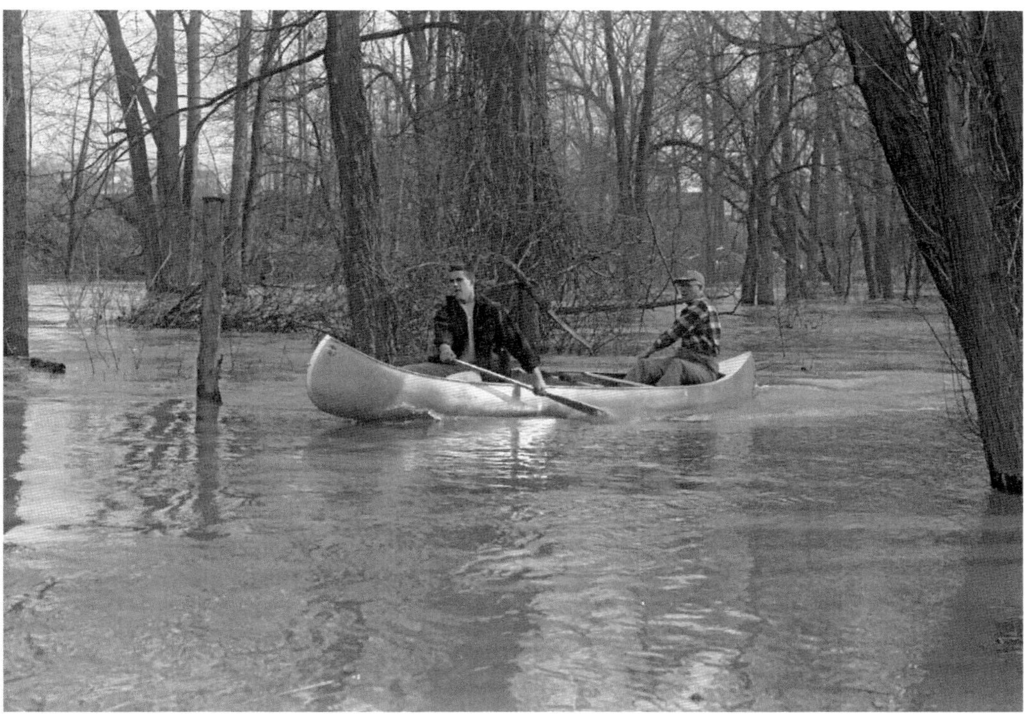

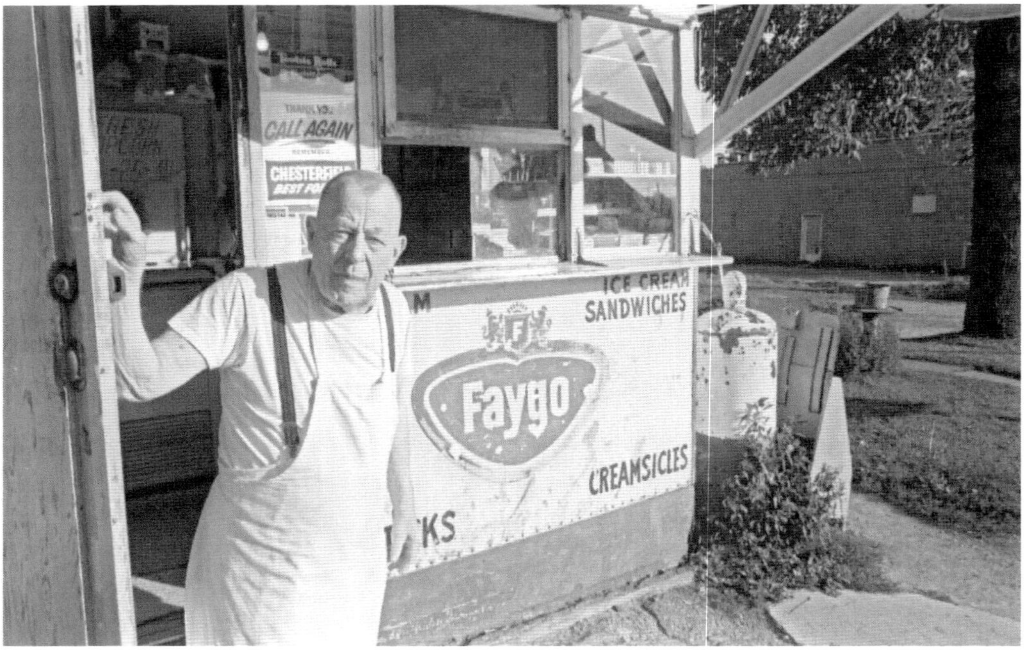

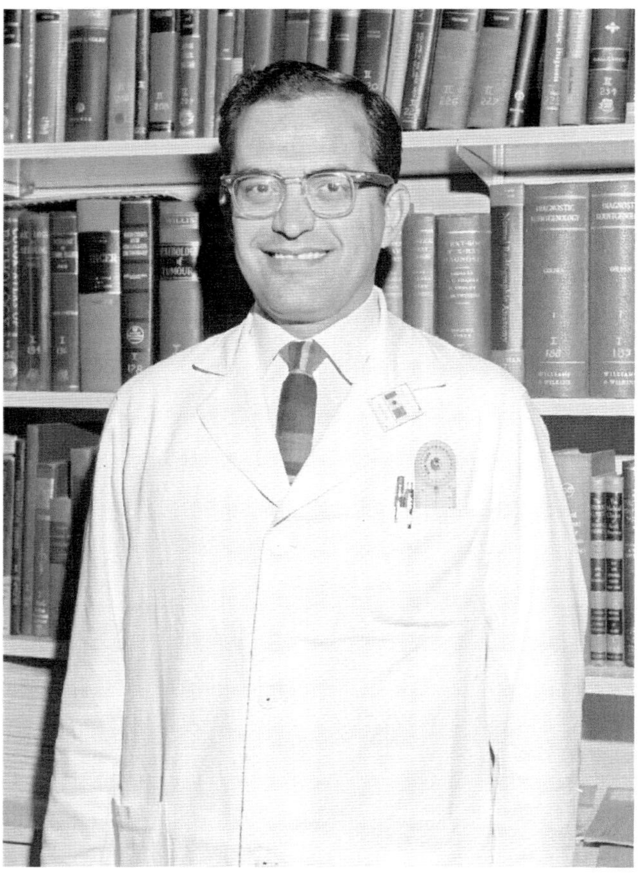

Herbert L. Hoffman

Although his business wasn't a large one, many longtime Mount Clemens residents remember Hoffman fondly. His popcorn stand on North Gratiot Avenue was a favorite stop for youngsters for 32 years. Hoffman set up shop in Mount Clemens in 1940 and made his own popcorn and roasted fresh peanuts daily until his retirement at the age of 75 in 1972. (Courtesy of the *Macomb Daily*.)

Victor Curatolo

The Detroit-born son of Sicilian immigrants, Curatolo earned degrees in pharmacy and medicine and then established the first radiology department and school of radiography at St. Joseph Mercy Hospital in Mount Clemens. During his 41-year tenure, the highly respected radiologist was known as a generous, larger-than-life character who served as a mentor to many health professionals. (Courtesy of the *Macomb Daily*.)

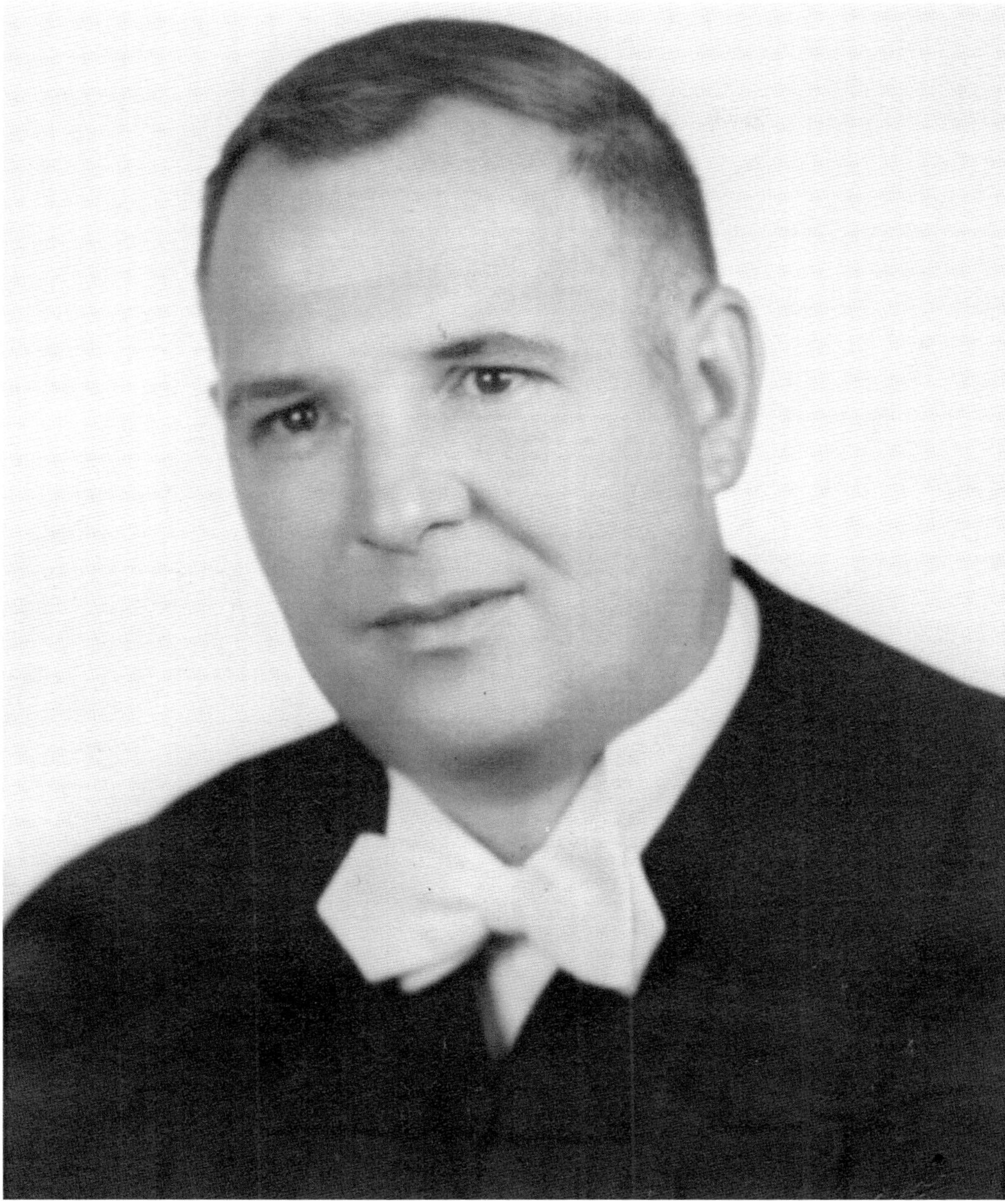

Frederick J. Roskopp

The Roskopp family arrived in Macomb County in 1853, and Frederick J. Roskopp was the fifth generation of his family to serve the Mount Clemens community. Roskopp was a career naval officer in the US Navy Reserve, an engineer for Chrysler Corporation, and after earning his law degree from Detroit College of Law, became senior staff counsel for Chrysler Corporation. His involvement in civic affairs included—among many efforts—service as a charter member of the Mount Clemens Public Library Board of Trustees, and a successful effort to preserve the historic 1859 Mount Clemens Grand Trunk Railway depot. Roskopp was especially pleased that the depot was acquired by the city of Mount Clemens in 1979 and placed on the National Register of Historic Places in 1981. (Courtesy of JoAnne Roskopp.)

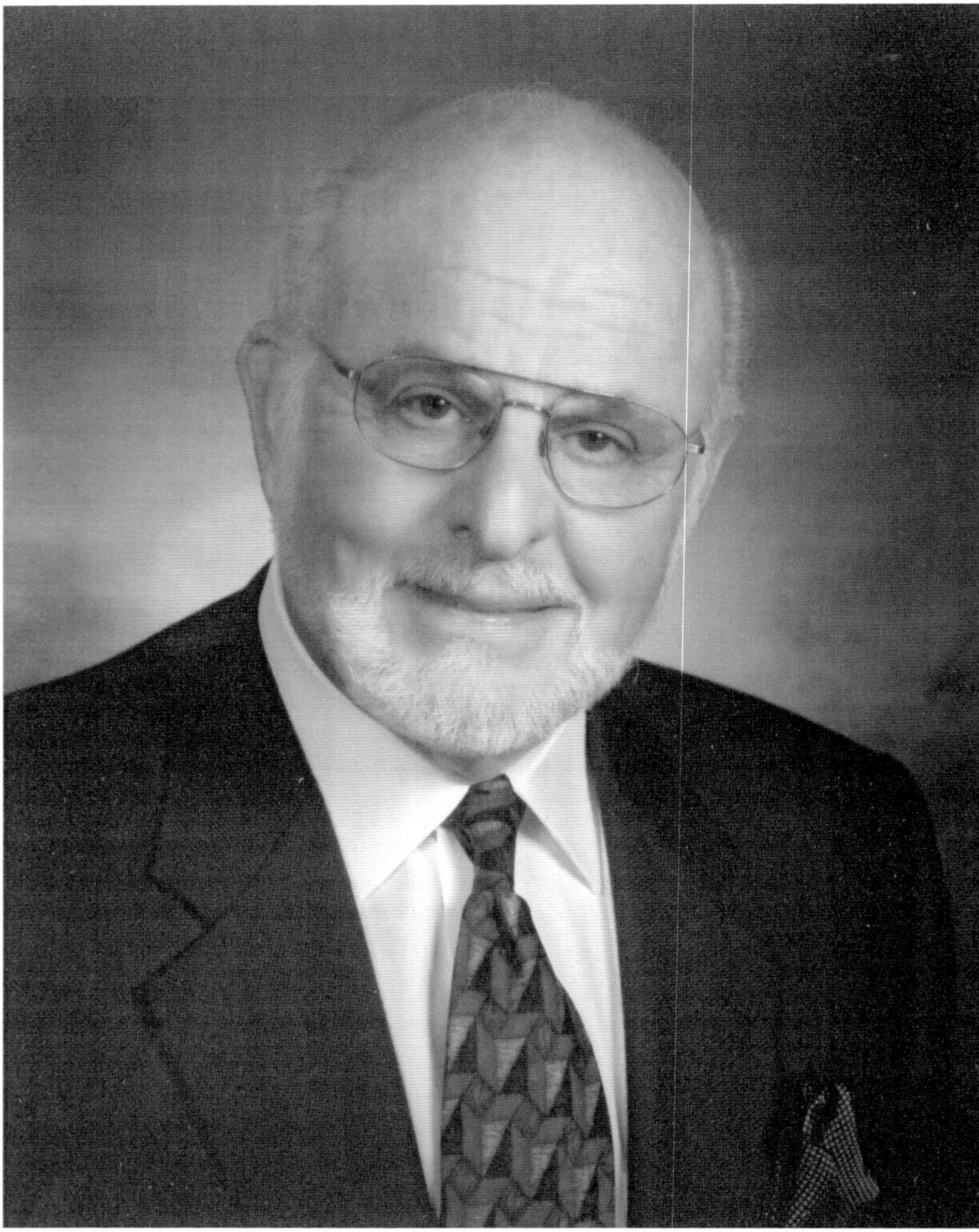

Gebran Syde Anton Jr.

When his father died in 1949, Anton took over his family's shoe shop in Mount Clemens, and in 1957 he opened the first of 13 menswear stores. He later ventured into real estate development and as his businesses prospered he shared his success with the community through major philanthropic and humanitarian gifts. With his wife, Suzanne, Anton has funded a mobile health clinic, a major addition to the Anton Art Center, and developed an endowment fund for a public art initiative. In 2010, Anton and partner Stuart Frankel donated a 25,000-square-foot downtown Mount Clemens building to Oakland University for use as a satellite campus. (Courtesy of Gebran S. Anton Jr.)

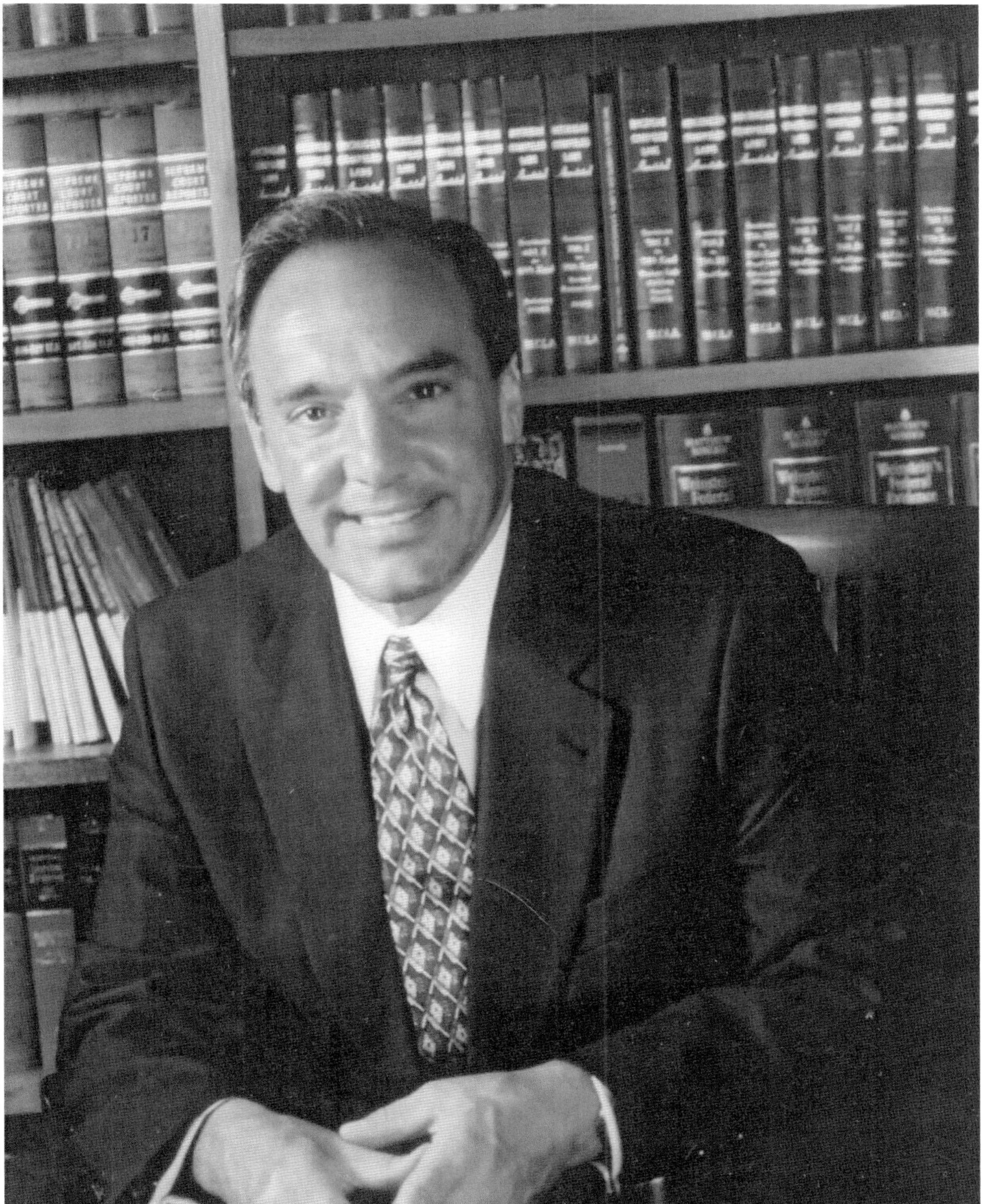

George Caram Steeh III

Mount Clemens High School and University of Michigan graduate George Caram Steeh III began his law career as an assistant prosecuting attorney and first served as a judge in Michigan's 41-B District Court. In 1990, he was elevated to the Macomb County Circuit Court, and in 1997 was nominated by Pres. Bill Clinton for a seat on the United States District Court for the Eastern District of Michigan. Steeh was the first of several federal court judges to hear a case challenging the constitutionality of the landmark Affordable Care Act of 2010. He was inducted into the Macomb Foundation's Macomb County Hall of Fame in 2011. (Courtesy of George Caram Steeh III.)

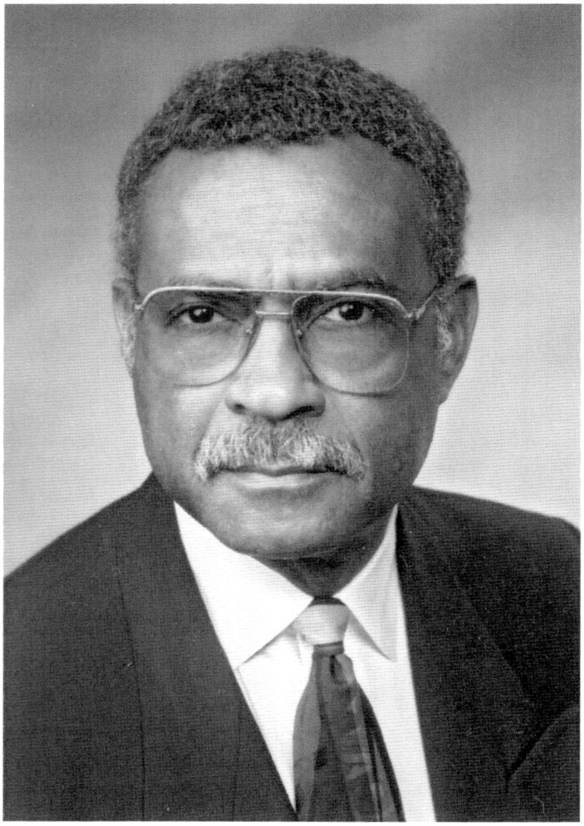

Harold C. Henry

In his position as a court reporter with the Macomb County Circuit Court, Henry has seen the need for strong community volunteers. Henry has served on the Mount Clemens City Commission, as vice president of the local NAACP chapter, and with local youth programs. He also served several terms on the Mount Clemens Public Library Board of Trustees. (Courtesy of Mount Clemens Public Library.)

Barb R. Dempsey

Mount Clemens's longest-serving woman mayor, Dempsey presided over a city commission faced with the greatest economic challenges in the community's history, including sharply declining revenues and necessary restructuring of city services. Here she is shown taking part in the annual Santa Claus Parade, a long-standing tradition for which she helped to garner stable private sponsorships. (Courtesy of Barb R. Dempsey.)

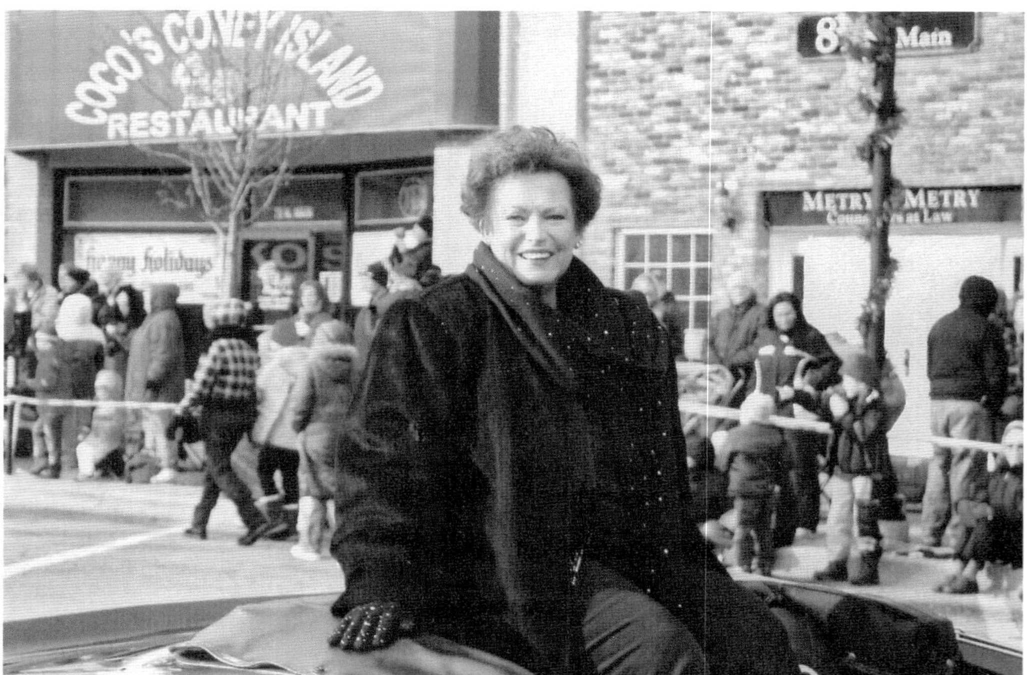

CHAPTER FOUR

Entertainers, Performing Artists, and Athletes

Some of the most famous names associated with Mount Clemens are found among the ranks of the entertainers, performing artists, and athletes who have called the Bath City home. In the 1880s, as acts playing Detroit theaters began to venture northward to Mount Clemens to entertain the bathhouse crowds, a theatrical colony of sorts began to develop. Musical comedy actors Sadie Hasson Dowling and her husband, Joseph J. Dowling, weary from a season on the road, came to Mount Clemens to rest between tours and decided to make the city their off-season home. So did juggler James DeWitt Cook, the Nelson Family of circus aerialists, burlesque dancer Amelia Price Churchyard, and many others. The citizens of Mount Clemens no longer had to travel to Detroit or beyond for top-notch entertainment—it came to their doorsteps.

With the professionals around for inspiration, there was no lack of aspiring performing artists among the hometown folks. Mount Clemens developed a civic chorus, symphony orchestra, musicale, and a high school music program that was the envy of many. From those organizations emerged a host of talented singers, musicians, and performers to impress the local audiences.

Performers of another stripe—the athletes—also made names for themselves in the pages of Mount Clemens history. Award-winning high school teams produced players who went on to college or professional fame, including John S. Pingel and Walter J. Weber, and the town fielded several semi-professional sports teams in its history. Told in the pages that follow are the intriguing stories of some of those Mount Clemens residents who saw their names in lights.

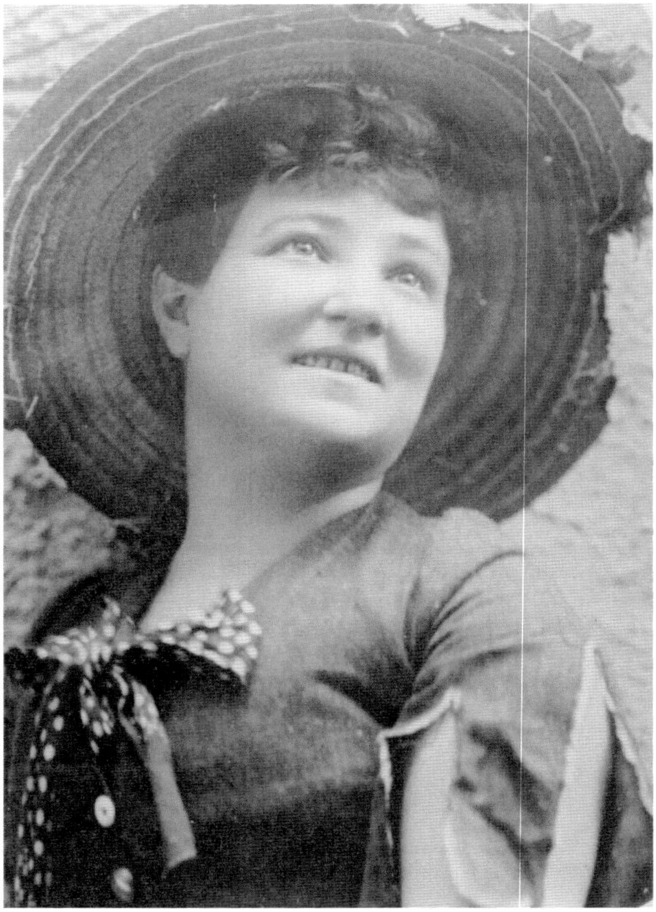

Sadie Hasson Dowling

Numbered among the entertainers who visited Mount Clemens for a respite and eventually adopted it as a permanent home was Sadie Hasson Dowling, a comic actress who starred in popular American stage dramas for over 30 years. Born Sarah Ann Berry in Amherstburg, Ontario, in 1856, Dowling started her career as a seamstress assistant with a theater company in Ohio. She recalled in a newspaper interview given late in life that she practiced singing the Negro spirituals that she heard backstage and availed herself of every opportunity to audition for work. At about the age of 20, she married performer William "Billy" Hasson and toured the Midwest with him in a variety act. Later, she married up-and-coming actor and producer Joseph Johnson Dowling and starred with him in his comic melodrama *Nobody's Claim*, a vehicle created especially for the Dowlings by playwright Edwin A. "Sweetie" Locke. The play was a great success and brought the couple to Mount Clemens, where they purchased a home in 1886. The Dowlings played to packed houses across the country for several years, but split up in a nasty divorce scandal in 1893. With her former husband touring on his own, Dowling, who had won their house in the divorce settlement, made the Bath City her permanent home and reared her two children in Mount Clemens. When she retired from the stage around 1901, Dowling lived quietly in Mount Clemens, occasionally granting an interview or participating in a benefit performance, but largely leaving behind the theatrical life for the final three decades of her life. When she died in 1937, she was buried in an unmarked grave in Clinton Grove Cemetery; in 2007, the Macomb County Historical Society placed a marker on Dowling's forgotten resting place, granting the actress one last curtain call. (Courtesy of Mount Clemens Public Library.)

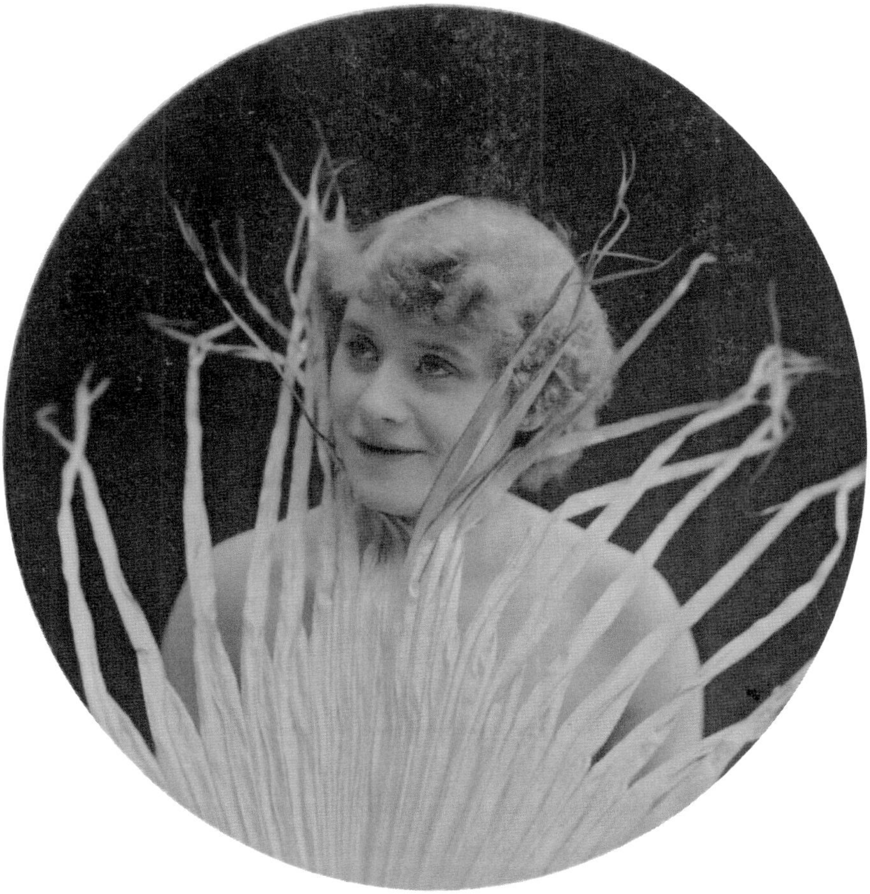

Amelia "Millie" Price Churchyard

Churchyard lived out the last decades of her life in relative anonymity as a resident of Mount Clemens, but her earlier days were anything but sedate. Born in London, England, in 1870, Amelia "Millie" Price began a stage career in the dance halls of London and perfected a high kick routine in which she kicked five or six inches higher than her head. She emigrated to the United States in 1888 and became a minor sensation on the burlesque stage using the name Millie Price, acting and dancing in many of the musical comedies popular during the era known as the "Gay Nineties." In 1891, while playing a theater in Denver, she met Clarence Merrill Dow, the young scion of a wealthy banking family, and married him the next day. The couple broke up on their honeymoon, after Churchyard was accused of wedding Dow for his fortune and his father refused to acknowledge the marriage. The story was carried in newspapers around the country for a time, and salacious details about the breakup were published. Churchyard went on with her stage career, dancing under the name Millie Price-Dow, until her divorce became final and she was married the following year, to William King Churchyard, a police commissioner in Buffalo, New York. Churchyard retired from the stage for a few years, but made a comeback in 1906, about the time that her husband was admitted to a state hospital for the insane. When he was discharged, about 1921, the couple relocated to Mount Clemens, where they spent the rest of their lives quietly and without fanfare, for a time serving as managers of the Cass Hotel. Churchyard died in Mount Clemens in 1947 at the age of 77, and was buried in an unmarked grave in Clinton Grove Cemetery, an obscure final curtain for the woman who was the first high-kicker on the American stage. (Courtesy of Billy Rose Theatre Division, New York Public Library for the Performing Arts, Astor, Lenox and Tilden Foundations.)

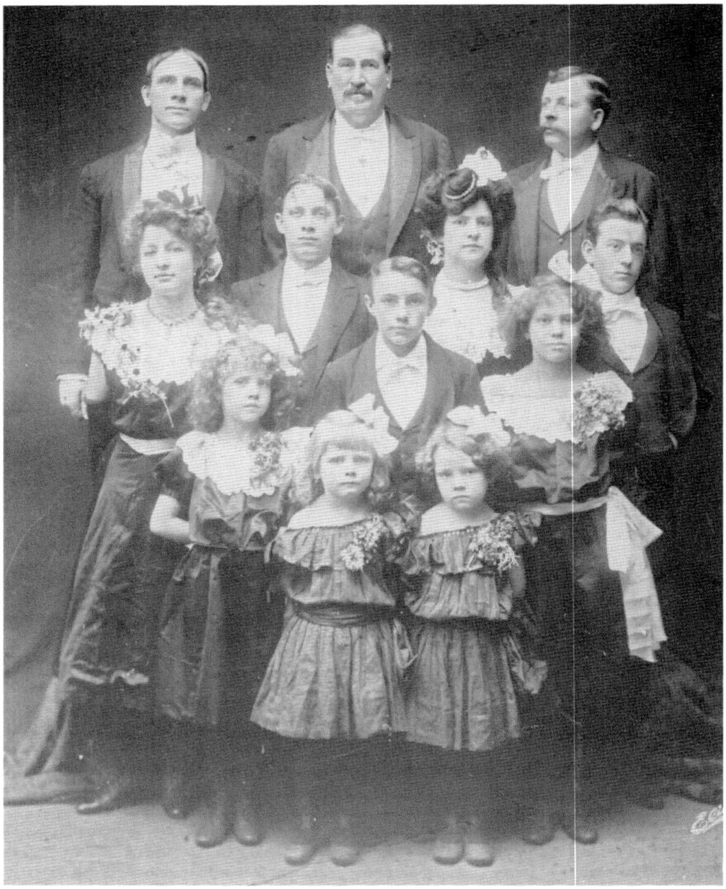

The Great Nelson Family

Numbered among the stars who are listed in the Circus Hall of Fame in Sarasota, Florida are the names of the members of the Great Nelson Family, a group of circus aerialists from Mount Clemens. The world-famous Nelsons were actually the Robert Hobson family; the elder Hobson began his circus career in his native England and adopted the stage name of Nelson from a former partner. He came to America in 1868 and developed an act that included his wife, Emma, and sons Arthur and Robert Jr., billing them as the Great Nelson Family. The act eventually expanded to include daughters-in-law and grandchildren, and the family by then known as the Flying Nelsons made Mount Clemens their permanent home in 1887. The Hobson residence on South Avenue had a specially equipped gymnasium in the basement that was used as an acrobatic training center for the troupe, and the family also owned and operated the Nelson Opera House in Mount Clemens. The Nelsons starred in every well-known circus in North America between 1910 and 1935, including Ringling Brothers, Barnum and Bailey, and Hagenbeck-Wallace. They even added movie credits to their record in 1928 when Hilda Nelson taught Lon Chaney to walk the wire in his film *Laugh, Clown, Laugh*, and doubled for actress Loretta Young in the same feature. Also in 1928, the entire troupe was featured in the MGM production entitled *Circus Rookies*. Even after the senior Nelson family members retired from the big top, the younger generations continued to perform together and individually for several more seasons. The family, described by one circus historian as "the most famous acrobatic act in the circus business," was inducted into the Circus Hall of Fame in 1969. Pictured here, left to right, (back row) are Arthur Nelson, Robert Nelson Sr., and Robert Nelson Jr., with unidentified members of the troupe about 1903. (Courtesy of Mount Clemens Public Library.)

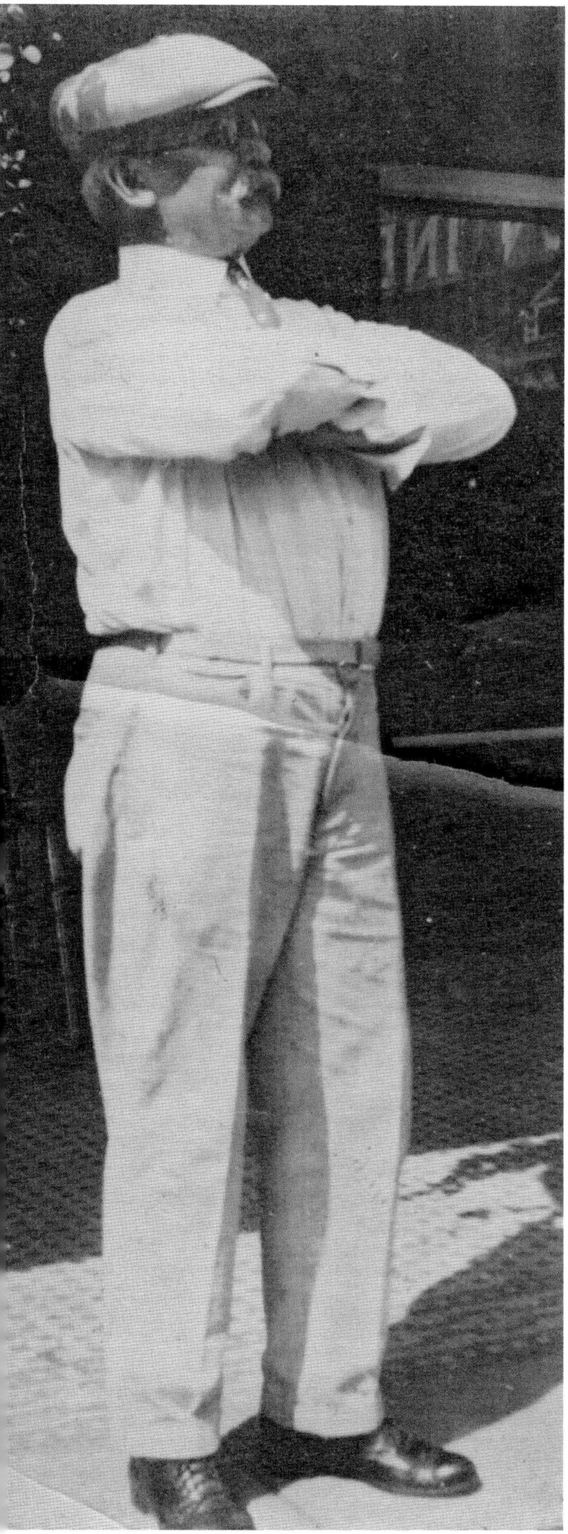

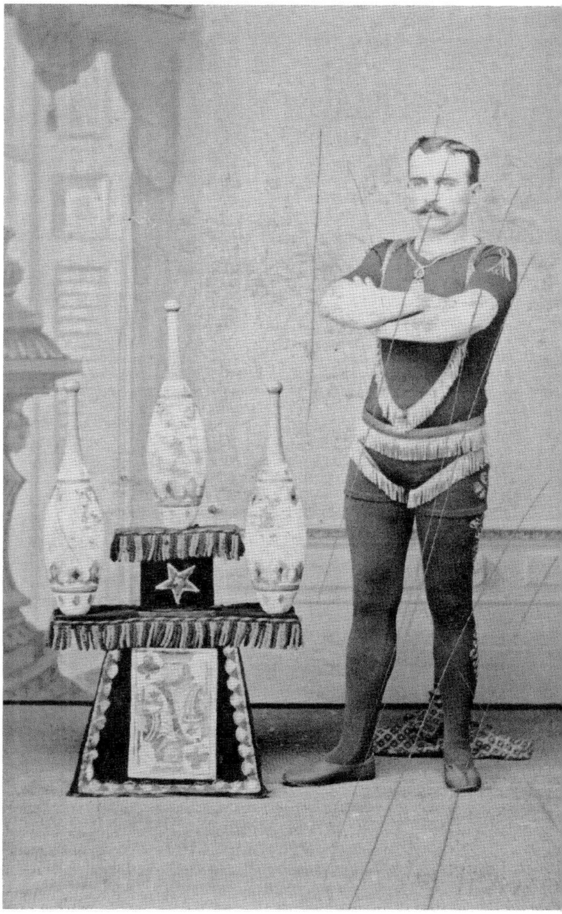

James DeWitt Cook

Between tours of the vaudeville circuit as the "King of Clubs" during the last quarter of the nineteenth century, Cook spent his off-season time relaxing with other show people in Mount Clemens's theatrical colony. Cook, a juggler, was the first to introduce American audiences to the Indian swinging club, a weighted prop originally designed as a strength-building tool. Although his family lived in Ohio, Cook decided to spend his retirement years with his friends in Mount Clemens. After leaving the stage in the late 1890s, he operated cigar and news stands in the Clementine Bath House and the John R. Murphy Hotel, where he was affectionately known as "Cookie." He is shown above in costume during his performing days, circa 1885, and at the Clementine in 1919 (left). (Courtesy of Mount Clemens Public Library.)

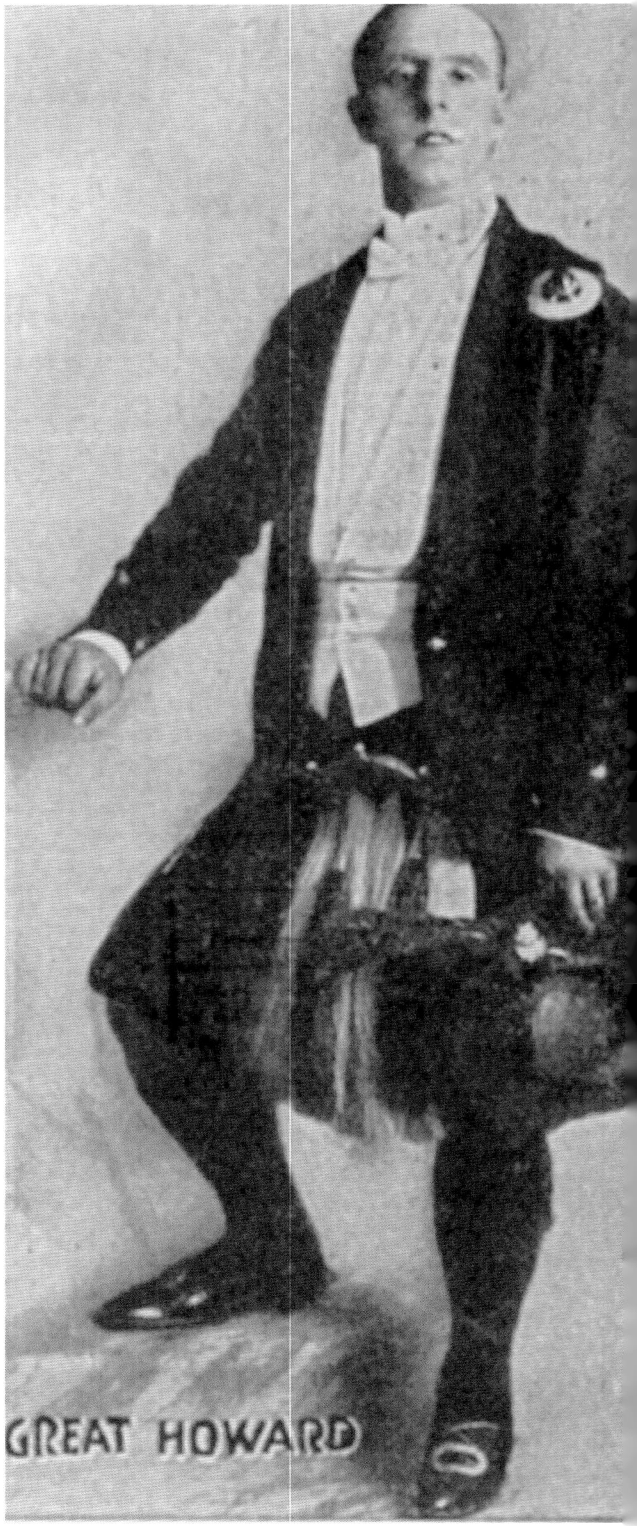

Frederick A. Howard Miller
Miller was born in London, England, in 1878 and trained as a physician in Scotland. After practicing medicine in South Africa for a few years, he emigrated to the United States and embarked upon a career as a singer and ventriloquist on the vaudeville stage. Miller settled in Mount Clemens in 1909, to be near his sister, Lydia Engel, who lived in the Bath City. As he toured the country, Miller billed himself as "The Great Howard," and performed his act with two dummies he called Scotty and Jimmy. Hearkening back to his earlier career, Miller used a doctor's office as a setting for his act, with his two dummies representing his patients. He was also a gifted songwriter and his act often featured his own original compositions, several of which were published as sheet music. RCA Victor recorded one of his hit songs entitled "Somewhere in France Is Daddy," a patriotic number composed during World War I. Other hit songs from Miller's pen, all of the "home and hearth" theme, were "I'll Be a Long Long Way from Home," and "If You Only Believed in Me." When at home in Mount Clemens, The Great Howard was well known for organizing and performing in benefit shows to raise money for charities, and for taking his act to schools, hospitals, and prisons. For one Red Cross benefit in particular, the *Mount Clemens Monitor* reported that Miller had canceled a week-long engagement at the "largest vaudeville theater in Chicago" in order to headline the Bath City's charity show. Miller was also an active member of the Presbyterian church, where he taught Sunday school and organized youth activities for boys. When Miller died at his home in Mount Clemens in 1930, the local newspapers eulogized him as "the world's greatest ventriloquist." (Courtesy of Mount Clemens Public Library.)

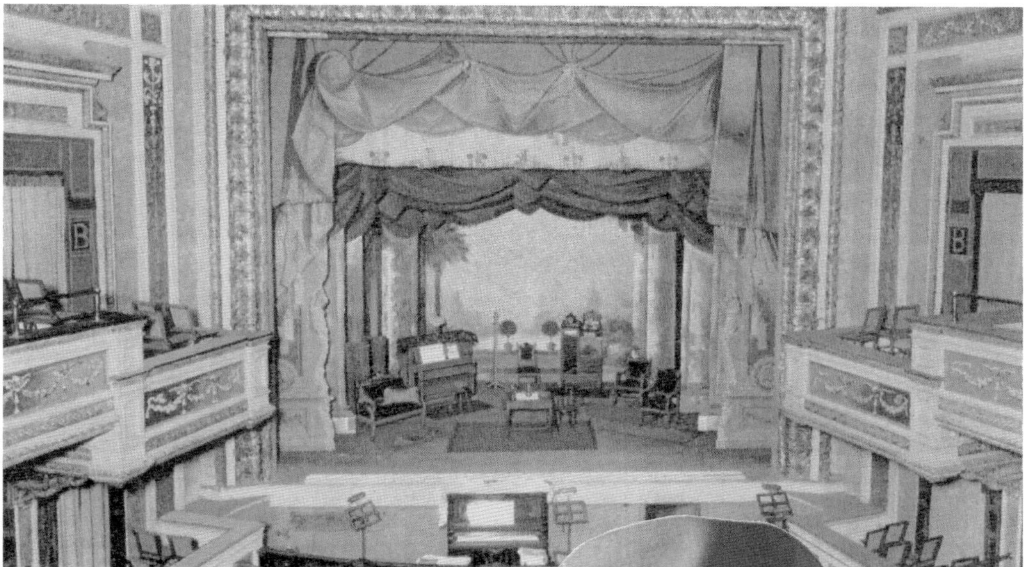

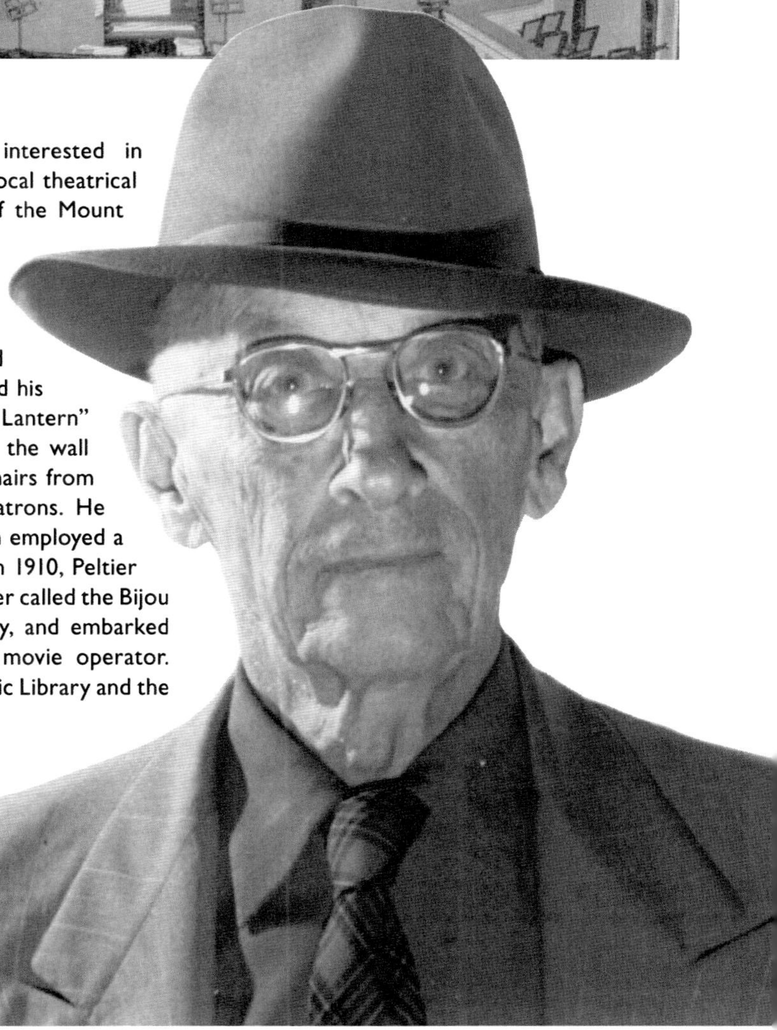

Robert George Peltier
Stage-struck as a youth and interested in acting, Peltier appeared in many local theatrical productions during the heyday of the Mount Clemens mineral bath industry. In 1905, he launched himself in the motion picture business when he opened the town's first movie theater in a rented downtown storefront. Peltier used his $300 in savings to buy a "Magic Lantern" projector, tacked a bed sheet to the wall for a screen, and borrowed 88 chairs from a local undertaker to seat his patrons. He played to packed houses and soon employed a projectionist and a piano player. In 1910, Peltier opened a large, modern new theater called the Bijou with partner Walter N. Trombley, and embarked on a three-decade career as a movie operator. (Courtesy of Mount Clemens Public Library and the *Macomb Daily*.)

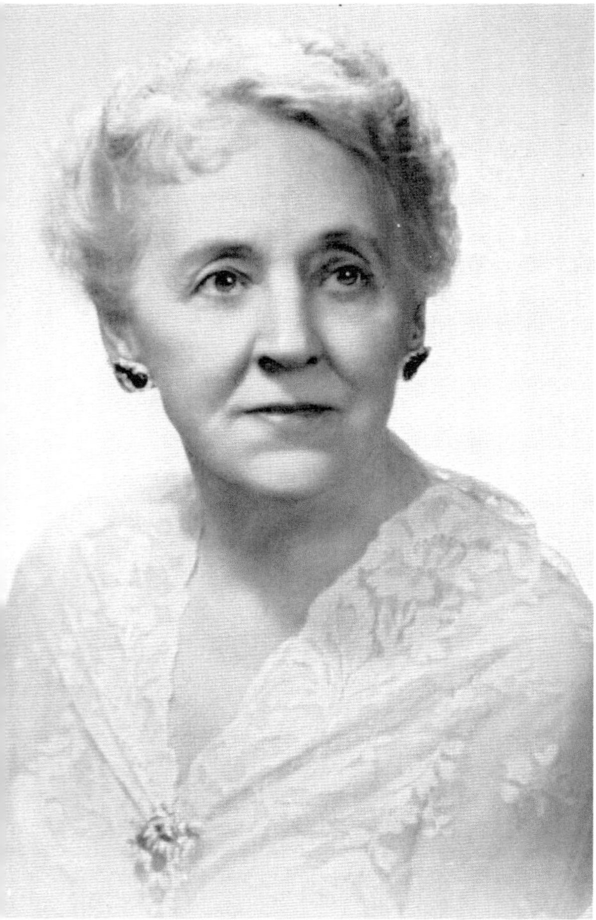

Maude Embrey Taylor Childs

After visiting the Mount Clemens mineral baths in 1905, Maude Embrey Taylor Childs married her physician, Dr. Harry F. Taylor, who championed her musical talent. An operatic soprano, Childs had performed at the funeral of Pres. William McKinley in 1901. After her husband's death in 1921, Childs remarried and embarked on a long career teaching music and directing church choirs. (Courtesy of the *Macomb Daily.*)

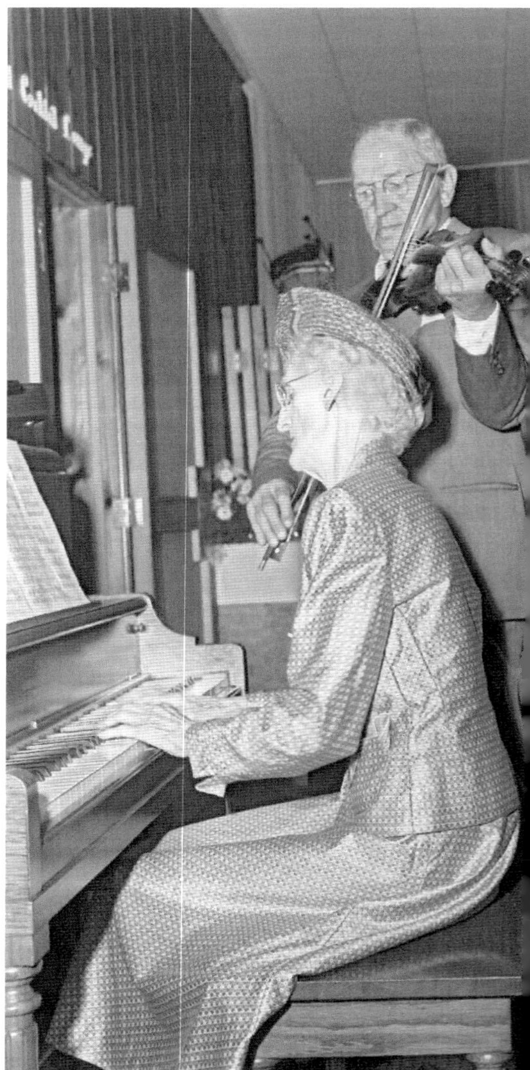

Pansy Metta Bell

For almost four decades, if a piano was played at a gathering in Mount Clemens, chances were that Bell was at the keyboard. Orchestra leader Fred Schock (right) invited Bell to come to Mount Clemens in 1917, and she played piano in the Bijou and Macomb Theaters, as well as for the Kiwanis and Rotary Clubs and area churches. (Courtesy of the *Macomb Daily.*)

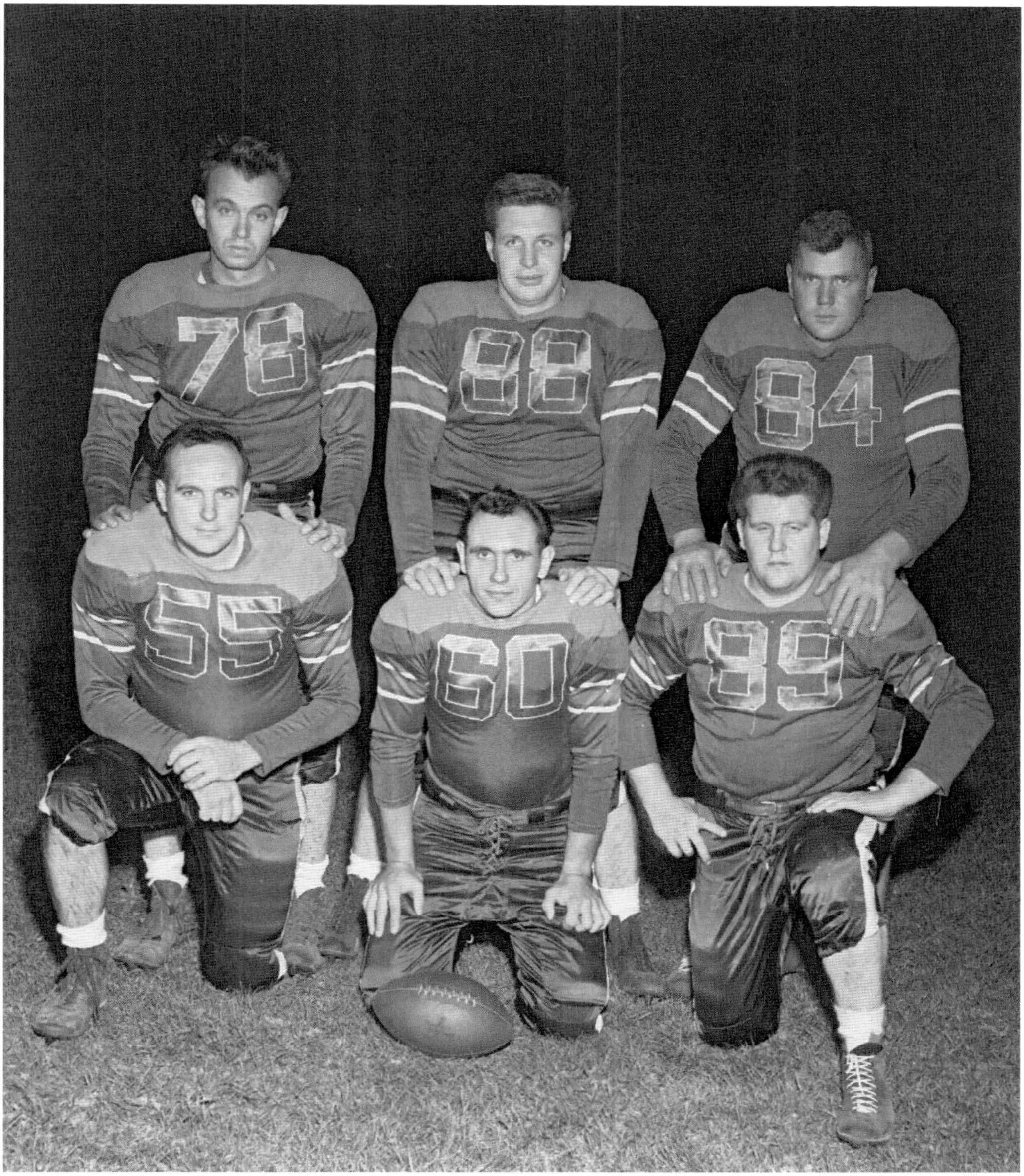

Mount Clemens Jugs

Mount Clemens boasted a semi-professional football team from 1948 to 1952 when a local sportsman's organization, the Juggle-Up Club, sponsored the formation of the Mount Clemens Jugs. Area athletes played on the squad, which had an impressive winning record in five seasons and advanced to the championship game of the newly formed Southern Michigan Football League in 1950. Shown here from the 1952 team are, from left to right (first row) quarterback Jack Sierens, end Clink Schroeder, and guard Bob Kolp; (second row) tackle Jim Kandt, tackle Bill Nicolai, and end Bob White. (Courtesy of the *Macomb Daily*.)

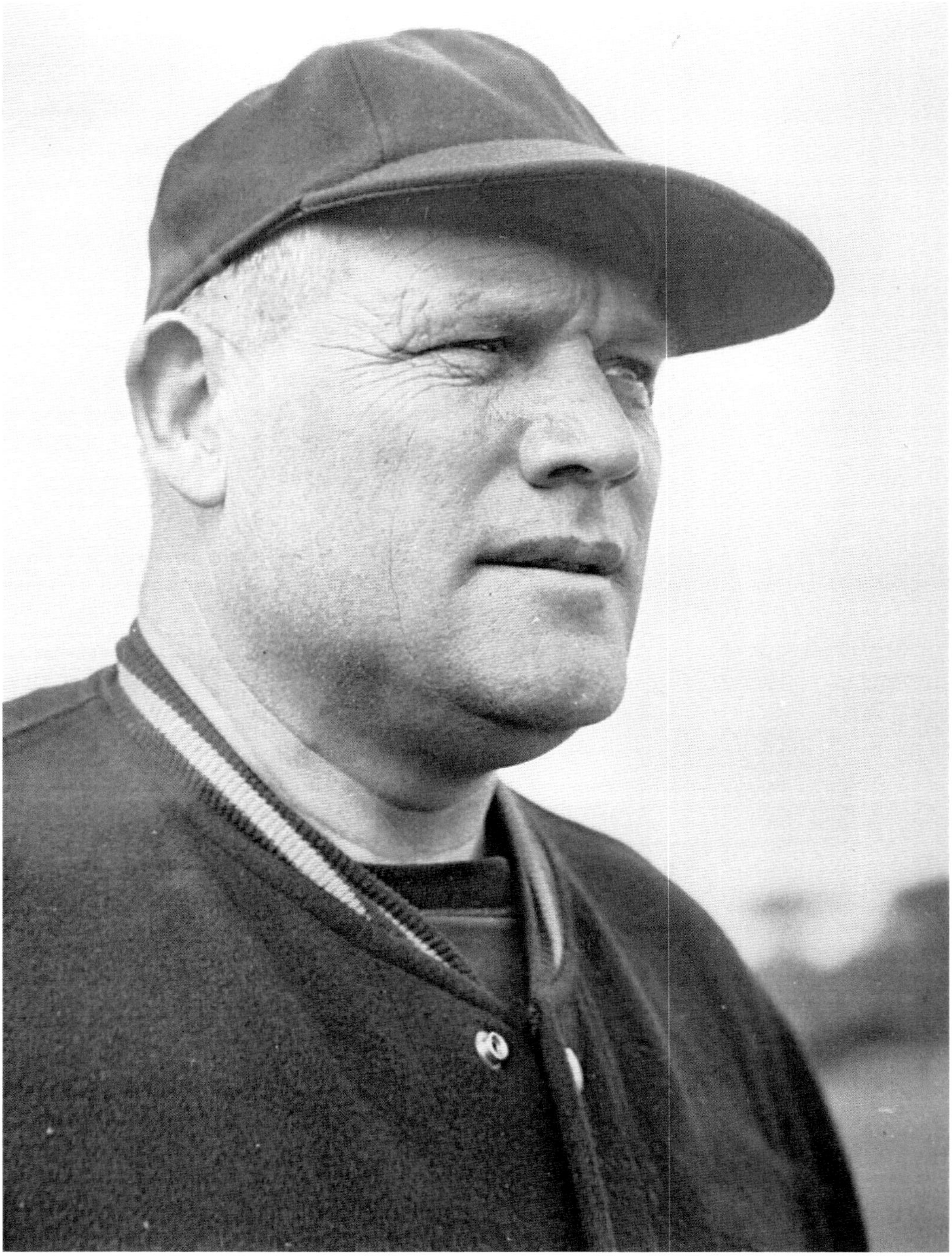

Walter J. "Wally" Weber

A Mount Clemens High School graduate, Weber played football for the University of Michigan and scored two touchdowns during Fielding H. Yost's final game as head coach in 1927. He later served as an assistant football coach for the University of Michigan for 28 years and provided color commentary on radio broadcasts with the legendary Bob Ufer. (Courtesy of the *Macomb Daily*.)

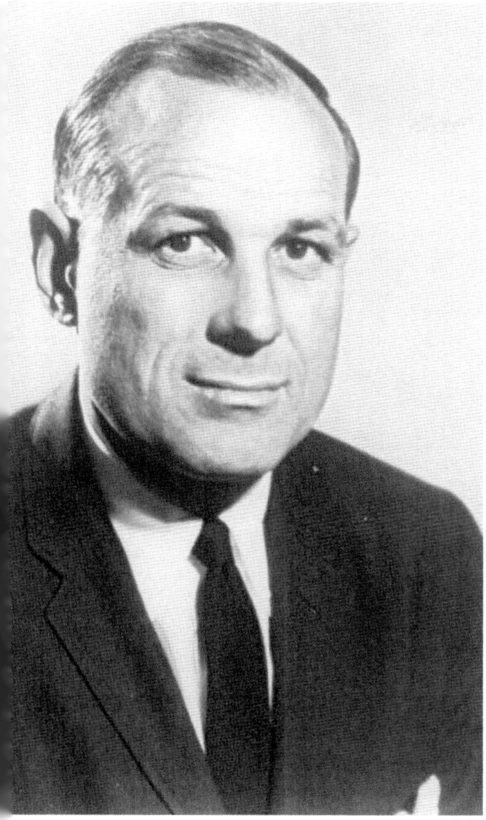

John Spencer Pingel

A star football player at Mount Clemens High School, Pingel earned an athletic scholarship to Michigan State University, where he was a record-setting All-America halfback who led the Spartans to their first bowl game in 1938. He played with the Detroit Lions before serving in the Army during World War II, and after the war became president of a prominent advertising agency. (Courtesy of the *Macomb Daily*.)

August Richard Maekelberghe

A man of diverse talents and abilities, Maekelberghe chose Mount Clemens as his home after leaving his native Belgium in 1932. Trained as a classical organist and proficient in eight languages, he found work as a church organist and as a radio announcer with WWJ in Detroit and made his home with the Joseph Miller family in Mount Clemens. In 1945, he embarked upon a 29-year career as the organist and music director at the historic St. John's Episcopal Church in Detroit. During this time, he composed hundreds of works for organ, piano, orchestra, and chorus, many of which were recorded by well-known artists. Maekelberghe died in his adopted home of Mount Clemens in 1975, but left a legacy of beautiful music by which he is still remembered. (Courtesy of the *Macomb Daily*.)

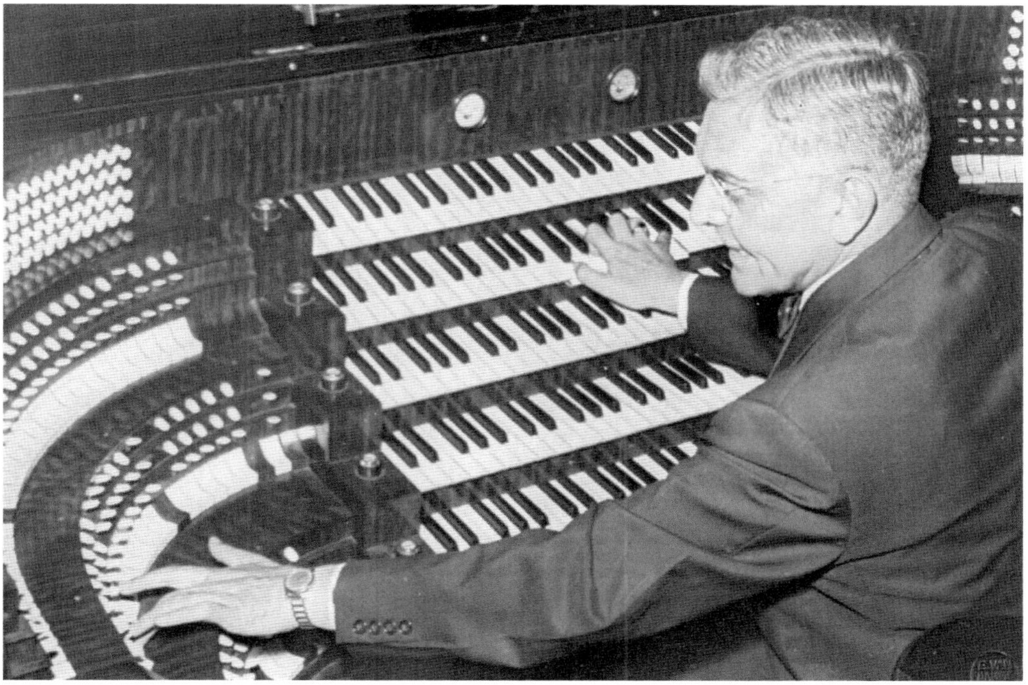

Rylma B. Strevel Marquardt

Golf and history were two of Marquardt's passions in life. At age 30, the Mount Clemens High School graduate was the 1953 Michigan Amateur Golf Champion, and she also competed in many national tournaments, including the US Women's Amateur and the US Women's Open. In a 1947 match, Marquardt played against famed Olympic medalist and LPGA champion Babe Didrikson Zaharias. When not on the links, Marquardt was known for her long service to the Macomb County Historical Society and the Alexander Macomb Chapter of the Daughters of the American Revolution, and for her hobbies of antique collecting and genealogical research. (Courtesy of the *Macomb Daily*.)

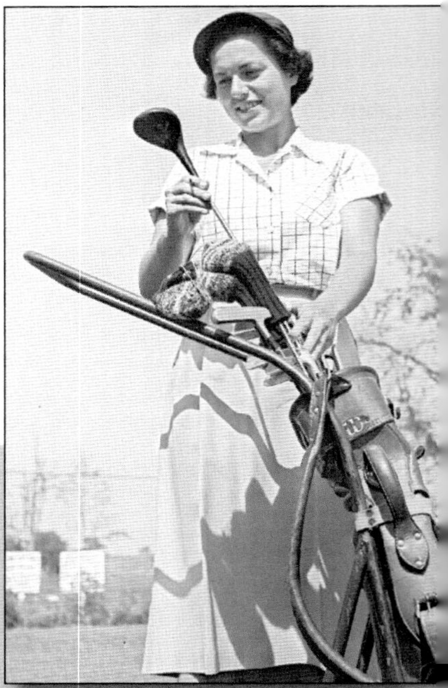

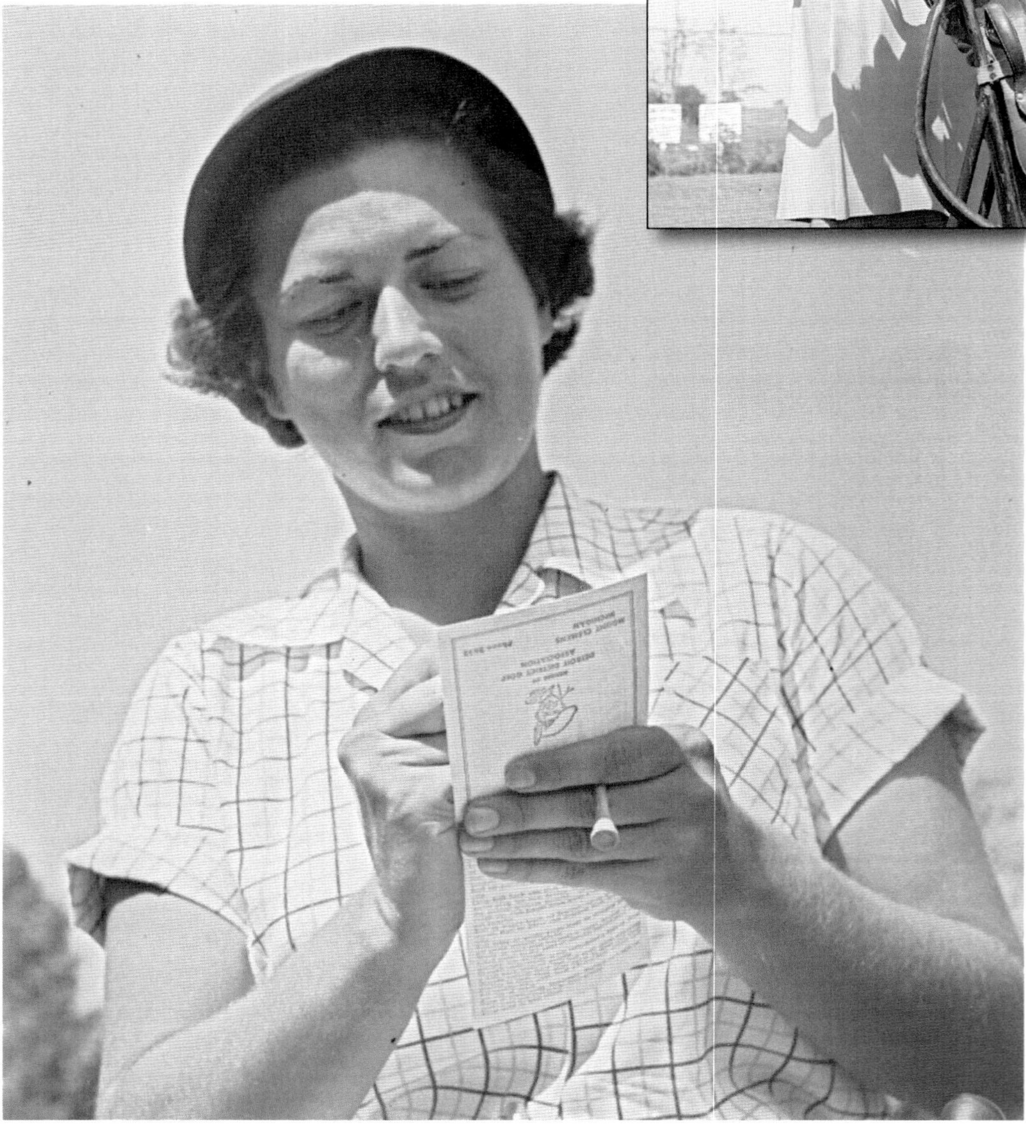

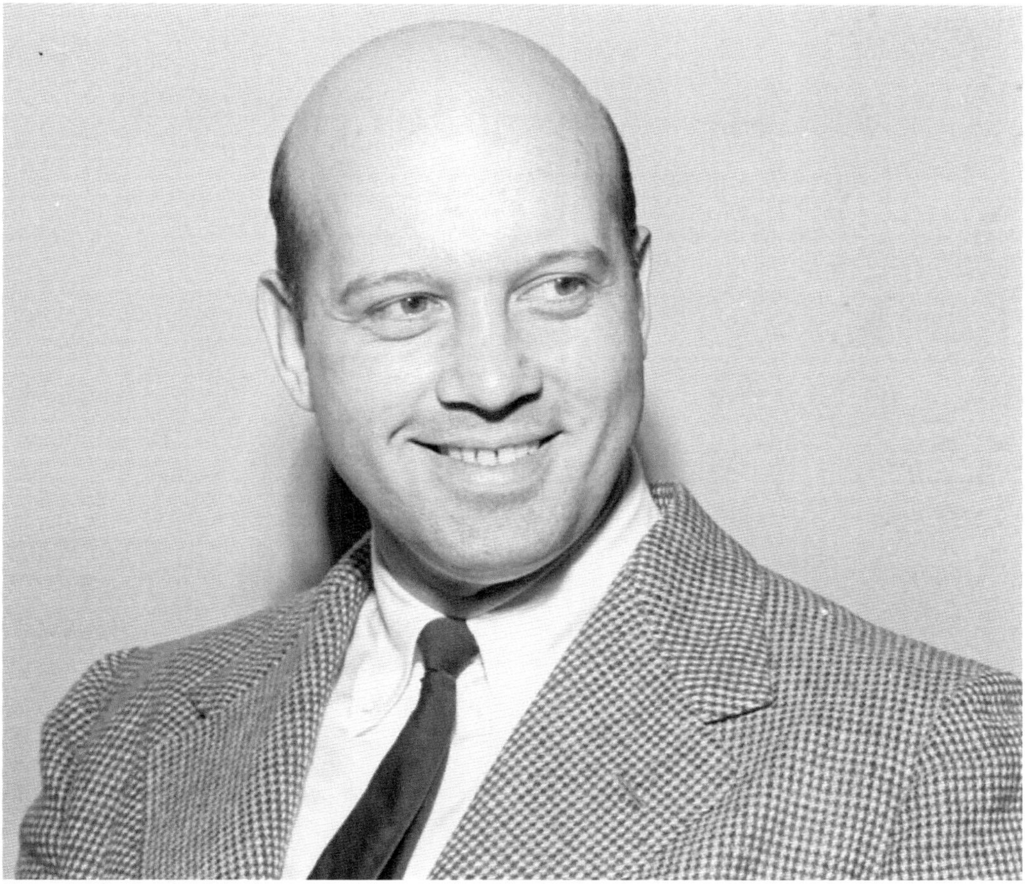

Victor Woodrow "Vic" Wertz

Wertz may be remembered by baseball fans as an All-Star slugger who played for the Detroit Tigers, Cleveland Indians, and other teams, but he is best known in Mount Clemens as the founder of the "Wertz Warriors," a group of volunteer sportsmen who have raised millions to underwrite the cost of the Special Olympics Winter Games in Michigan. Born in 1925 in Pennsylvania, Wertz began his professional baseball career in 1947 as an outfielder with the Detroit Tigers, was known as a strong hitter, and was elected to the All-Star team three times. The most memorable moment of his baseball career came during the 1954 World Series opener, in which Wertz hit a 455-foot drive into center field—a certain home run in most parks—only to watch in shock as Giants outfielder Willie Mays made a spectacular over-the-shoulder catch on the warning track to snuff out the Indians' chance to take a three-run lead. In 1955, while playing with the Indians, Wertz contracted polio and was hospitalized—an event that changed his outlook and the course of his life. Following his recovery from the near-fatal disease, he played ball for a few more years, retiring in 1963. Wertz then turned his attention to the thriving beverage distributorship that he had founded in Mount Clemens in 1955, as well as to the philanthropic work that he had envisioned during his earlier hospital stay, when he had decided to use his fame and resources to help those less fortunate than he. Wertz was a successful Mount Clemens business leader and major contributor to charities such as the Boys and Girls Clubs, Easter Seals, March of Dimes, and Special Olympics, to name a few. For three decades, the 900-mile Macomb-to-Mackinac snowmobile endurance ride that he founded to raise funds for the Special Olympics has been a popular winter event. Wertz died at the age of 58 during cardiac bypass surgery in 1983, but left behind an enduring legacy of care for his community. (Courtesy of the *Macomb Daily*.)

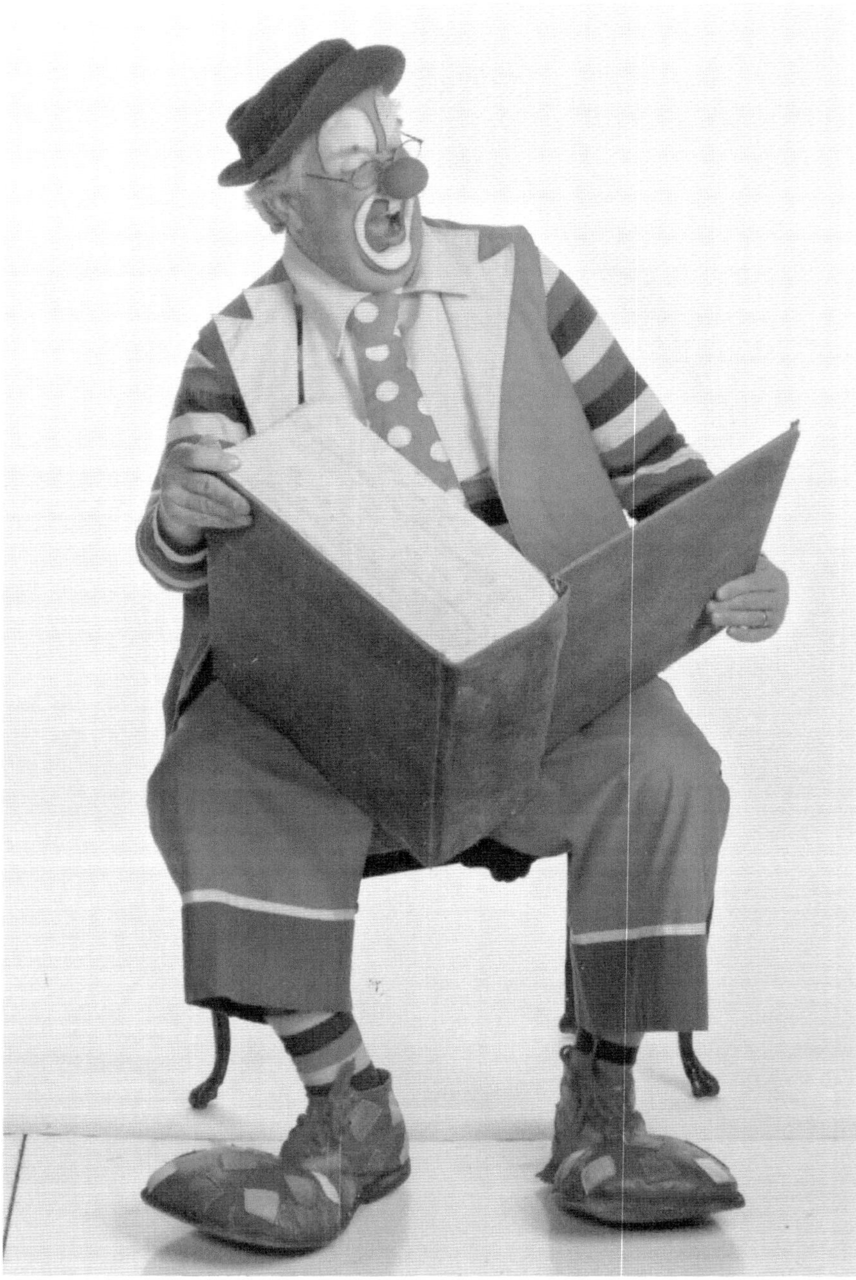

Ross Champion

Lifelong Mount Clemens resident and former landscape designer Ross "Rosco the Clown" Champion started clowning for fun in 1978, but in 1990 decided to make it his primary occupation. Michigan audiences have enjoyed Rosco's humor, magic, and balloon art for three decades, while local children have benefited from Ross Champion's volunteer service with the Mount Clemens Board of Education, Macomb YMCA Board of Directors, Macomb County Historical Society, and the Kiwanis Club of Mount Clemens. Champion also serves as a spokesperson for the Macomb Literacy Partners and promotes childhood literacy through his "Read to Me, Rosco" programs. (Courtesy of Ross Champion.)

CHAPTER FIVE

Educators and Communicators

Ask almost any adult to recall his or her most vivid memories of childhood, and those memories will invariably include the teachers and coaches who wielded influence in that person's life. Other prominent memories frequently center on stories that were read in youth, often at the behest of a respected teacher, librarian, or coach.

The citizens of today have beloved schoolteachers like Louisa "Loa" Green and Adelaide C. Schwark to thank for the knowledge they hold as adults. They may thank teachers like Charles Bernard McGhee and Isabel M. Miller for their appreciation of music and culture and the development of their performing abilities, while coaches like Walter A. Olsen and Ernest J. Buckholz inspired some of them to athletic achievement. Sometimes feared in childhood, but usually respected and remembered fondly in adulthood, these mentors are recognized—often in hindsight—for the significant role they played in shaping their former students' success.

Much of the history and culture of Mount Clemens would be lost to future generations were it not for the educators and communicators who chronicled it and passed it on from their hands to the next. Local journalists Edgar D. Racine, Desmond A. Arnsby, and Dorothy M. Magee skillfully recorded the history of Mount Clemens in the pages of the *Daily Monitor-Leader* and *Macomb Daily* newspapers. Over the decades, teachers, librarians, historians, and journalists such as these have been the custodians of the Bath City's collective memory, and their efforts have ensured that the tales of old Mount Clemens will be accessible for years to come.

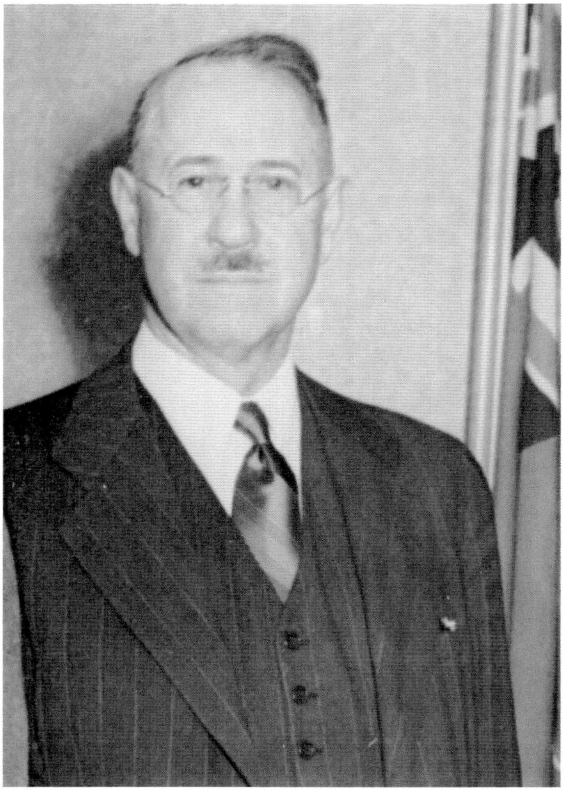

Lucius Wade Fast

Mount Clemens's longest-serving superintendent of schools was Lucius Wade Fast, who came to the Bath City in 1919 and led the school district until 1948. He was active in the community as a charter member of the Mount Clemens Rotary Club, and as a Boy Scout leader. In 1960, L. Wade Fast Elementary School was dedicated in his honor. (Courtesy of the *Macomb Daily.*)

Louisa "Loa" Green

In 1945, Donaldson Elementary School in Mount Clemens closed its doors to mark the passing of Green, who had taught at the school since 1911 and also served as its principal. In 52 total years of teaching, Green was described as having seen "hundreds of her former pupils rise to places of trust and accomplishment." (Courtesy of Macomb County Historical Society.)

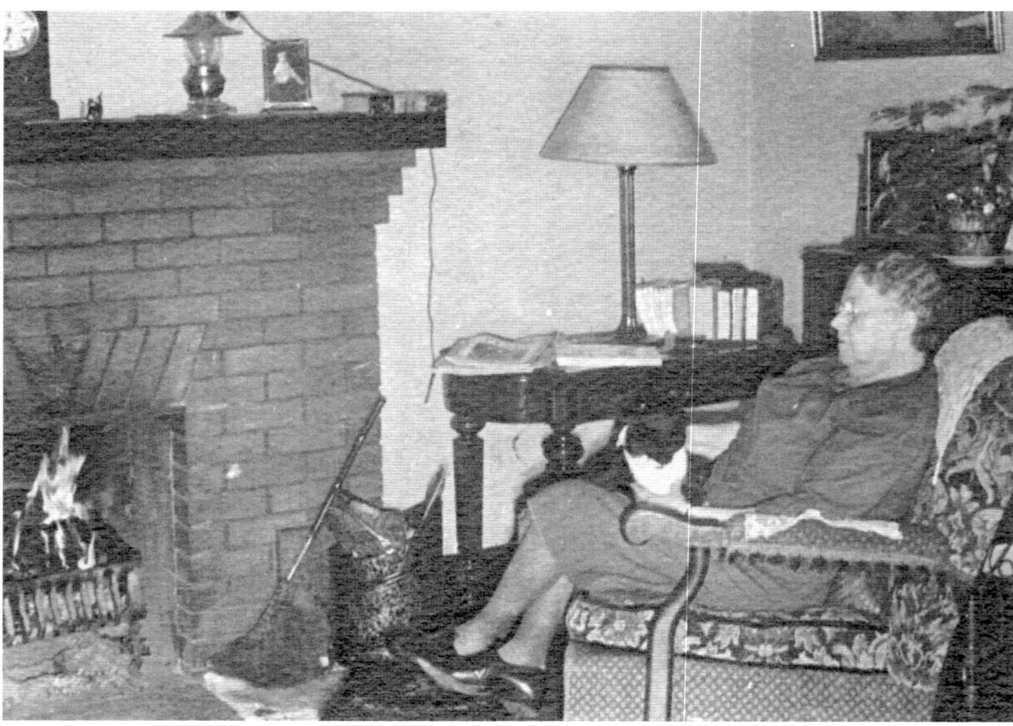

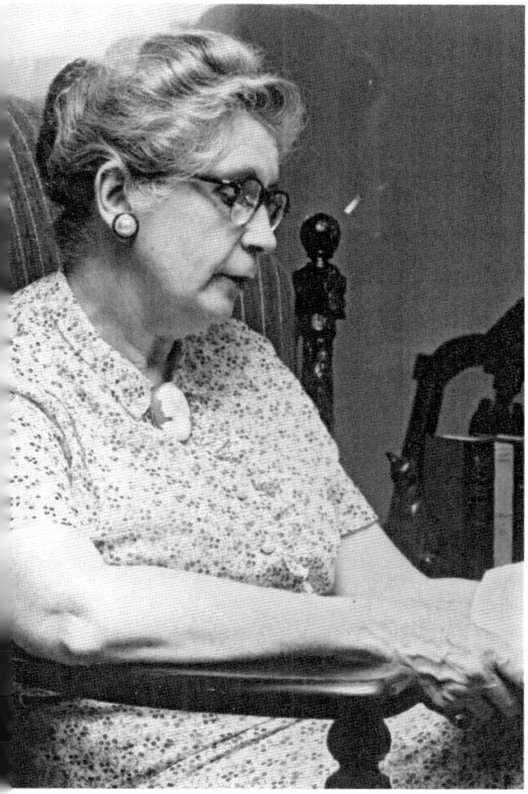

Ann Alexis Steele Crocker
Remembered by many who knew her as children as a formidable presence in the public library, Crocker was a guardian of knowledge in Mount Clemens for three decades. Crocker, the daughter of former Mount Clemens mayor George Martin Crocker, was appointed head librarian at Mount Clemens Public Library in 1926 and served in that position until 1956. (Courtesy of the *Macomb Daily*.)

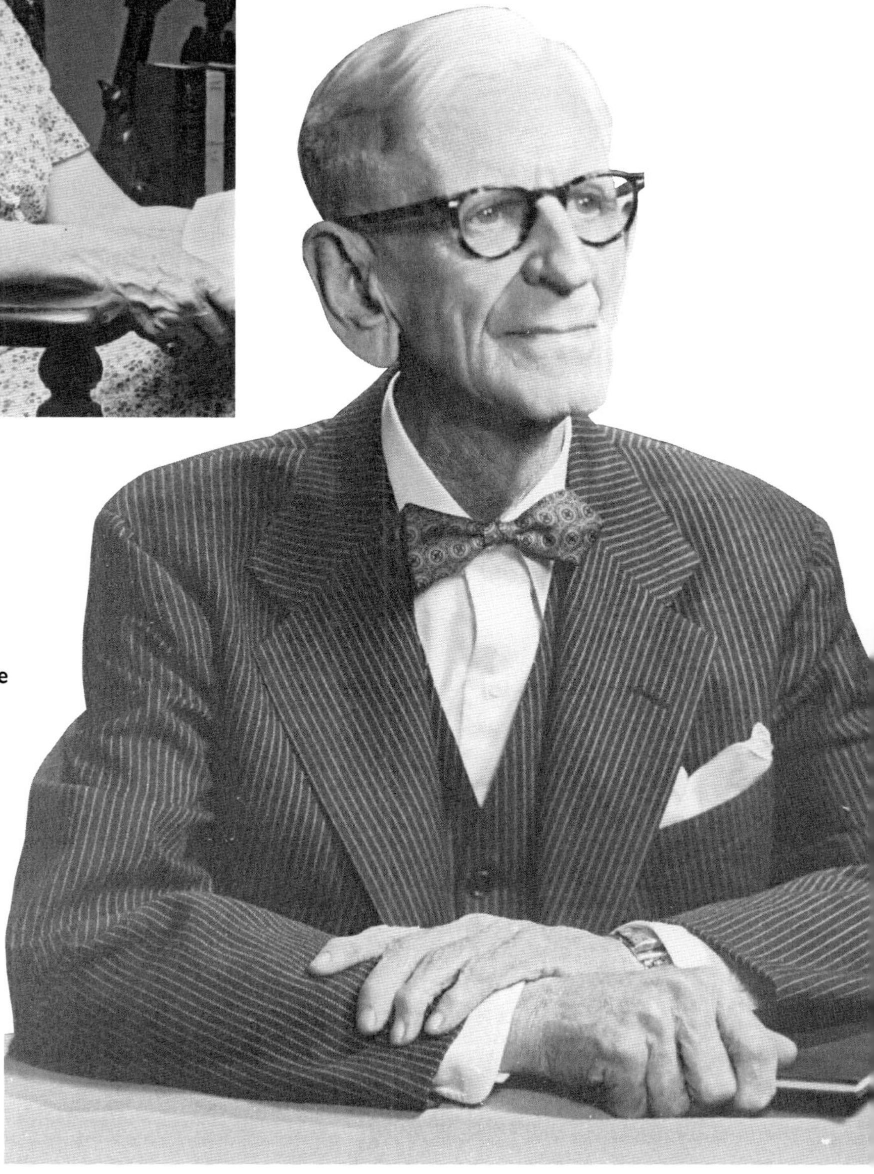

Will L. Lee
For over half a century, Lee served as a teacher and administrator for the students of Macomb County. He was elected as county school superintendent in 1914 when 4,500 pupils were enrolled in Macomb's public schools, and held the post until his death in 1953. Widely respected, Lee was regarded as the "dean" of the state's school superintendents. (Courtesy of the *Macomb Daily*.)

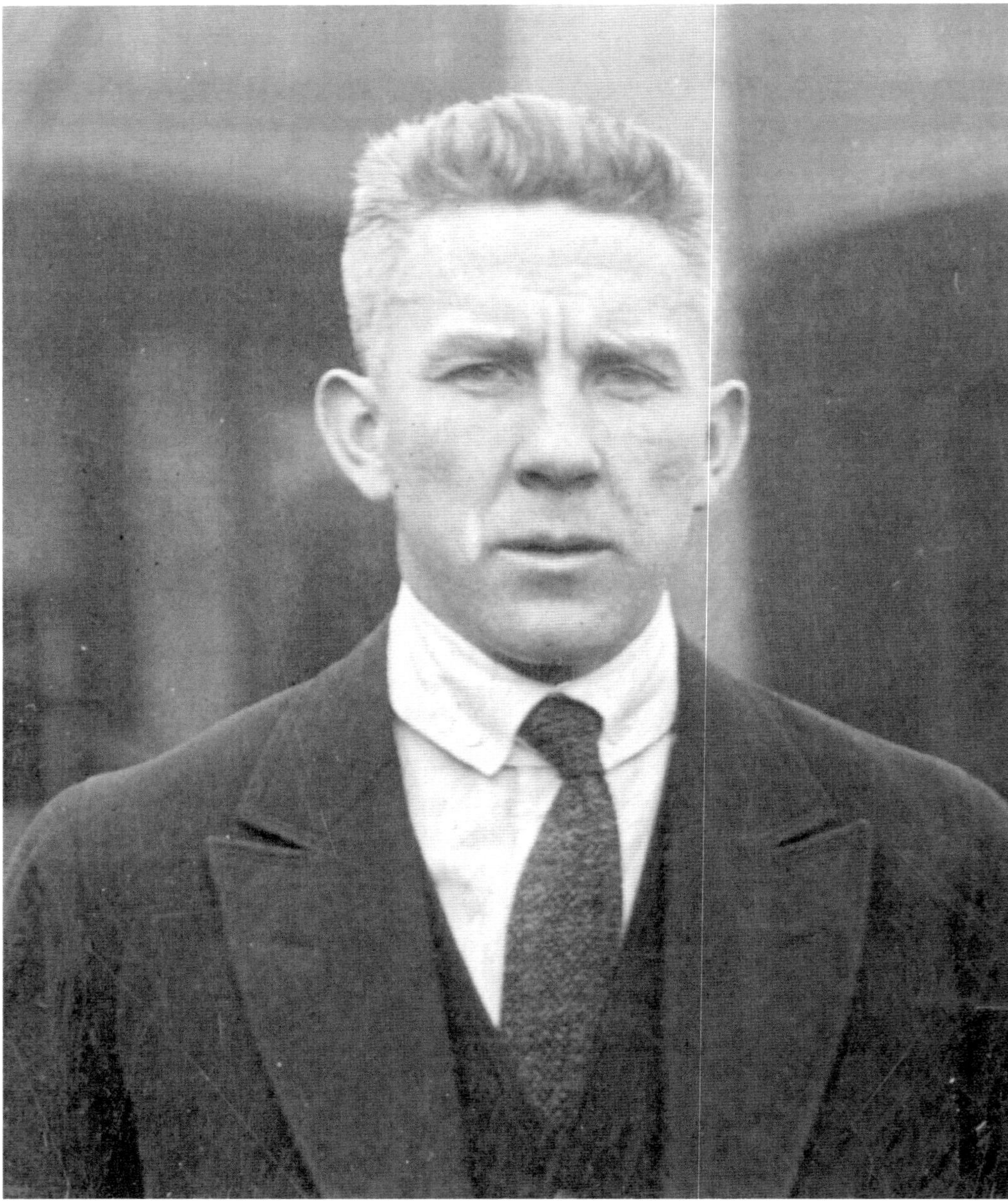

Walter Adam Olsen

Former Mount Clemens High School football coach Walter Adam Olsen is seen here (above right) enjoying a reunion in 1958 with some of the star players from his championship teams. Shown (from left) are James C. Daner, Harry "Hatchet" Haller, George "Sam" Rastigue, Harry "Jake" Lefurgey, Olsen, and Edgar D. Racine. Olsen, himself a star player in football, basketball, and baseball at Western Michigan University, coached Mount Clemens High School football from 1920 to 1934 and then spent two seasons as the school's athletic director. During his tenure as coach, his football teams compiled an impressive record of five undefeated seasons. In 1959, the city of Mount Clemens named a public park in the esteemed coach's honor. Seen at the dedication (below right) are (from left) R. Harvey Millar, Olsen, and mayor Harold Lindsey. (Courtesy of the *Macomb Daily*.)

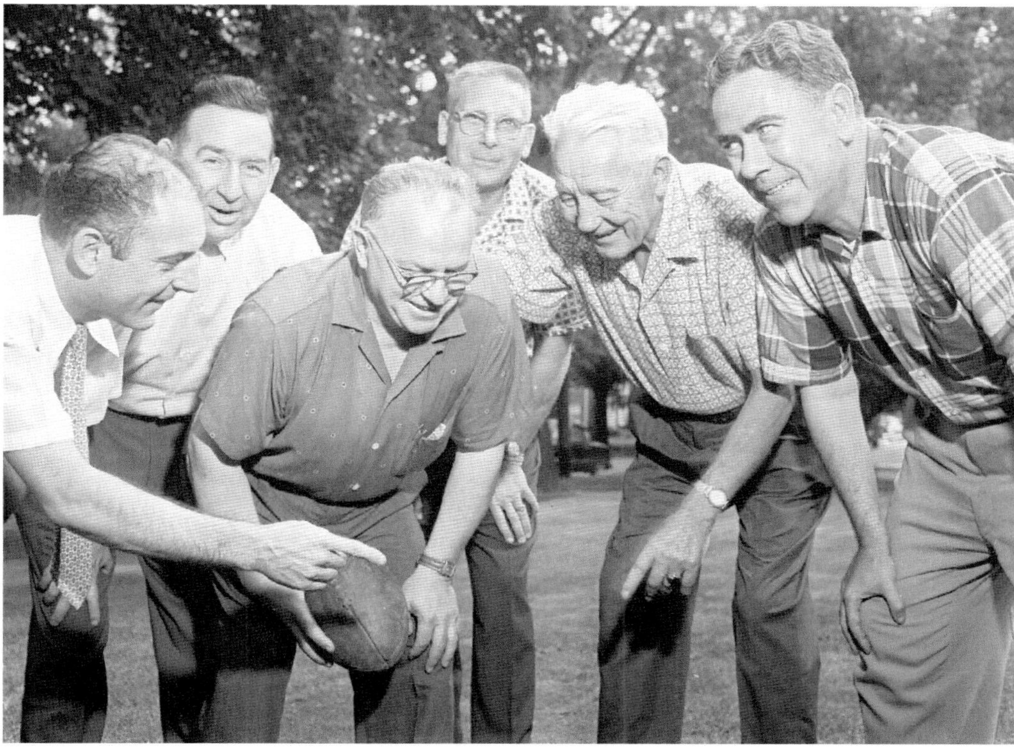

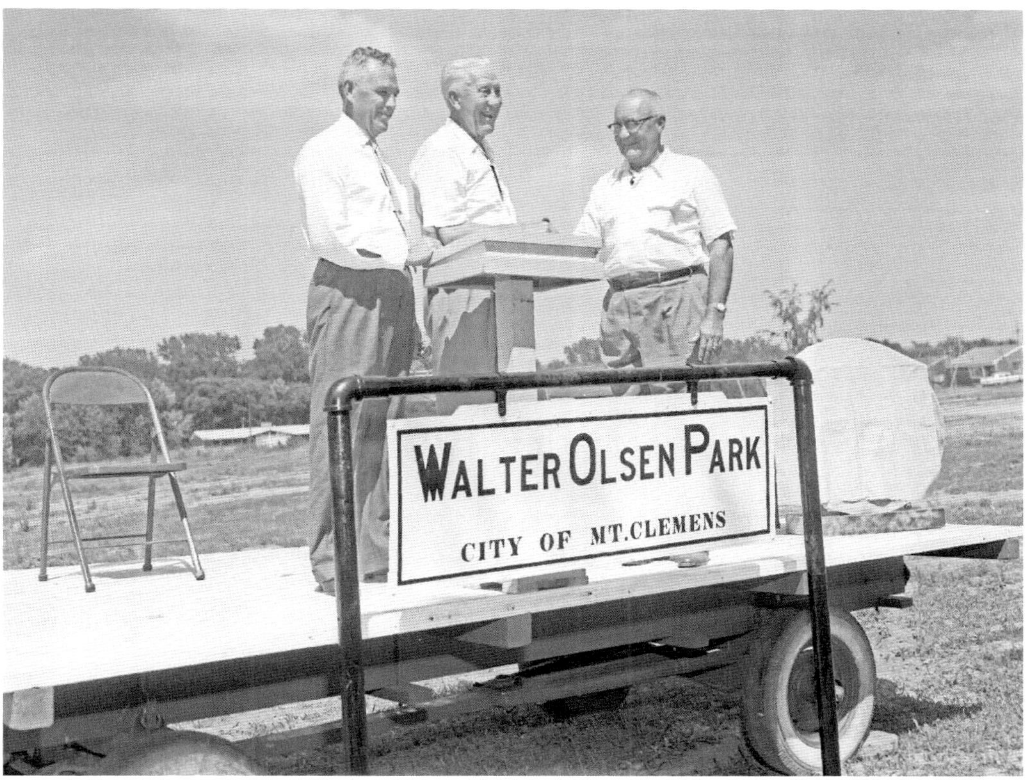
WALTER OLSEN PARK
CITY OF MT.CLEMENS

Miriam Altman

Generations of children who visited Mount Clemens Public Library were well acquainted with Altman, shown here at the library circulation desk in 1948. A graduate of the University of Michigan, she began her career with the library in 1942 as assistant to head librarian Ann A.S. Crocker and was appointed library director in 1956 upon Crocker's retirement. It was during Miriam Altman's tenure as director that the library moved from an overcrowded building to a modern and spacious facility on Cass Avenue, and greatly expanded its range of services to the public. In announcing her retirement in 1973, the *Macomb Daily* commented that the library "achieved its greatest stature for service during the incumbency of Miss Miriam Altman." (Courtesy of the *Macomb Daily.*)

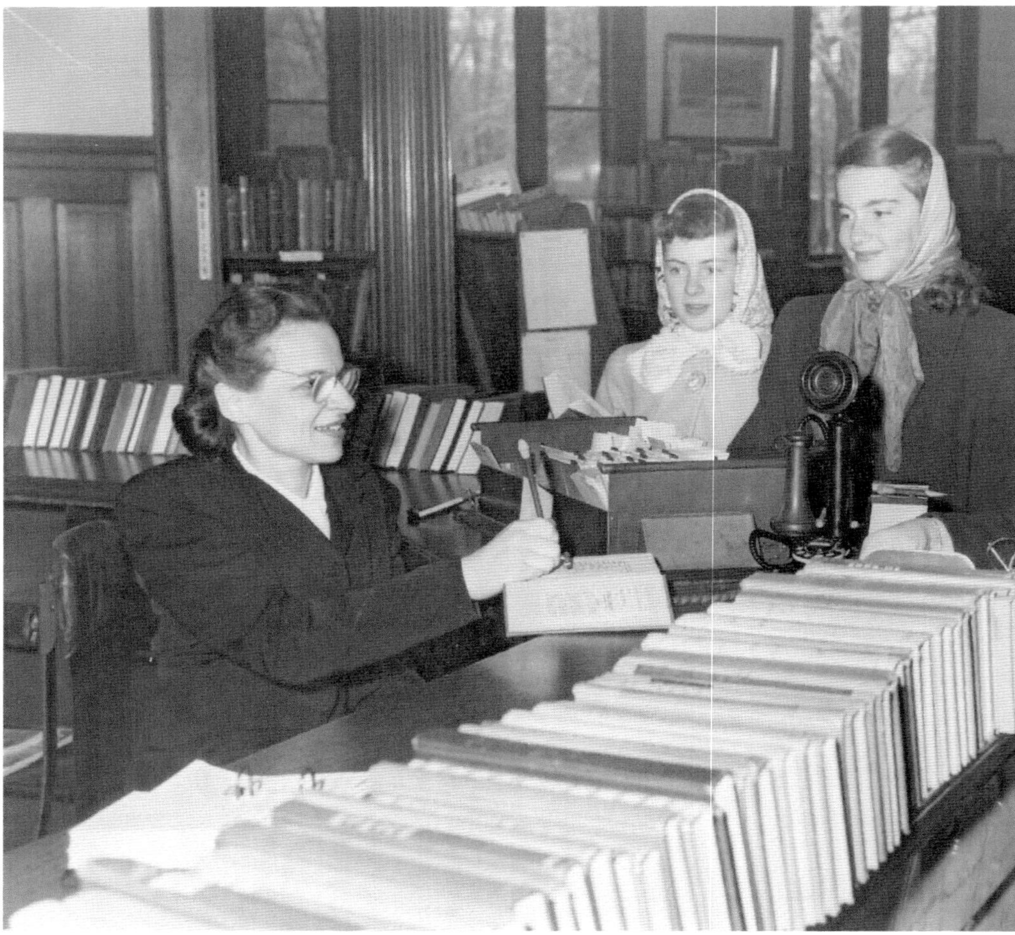

Mark Thompson McKee Sr. (RIGHT)

Seven US presidents were numbered among McKee's acquaintances, from William McKinley to Harry S. Truman. McKee left a job as a traveling formaldehyde salesman in 1923 to join his brothers, Paul and Max, in the newspaper business when the trio purchased the weekly *Mount Clemens Monitor.* The brothers eventually merged the *Monitor* with other local newspapers to form a daily paper that became known as the *Macomb Daily.* With his brothers, McKee also invested in transportation companies, especially shipping and railroad lines, and developed many national and international business contacts. McKee served as a member of the board of directors of Pan American Airlines from 1939 until 1982. (Courtesy of the *Macomb Daily.*)

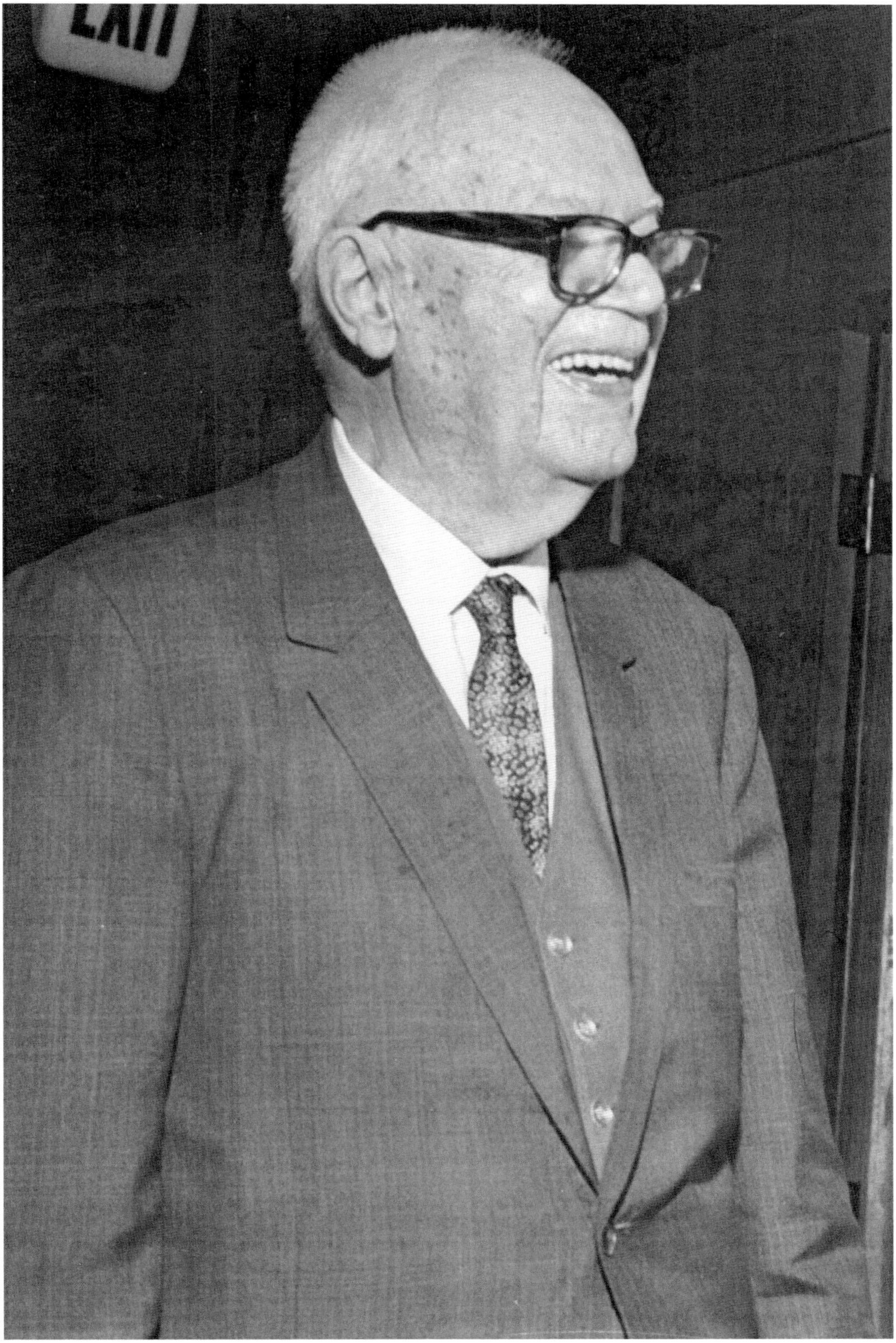

William L. Berkhof

While serving as superintendent of Mount Clemens Community Schools from 1948 to 1968, Berkhof led an ambitious 20-year construction program that expanded and modernized the school district's aging and inadequate facilities, and replaced an overcrowded public library building. The University of Michigan graduate also made lasting contributions in many areas of community life, by helping to found the Macomb County Child Guidance Clinic, the Art Center, and the Mount Clemens Symphony Orchestra. He was an active member of the Mount Clemens Rotary Club, serving as its president and also as a Rotary district governor. (Courtesy of the *Macomb Daily*.)

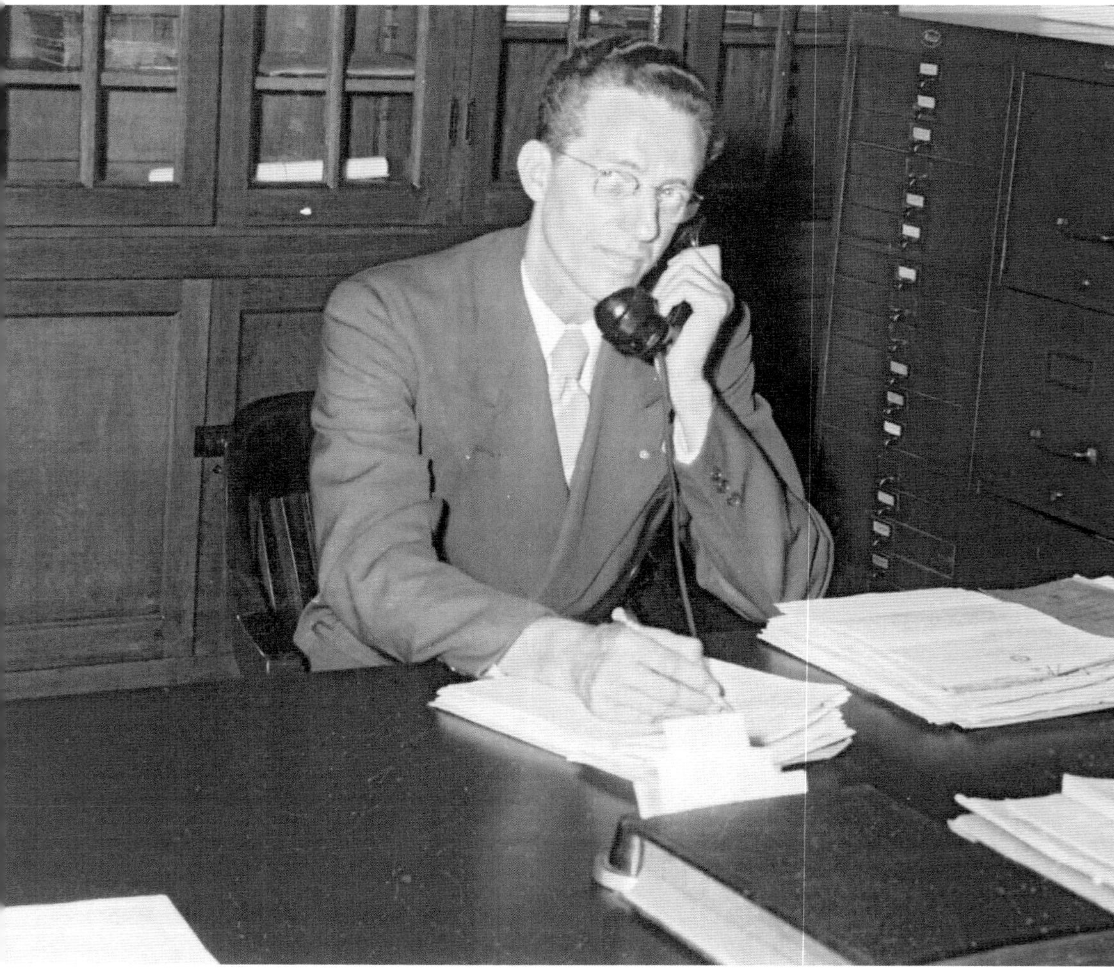

Desmond A. "Des" Arnsby (RIGHT)

Arnsby was born in Ireland and began his journalism career in London, Ontario, before coming to Mount Clemens to join the *Daily Leader* as a police beat reporter in 1929. Except for a two-year stint with the Associated Press, he spent the rest of his career in Mount Clemens working for the *Leader* and its successor newspapers. In 1950, he penned a series of articles on the loneliness of soldiers stationed at nearby Selfridge Air Force Base, an effort that spurred the formation of the first successful Military-Community Relations Committee in the nation. The following year, Mount Clemens's effort to support its local military base was the subject of a theatrical short film that was released nationwide and featured Arnsby as narrator. (Courtesy of the *Macomb Daily*.)

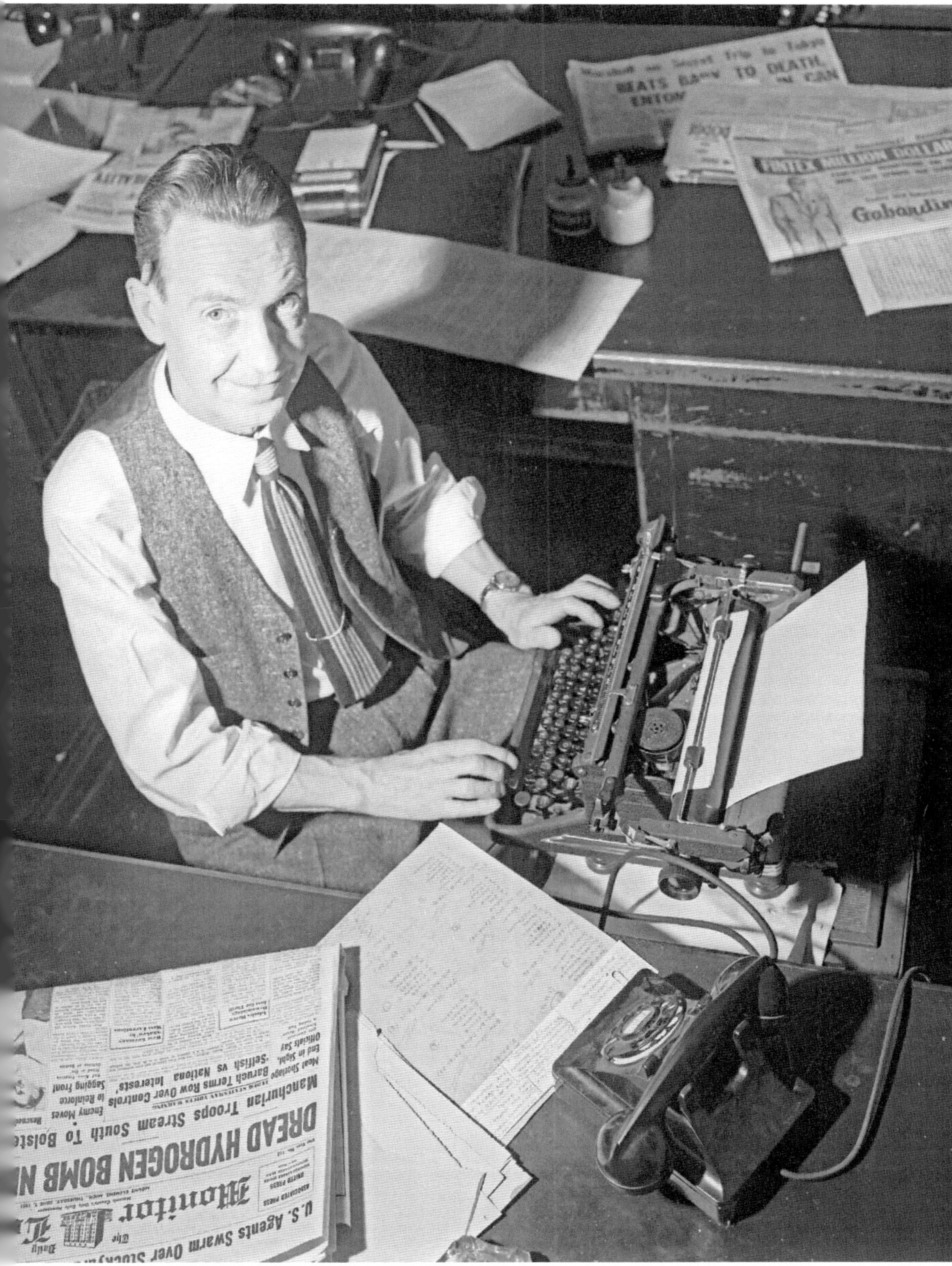
DREAD HYDROGEN BOMB
Manchurian Troops Stream South To Bolste
U.S. Agents Swarm Over Stocks
BEATS BABY TO DEATH
Gabardine

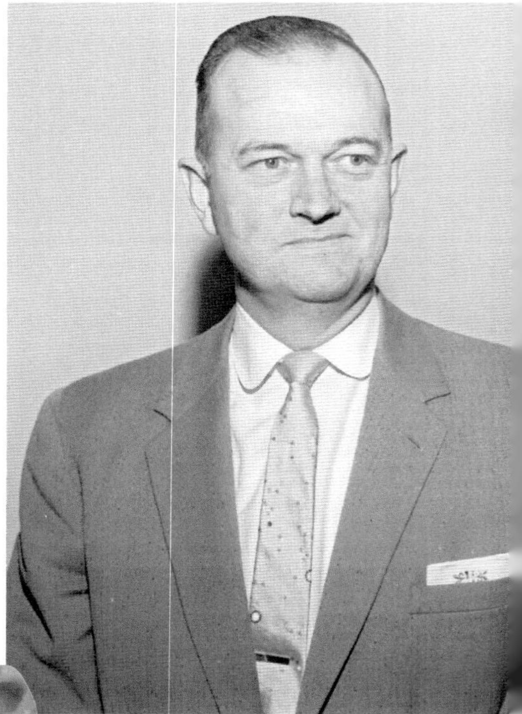

Harold E. Jones

As principal of Mount Clemens High School from 1947 to 1973, Jones was well known to an entire generation of students. He led the high school staff during a time when the school district was expanding and a $4 million building project added 44 classrooms, a new swimming pool, a gymnasium, and a planetarium to the campus. (Courtesy of the *Macomb Daily*.)

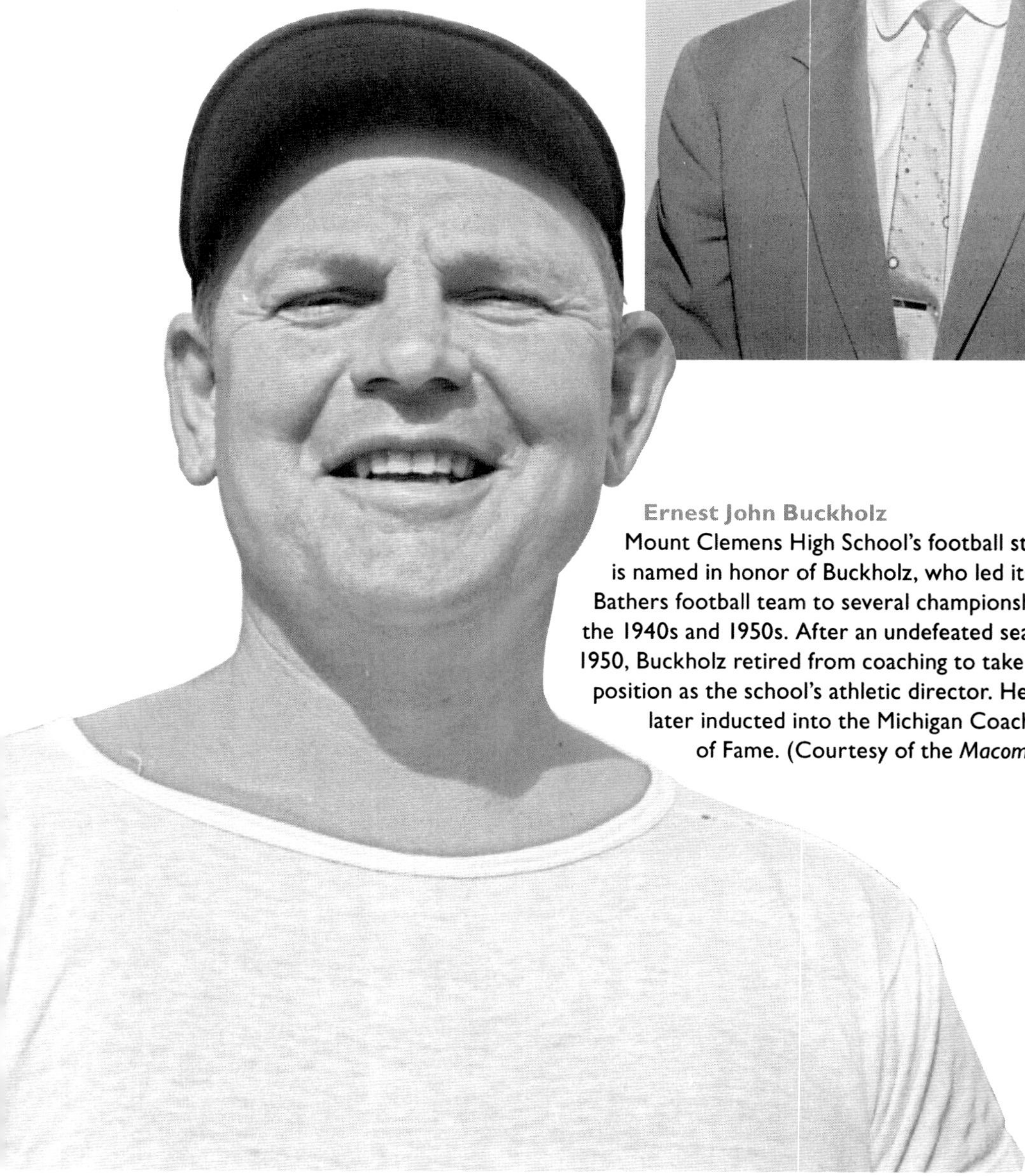

Ernest John Buckholz

Mount Clemens High School's football stadium is named in honor of Buckholz, who led its Bathers football team to several championships in the 1940s and 1950s. After an undefeated season in 1950, Buckholz retired from coaching to take a new position as the school's athletic director. He was later inducted into the Michigan Coaches Hall of Fame. (Courtesy of the *Macomb Daily*.)

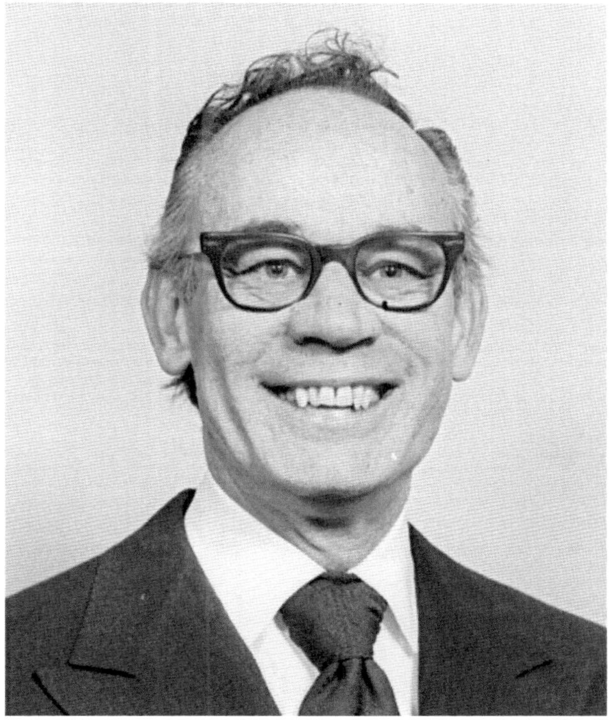

Charles Bernard McGhee
For more than three decades, much of the choral music that was heard in Mount Clemens was produced under the baton of McGhee. The director of music education for Mount Clemens Community Schools also served as director of the community's civic chorus and three of its local church choirs. McGhee also founded the Mount Clemens Symphony Orchestra Association. (Courtesy of the *Macomb Daily*.)

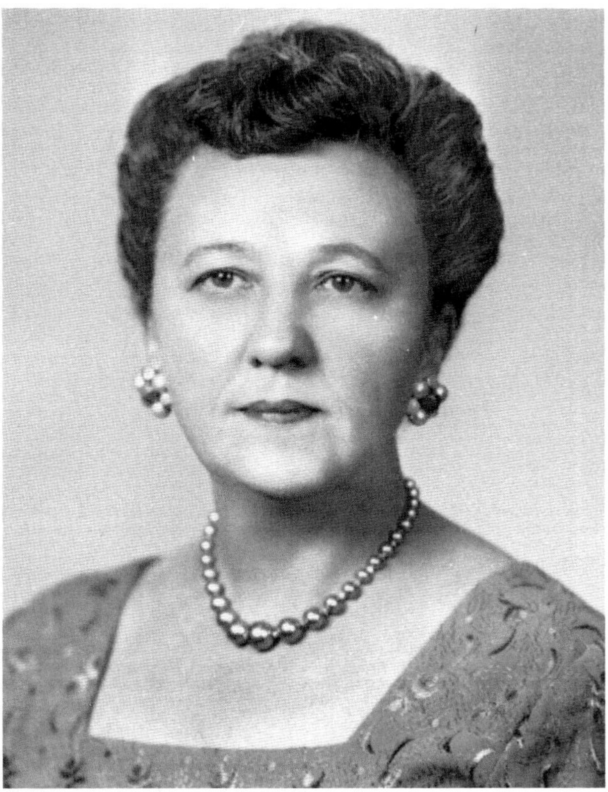

Isabel M. Miller
Miller devoted her long and active life to the teaching and enjoyment of music. An accomplished student of piano and voice, she earned a master's degree in music, taught music in the Detroit Public Schools and at Wayne State University, and directed the nurses' choirs of several Detroit area hospitals. She died in 2010 at the age of 101. (Courtesy of the *Macomb Daily*.)

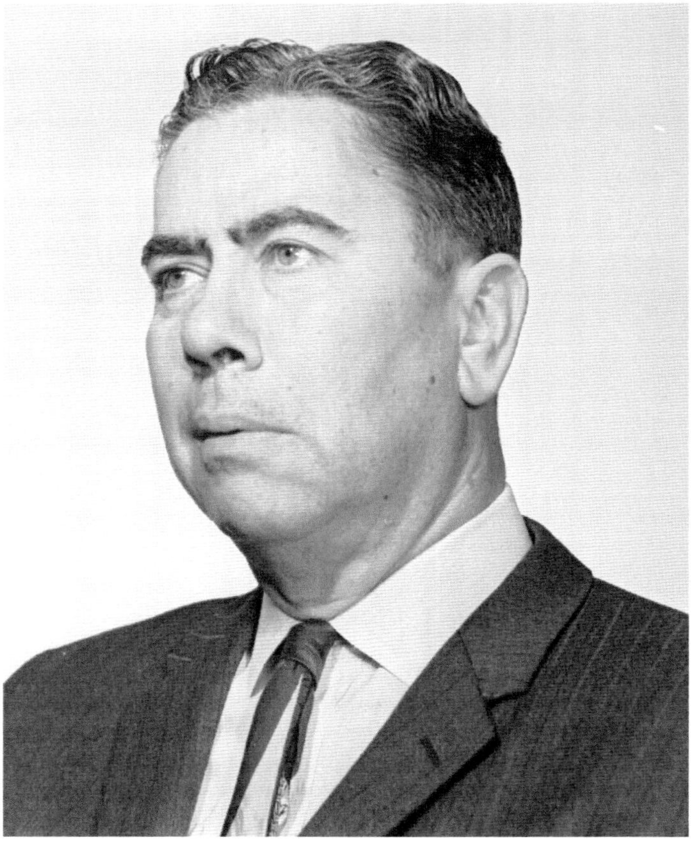

Edgar Donaldson Racine
Everyday life in Mount Clemens as well as stories of the community's long history were captured and preserved in print by Racine, longtime columnist and editor of the *Macomb Daily* and its predecessor, the *Daily Monitor-Leader.* Racine was a Mount Clemens native with family ties to the town's pioneer days, and he regularly capsulized local history lore for his readers in his weekly column entitled "Down Memory Lane." With his wife, Kathleen, who was a teacher at Mount Clemens High School, Racine lived in a historic home on Cass Avenue, shown below. (Courtesy of the *Macomb Daily.*)

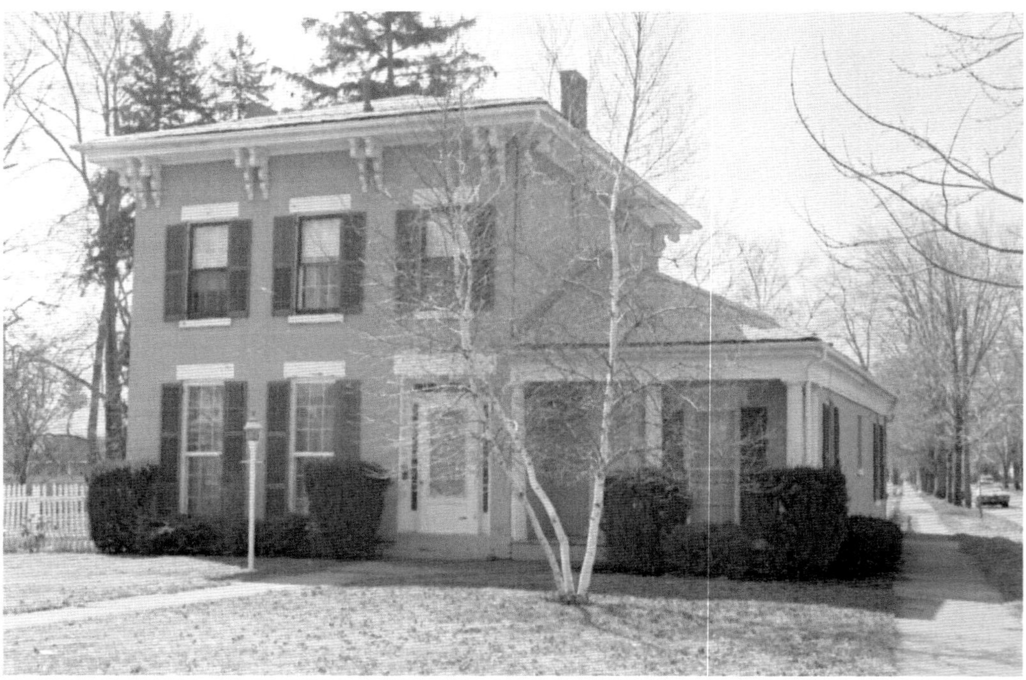

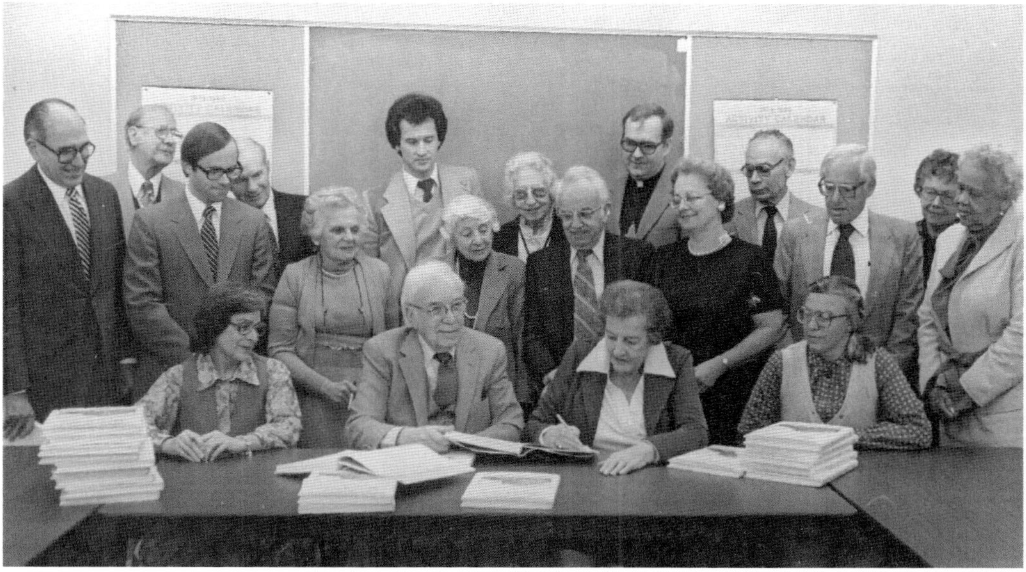

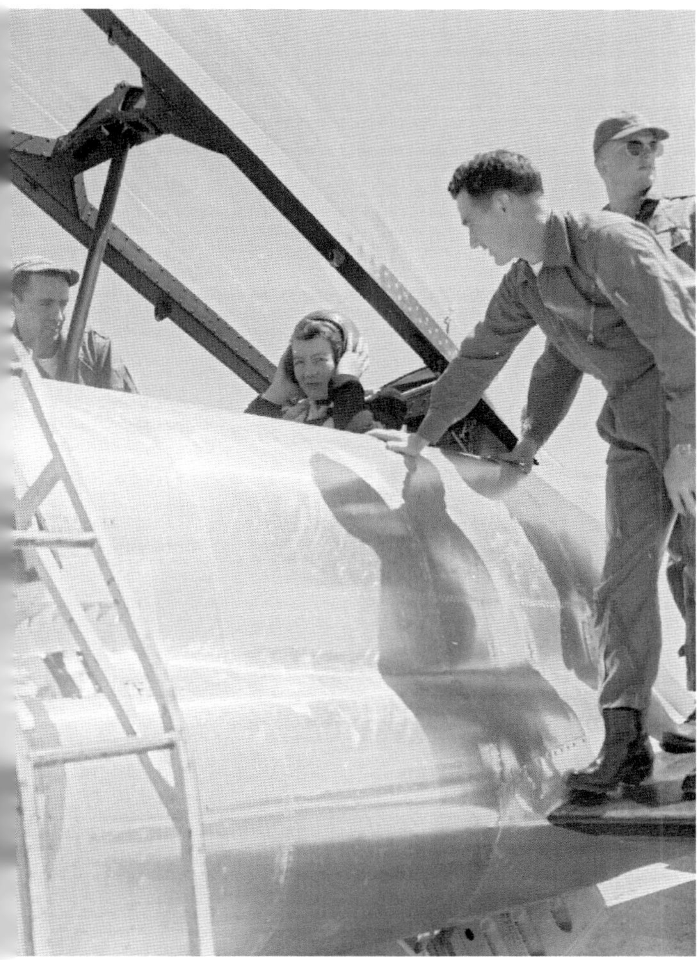

Dorothy McPherson Magee
Magee began her 29-year career at the *Macomb Daily* in 1948 as a secretary with the newspaper's predecessor, the *Daily Monitor-Leader*. Over the years, she served as a general assignment reporter, telegraph editor, women's editor, church editor, and features editor. A talented reporter and writer with an intrepid spirit, Magee is shown (left) preparing to take a flight in a jet fighter in 1950. She received special permission for the flight, and was one of the first women ever to ride in a military jet. Magee also edited a history of Mount Clemens published in 1980 by the Bright Future For Mount Clemens Committee, and is seen above (seated, third from left) with the committee celebrating the book's publication. (Courtesy of the *Macomb Daily*.)

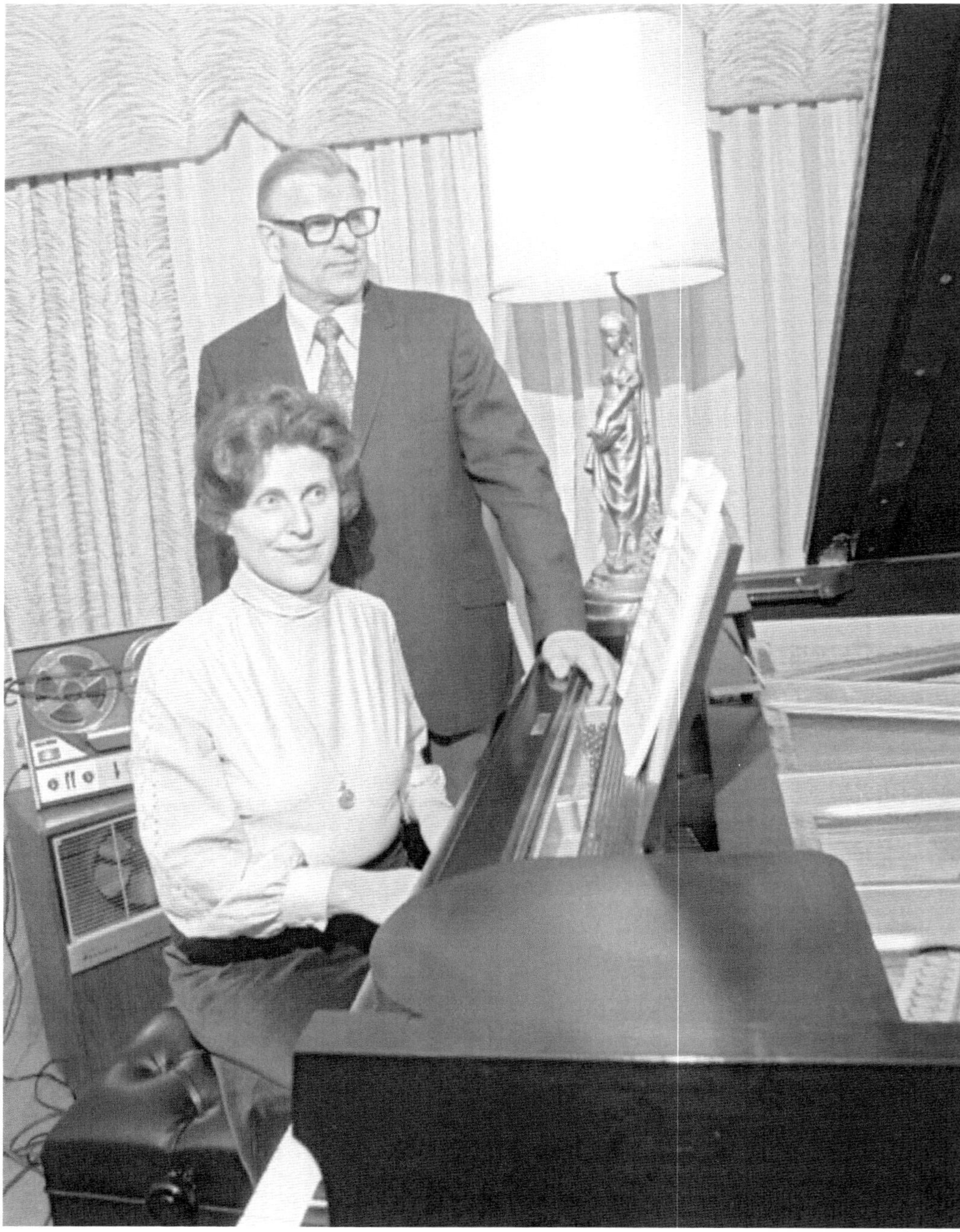

Adelaide C. Schulte Schwark

For 37 years, Schwark was a beloved and respected teacher at St. Mary's Catholic School in Mount Clemens, where she also served as vice principal. Schwark was known for her exacting standards and high expectations of her pupils and is fondly remembered by the many students whose lives she touched. The mother of four sons and four daughters was also an avid gardener and musician. Both Schwark and her husband, Martin, held college degrees in music and were talented pianists. The couple, shown here at the keyboard, often performed duets together. (Courtesy of the *Macomb Daily*.)

CHAPTER SIX

Innovators and Rebels

In any community, there are those who cannot be neatly categorized—those who may be considered by their contemporaries to be a little too eccentric, unconventional, or idealistic. Some possess gifts of genius and inspiration that are poorly understood by those around them, and they are labeled by history as "ahead of their time." Others harbor a defiant, independent streak that prevents them from fitting into society's accepted norms, making them virtual outcasts.

The stories of individuals such as these are rarely neat and tidy. A look beneath the glaring headlines usually reveals complexities not acknowledged by the community. In Mount Clemens's history, one may find a dedicated nun, known to the outside world as a pediatric nurse, who in her private moments was an inventor working on the development of a product now recognized around the world. At the other end of the spectrum is found the town's most notorious brothel operator, who also happened to be—on the sly—one of its most generous local philanthropists.

These are the innovators and rebels—the geniuses and nonconformists—who are the stuff of local legend. The flamboyant ones are recognized chiefly for the headlines they made or the back fence gossip they generated. Others who shunned the spotlight are generally overlooked by history, their contributions all but forgotten. Told here are some of those stories that never made the headlines, brought into specific relief through the passage of time.

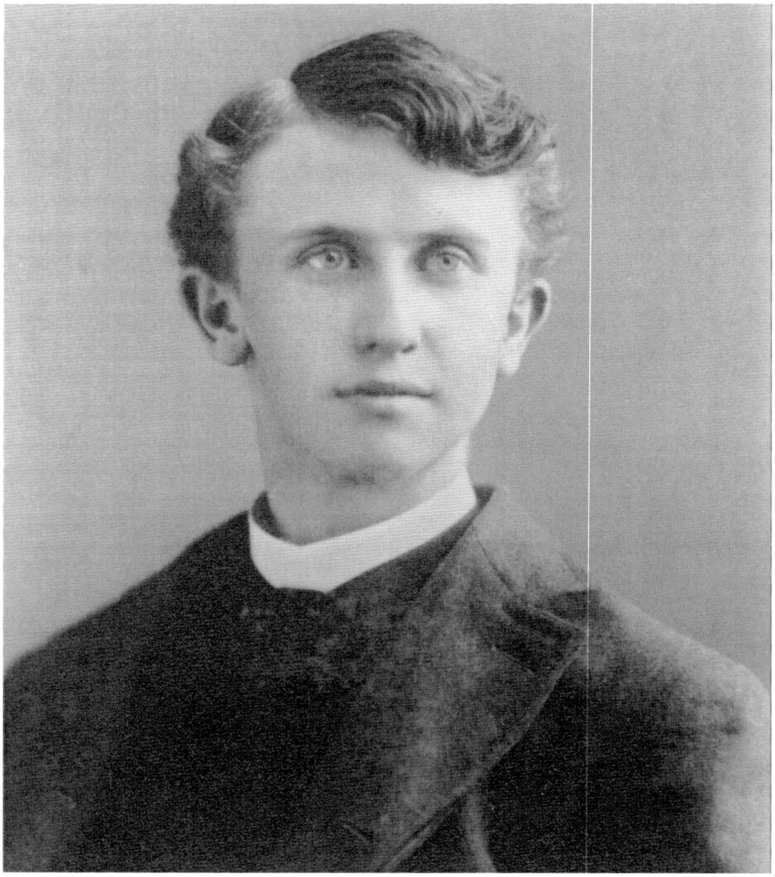

Franklin Harold Hayward

As a young teenager, Hayward was already drawing charcoal and crayon portraits, many of which were displayed in the store windows of local merchants. At the tender age of 17, he opened a studio in downtown Mount Clemens and sought commissions for his artwork. His parents encouraged him to develop his talent by studying with established artists, and in 1886 he won two first prizes for work he exhibited at the Michigan State Fair. Hayward moved to Chicago to study and work for several years, then traveled abroad where he entered the Paris art academy of James McNeill Whistler; he also studied with other renowned painters based in Paris and toured widely in Europe. Upon returning to Mount Clemens in 1901, Hayward opened an academy and studio and produced a large number of portraits, landscapes, and still life studies. He captured on canvas the likenesses of numerous residents of Mount Clemens, from business leaders and circuit court judges to an old fisherman for whom he had a particular affinity. Determined to make a living solely from his art, Hayward was destined to endure financial difficulties, which were made worse in his later life and career by the economic conditions of the Great Depression. In addition, his family relationships were strained and sometimes exceedingly turbulent, and he was regarded as something of an eccentric personality. Although he had become by that time a well-known artist with a strong regional reputation, he was living in dire circumstances at the end of his life and subsisted primarily on handouts from friends and students. A newspaper interview published not long before his death quoted him as saying "I want to work until the last hour that I live." Hayward died in Detroit in 1945 and was buried in Clinton Grove Cemetery near his hometown of Mount Clemens. His work hangs in museums, state capitol buildings, and halls of justice around the country. (Courtesy of Mount Clemens Public Library.)

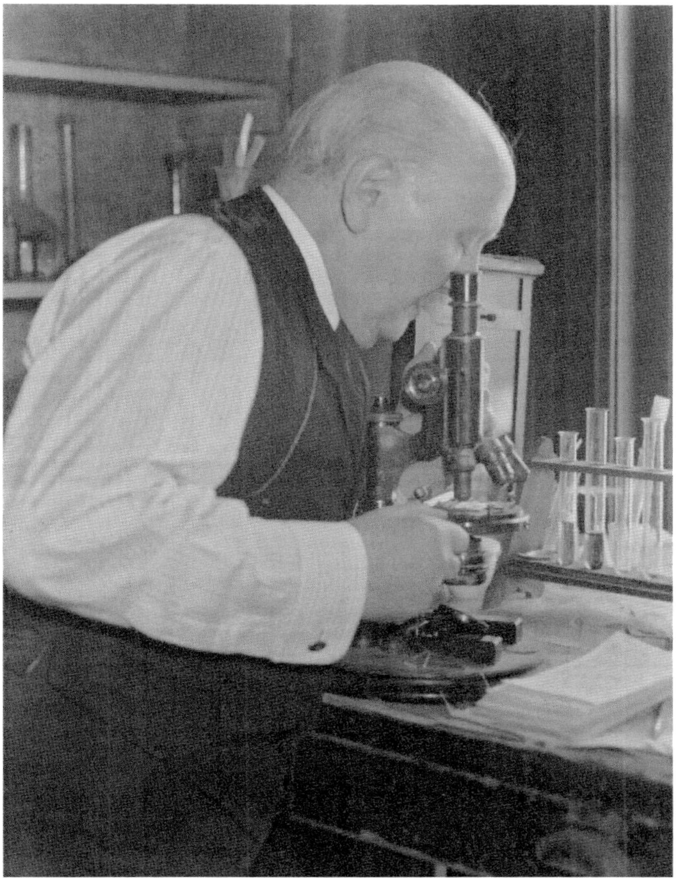

John Meyer

Mount Clemens bathhouse operators often quoted a chemical analysis completed by local druggist John Meyer to tout the efficacy of the mineral water they pumped from the ground. The German-born Meyer had come to Mount Clemens in 1879 and published a breakdown of the elements found in the town's mineral water in 1905. The front window of his pharmacy displayed a large glass jar containing 125 pounds of solids that he had distilled from the 65 gallons of water used to give one mineral bath. Ever a Bath City booster, Meyer also bottled and sold a medicinal product he called Lithiated Mount Clemens Aperient Water, but in 1917 the federal government found it to be adulterated with mold and bacteria and fined him for selling it. (Courtesy of Macomb County Historical Society and Mount Clemens Public Library.)

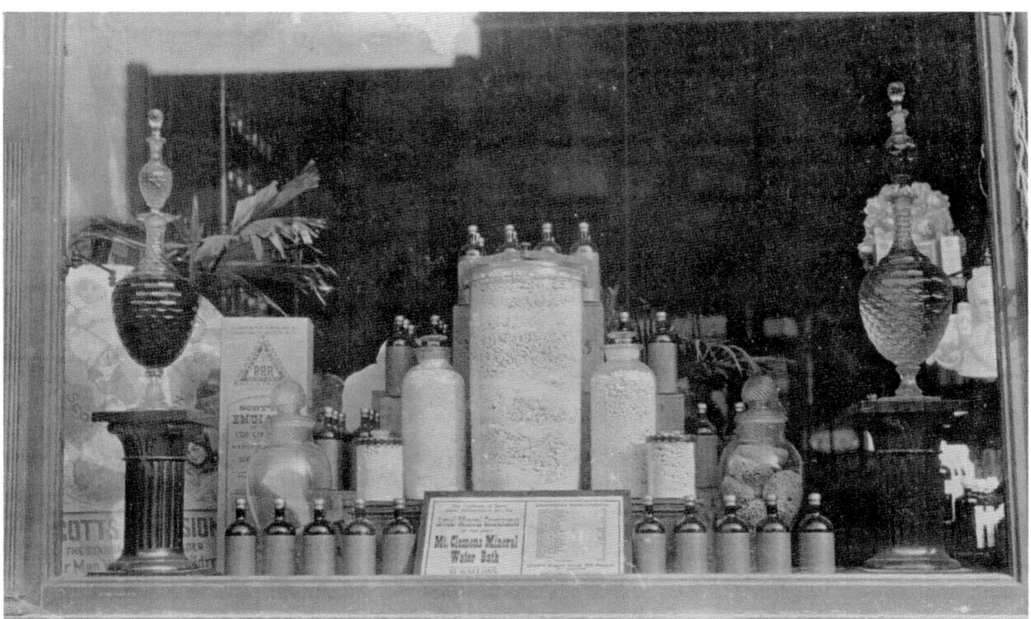

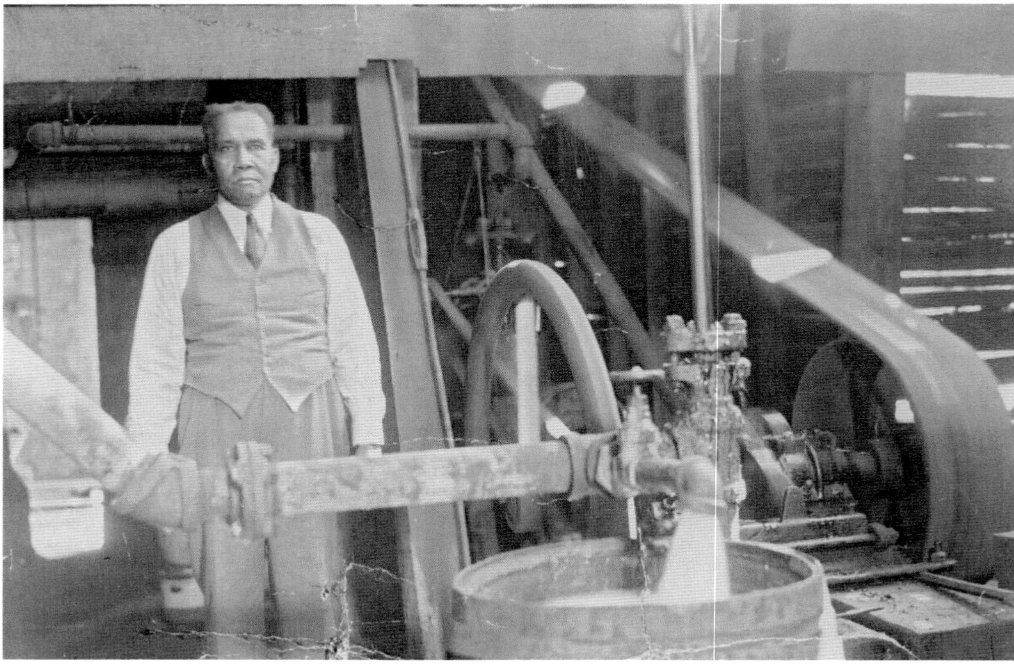

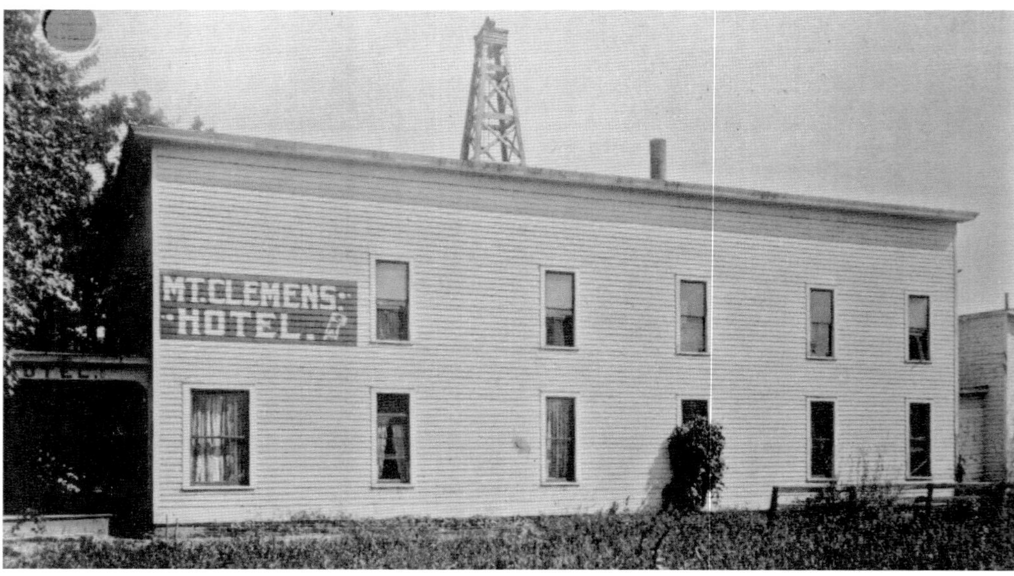

Henry John Lightbourne

Lightbourne learned the blacksmith trade in his native Jamaica, worked on the Panama Canal construction, and shod horses for the mounted police in Alberta, Canada, before coming to Detroit to take a job in an auto factory. In 1920, he left Detroit and purchased the Mount Clemens Hotel and Bath House, the only bathhouse in the city at the time that served people of color. Lightbourne was also an avid inventor, and while living in Detroit in 1919, he devised a design for a tire protector—an early version of a tire stud, of sorts—which he successfully patented. Although the hotel shown above burned in 1929, the bathhouse stood until 1965, when Lightbourne's property was acquired for a road project. (Courtesy of Mount Clemens Public Library.)

William Thomas Moxon

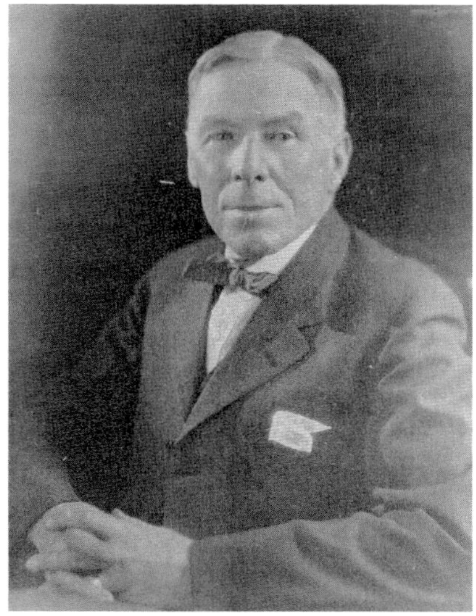

English-born William Thomas Moxon came to the United States in 1881 and shortly thereafter to Mount Clemens, where he made his home. The pharmacy clerk founded his own business in 1891 when he devised a medicine called Moxon's Liniment, a treatment that was advertised as making "cripples dance with joy." The nationwide success of the product allowed Moxon to move into a large new store at 65 North Walnut Street in 1893. A leader among patent medicine producers in Mount Clemens, the company ran into trouble in 1936 when the FDA judged it in violation of the Federal Caustic Poison Act. Upon analysis, the government found Moxon's Liniment to consist primarily of ammonia and concluded that claims about its curative power were false and misleading. (Courtesy of Macomb County Historical Society and Mount Clemens Public Library.)

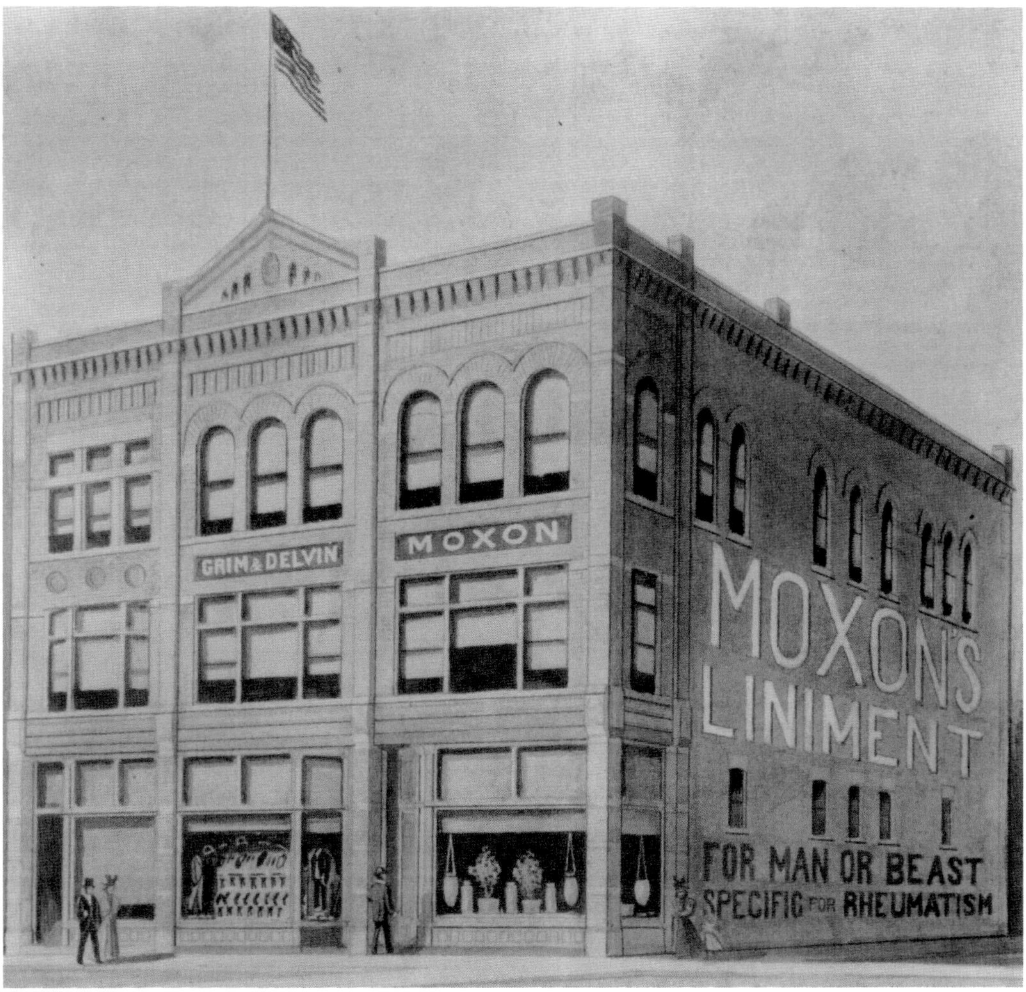

Mary "Mae" McKenna

Of all of the colorful characters in Mount Clemens history, few can claim the title of "legendary" more appropriately than McKenna. Abandoned at a foundling home in New York City soon after her birth in 1880, McKenna was reared by the August Wolters family in Sheboygan, Wisconsin, and grew up using the name Mary Wolters. While living in Wisconsin, she met and married a salesman named Henry Collins, and the young couple relocated to Omaha, Nebraska, where Collins died suddenly in 1918. For reasons not recorded in history, the widowed McKenna moved from Omaha to Mount Clemens after her husband's death, paid cash for a house at 35 Park Street (shown below), and used it as the base for a rather spectacular career as a brothel operator. McKenna's business was highly successful and was said to have catered to many of the town's power brokers, a situation that may have kept her out of jail on several occasions. Her only real trouble with the law came when she was arrested for Prohibition-era liquor law violations, and she served two terms in the Detroit House of Correction for selling and serving illegal spirits. When not flirting with the law, McKenna was known for her quiet generosity to charitable causes. A nominal Roman Catholic, she donated—often through a third party—to charities affiliated with the church, and to the Girl Scouts and other children's organizations. A local merchant remembered that during the years of the Great Depression he would occasionally receive a telephone call from McKenna, advising him that she was sending a group of neighborhood children to his store to be fitted with new shoes. After the children had departed, McKenna would quietly stop in to pay the bill. So well known was Mount Clemens's famous madam that when she died in 1944, her death was reported for soldiers overseas in *Yank Magazine*, and she was eulogized in the *Detroit Free Press* as the "Queen of Vice." Having no local family, McKenna was buried in her childhood home in Wisconsin, under the name Mary Wolters. (Courtesy of City of Mount Clemens.)

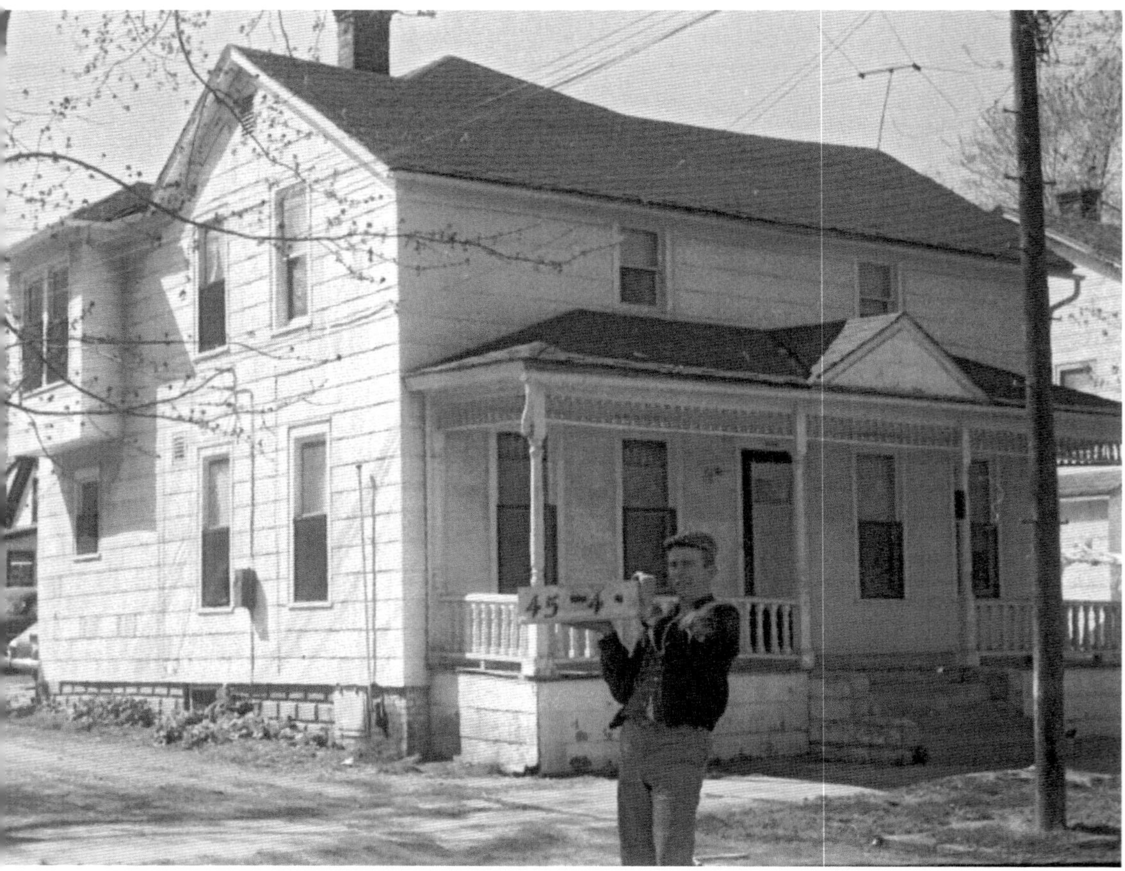

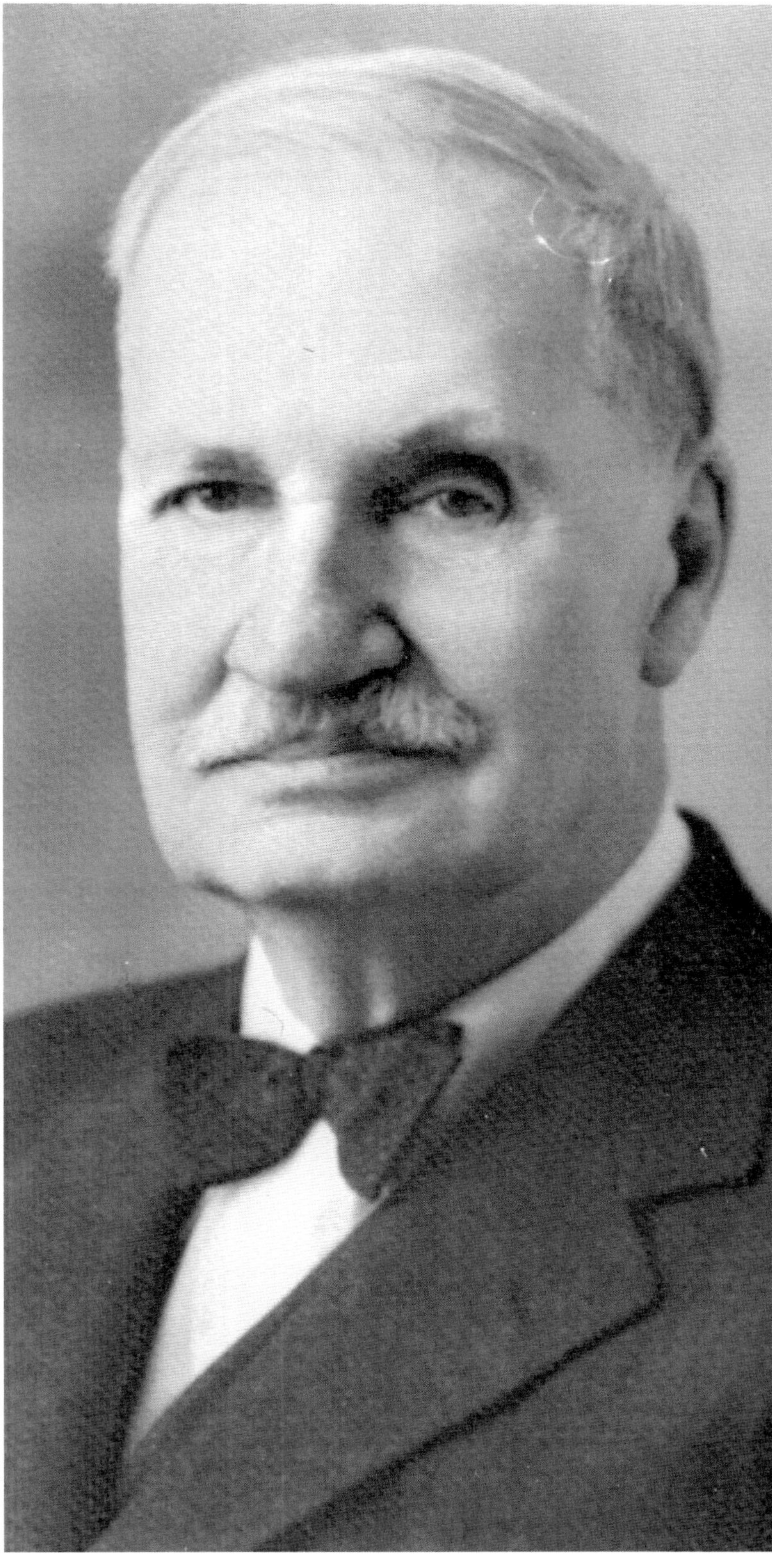

Alfred Copony
Inventor and engineer Alfred Copony was born in Vienna and came to Mount Clemens in 1920. He had worked as a master car builder for the Grand Trunk Railway system until 1913, and during that time he invented a device to load automobiles onto railroad cars. Copony registered the first US patent for the auto loading mechanism, and with it launched the Copony Auto Loading Company in Detroit. Copony held more than 100 other patents and also used his expertise to advise the Austrian consular service on trade matters. When he settled in Mount Clemens, he founded a company that later became known as the Mount Clemens Metal Products Company, and he helped to organize the Macomb County Engineering Society. (Courtesy of the *Macomb Daily*.)

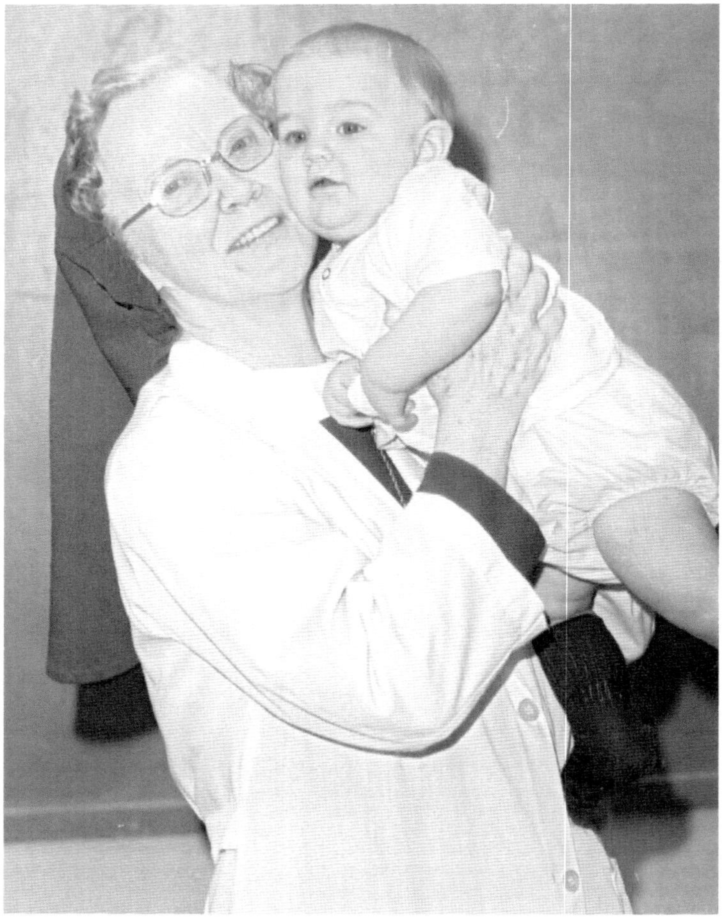

Sr. Redempta Wittberg

Ethel Magdeline Wittberg was born in Cincinnati, Ohio, and earned her degree in nursing in 1940 from the College of Mount St. Joseph. She entered the congregation of the Sisters of Charity the following year, taking the name Sr. Redempta. She served as a nurse, and later as director of nursing services at St. Joseph Mercy Hospital in Mount Clemens from 1943 until 1953, was transferred to an infant and maternity center in Cincinnati, and then returned to Mount Clemens in 1971 to serve as St. Joseph's supervisor of pediatrics. Sr. Redempta earned a reputation for experimentation and development of new tools to assist her in the care of infants, so when Procter and Gamble wanted to develop a marketable disposable diaper in the late 1950s, researchers at the Cincinnati-based company contacted her for assistance. "I was using cloth diapers at the time because I was disgusted with paper diapers," Sr. Redempta recalled later. "I told the researcher I was willing to work on the development of a usable paper diaper." And so she did. For the next two years, under cloak of secrecy, Sr. Redempta worked with Procter and Gamble, personally developing the shape, paper, padding, and glue for the new product that was known as "Pampers" when it was released to the public in 1961. At the company's request, Sr. Redempta signed over her patent rights to Procter and Gamble, and was reimbursed with enough money to have two nursery rooms soundproofed. Although she enjoyed the challenge of the diaper project, she wasn't entirely convinced of its value at first. "My attitude at the time was that only a lazy mother would use that type of diaper," she later recalled in a newspaper interview. Sr. Redempta died in 2010 at the age of 98, just as Procter and Gamble was preparing to celebrate the 50th anniversary of its iconic diaper product. (Courtesy of the *Macomb Daily*.)

CHAPTER SEVEN

Heroes

As Mount Clemens approaches its bicentennial, the town can boast thousands of homegrown heroes who have served their neighbors as soldiers, sailors, airmen, marines, police officers, firefighters, and medical first responders. The Bath City has been represented in the nation's armed forces in all of the major and minor conflicts of the last 200 years, from the Civil War to the war on terrorism. Many local families lost sons and daughters on the field of battle, and some whose loved ones went missing were even denied the privilege of laying those heroes to rest.

The common threads in all of the stories of Mount Clemens's heroes are the commitment, courage, duty, honor, and sacrifice found not only in those who served but also in those they left behind. These concepts were not just pretty words for people like Donald E. Odell, who survived a hellish imprisonment in North Vietnam's infamous "Hanoi Hilton," or for Ralph E. Bennett, who went from the football fields of Mount Clemens High School and Michigan State University to a Japanese prison at Corrigedor in the Philippines.

Those who kept peace and order at home were likewise prepared to make substantial sacrifices for the principles they cherished. In the pages of Bath City history are found the names of men who died defending their neighbors' lives or property, including fire chief Edward J. Sawitzky and patrolman Robert J. Ahrens. Also recorded is the courage of attorney Kenneth N. Sanborn, who risked irreparable harm to his professional career in defense of freedoms he held dear.

The few heroes whose stories are told here stand to represent all of the many heroes who have called Mount Clemens home.

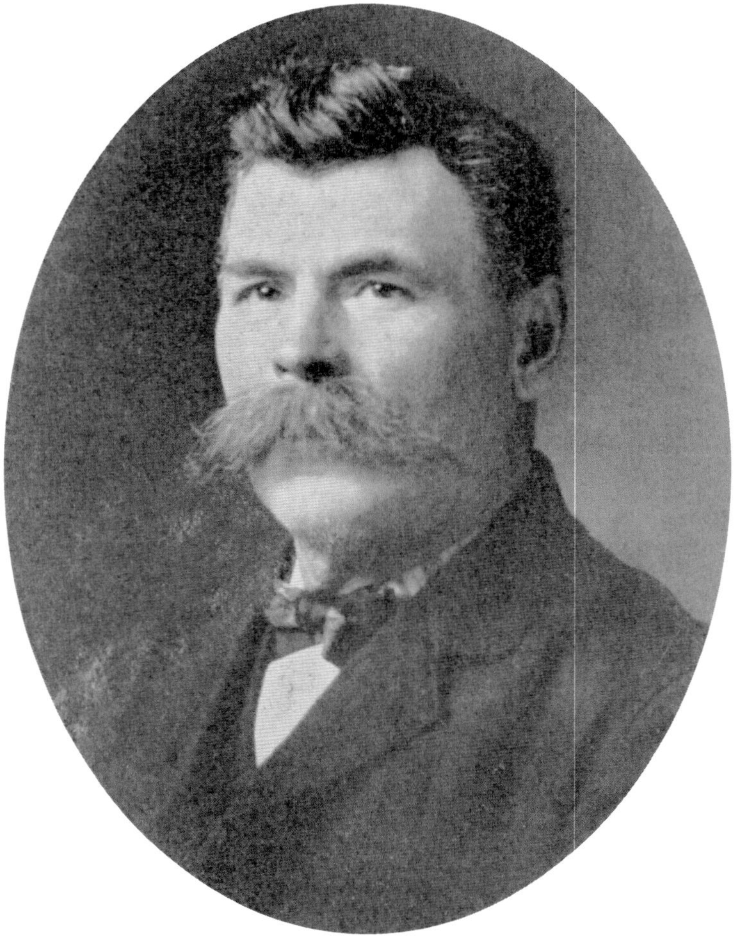

Gilbert LaCroix

As the last local veterans of the Civil War passed from the scene, it was their comrade in arms, Gilbert LaCroix, who kept their memories alive in the minds of the people of Mount Clemens. Born into one of Macomb County's pioneer families, LaCroix followed the tradition of his father and grandfather and worked on the boats plying the Clinton River and the Great Lakes. When the Civil War broke out, he enlisted in the Fifth Michigan Volunteer Infantry and was involved in 14 battles over the course of his term of service, including the battle of Gettysburg, where 105 men from his regiment were killed in the span of a single hour. He was also present at Appomattox Court House to witness the surrender of Confederate commander Robert E. Lee. Upon his return from the war, LaCroix resumed sailing as a lake boat captain and was also part-owner of a fleet of 10 vessels. With partner Oliver Chapoton, he built the steamer *City of Mount Clemens*, and later was the owner and master of the passenger steamer *Mascotte*, which carried Bath City visitors on excursion tours of Lake St. Clair. When a Grand Army of the Republic post was organized among the Civil War veterans of Mount Clemens in 1884, LaCroix took an active role in the post, over the years attending the funerals of every one of its 132 members. He served as the last post commander, accepting the solemn duty to disband the group and return its colors to the state capital in 1925 when only a handful of men remained to answer roll call. When Gilbert LaCroix died in 1938 at the age of 92, he was the last Civil War veteran in Mount Clemens and the oldest active member of the Old Crowd, having attended the annual reunion of the group only a few weeks before his death. (Courtesy of Mount Clemens Public Library.)

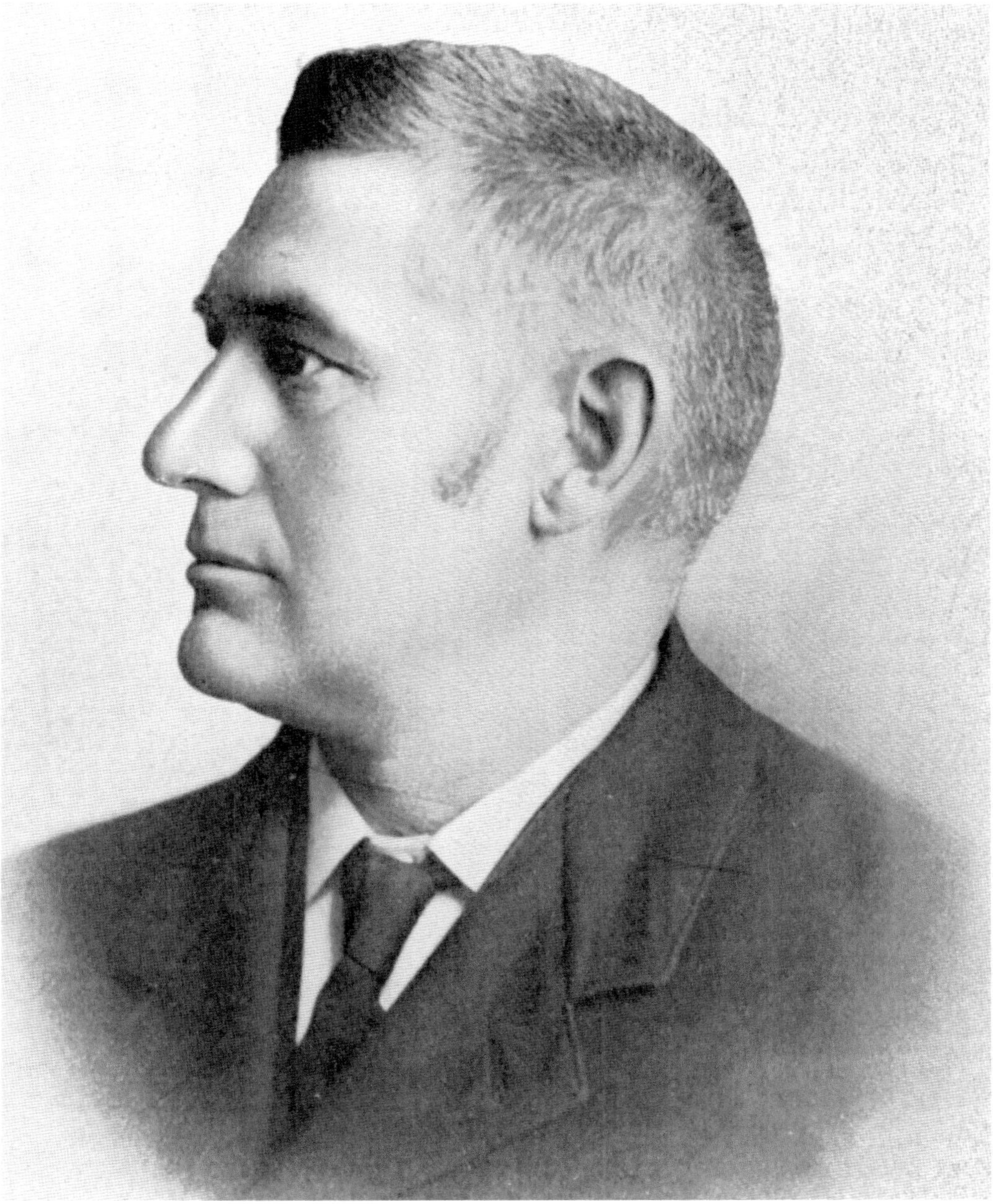

Joachim Matthews
Macomb County sheriff Joachim Matthews traveled to nearby Harrison Township on December 1, 1910 to arrest an immigrant farmer on charges of animal cruelty. As he stood on the porch of the farmer's home, a gunshot blasted through the front door, wounding the sheriff. Matthews drove himself back to Mount Clemens in his buggy, where he collapsed on the floor of the county jail; he died of his wounds a short time later. Investigators found that the shot had been fired by the farmer's son at the behest of the boy's mother, who spoke no English and thought a robbery was in progress. Meanwhile, businesses were closed on the day of Matthews's funeral, and the *Mount Clemens Monitor* reflected that the sheriff had discharged his duties "intelligently, faithfully, and unafraid." (Courtesy of Mount Clemens Public Library.)

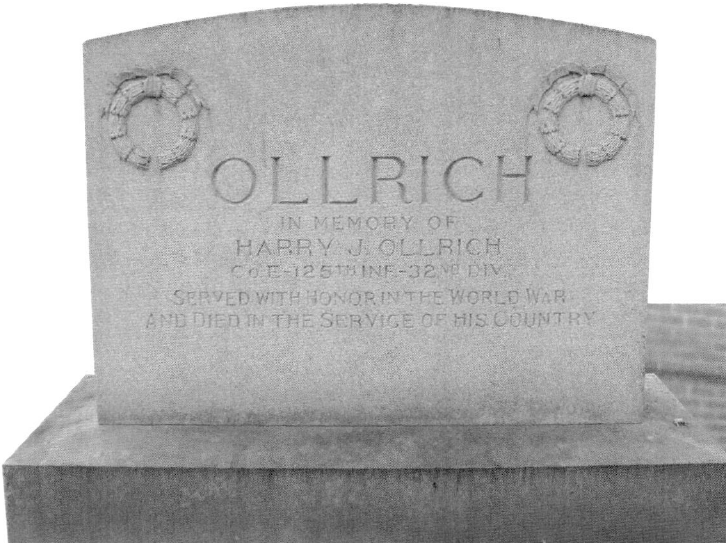

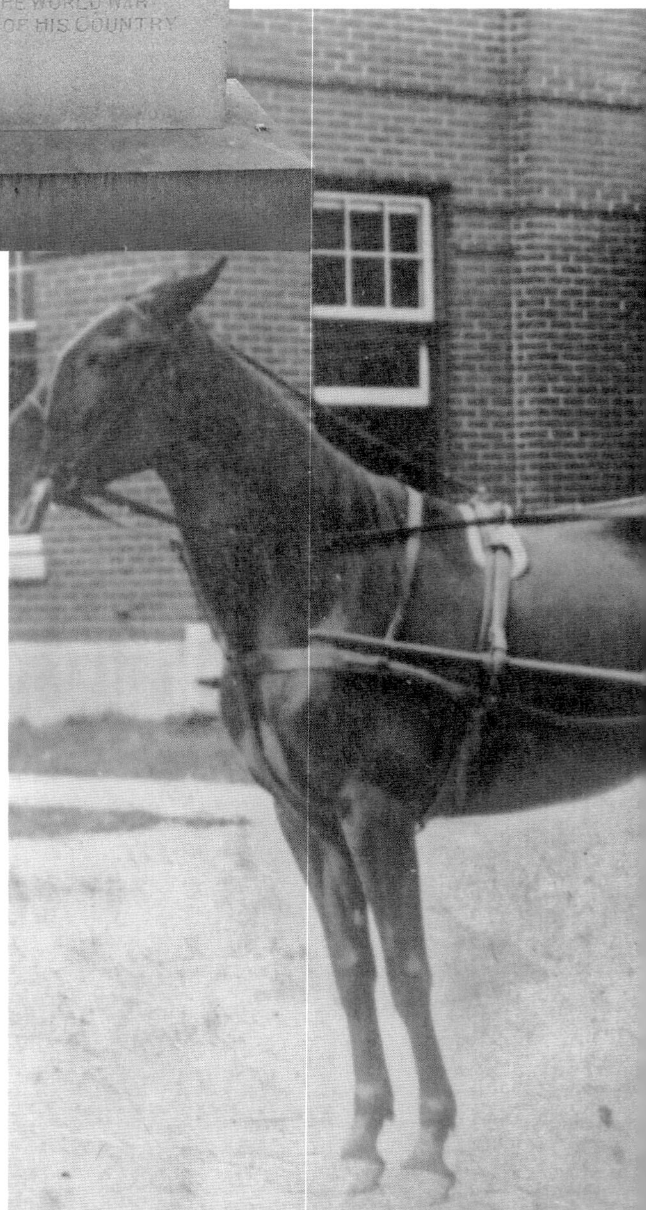

Henry John Ollrich

World War I was raging when Ollrich volunteered for service in 1917. A member of the 125th Infantry, Private Ollrich was part of the Allied advance from Cièrges to Fismes, France, in the summer of 1918 and was assigned to courier messages through enemy barrages. On August 4, 1918, Ollrich was killed in action while attempting to deliver an important message to the battalion commander across a shell-swept zone. He was posthumously awarded the Distinguished Service Cross for extraordinary heroism in action. Ollrich's remains were returned to his family in 1925 and were interred at Clinton Grove Cemetery. Ollrich was the first citizen of Mount Clemens to be killed in service during World War I, and the community's American Legion post was named in his memory. (Photograph by Deborah J. Larsen.)

Edward John Sawitzky

Sawitzky (shown below standing in front of the fire hall next to Chief Joseph Rosso, who is seated in the buggy) joined the Mount Clemens Fire Department in 1910. He was promoted to fire chief in 1917, succeeding Chief Rosso. Responding to what appeared to be an ordinary structure fire at 54 East Broadway on the evening of January 26, 1929, Sawitzky was overcome by noxious gases and smoke and was rushed to St. Joseph Mercy Hospital. He waged a three-day battle for his life, but ultimately succumbed after suffering a heart attack on the fourth day after the fire. To this date, Sawitzky is the only Mount Clemens firefighter to lose his life in the line of duty. (Courtesy of Mount Clemens Public Library.)

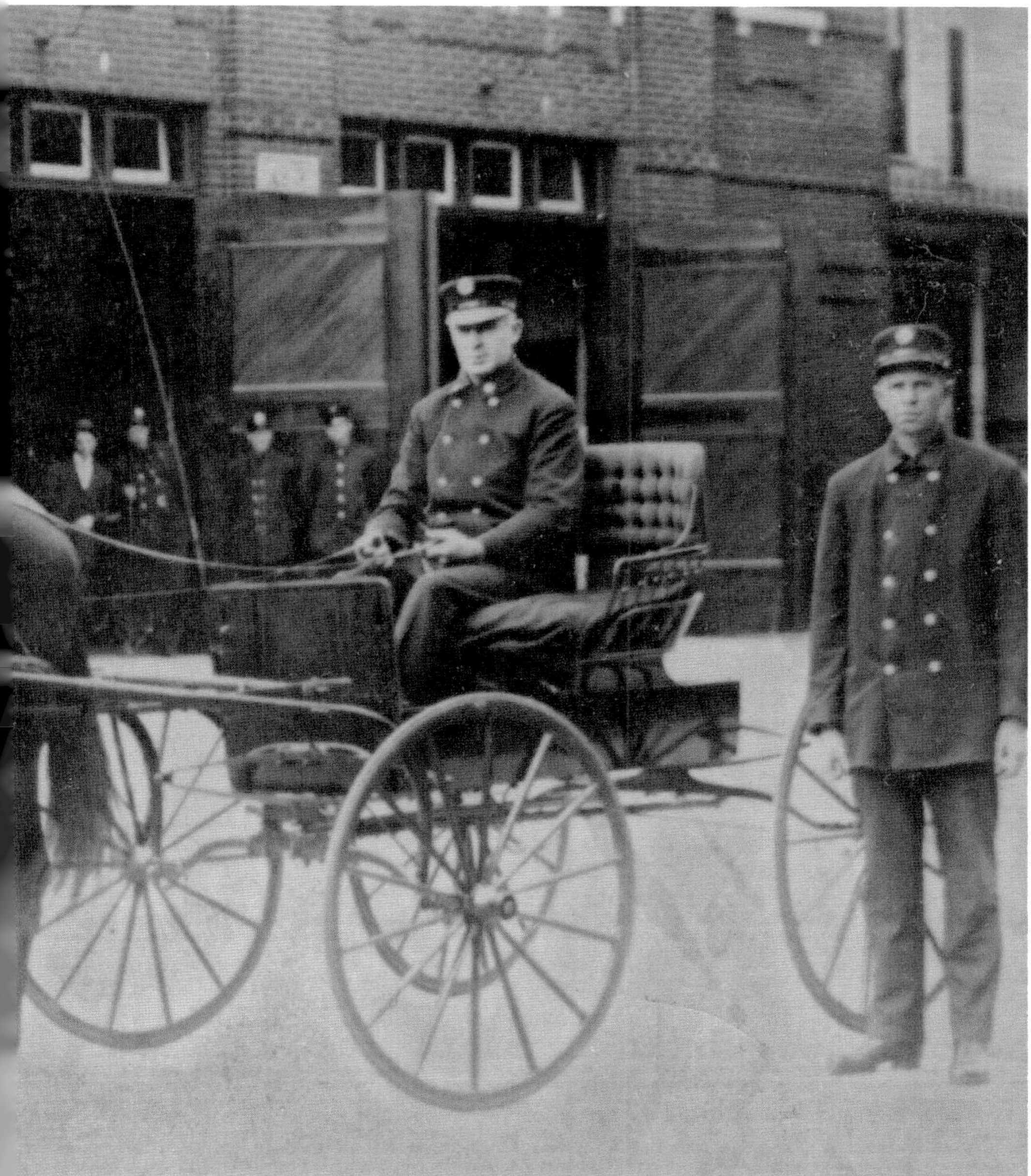

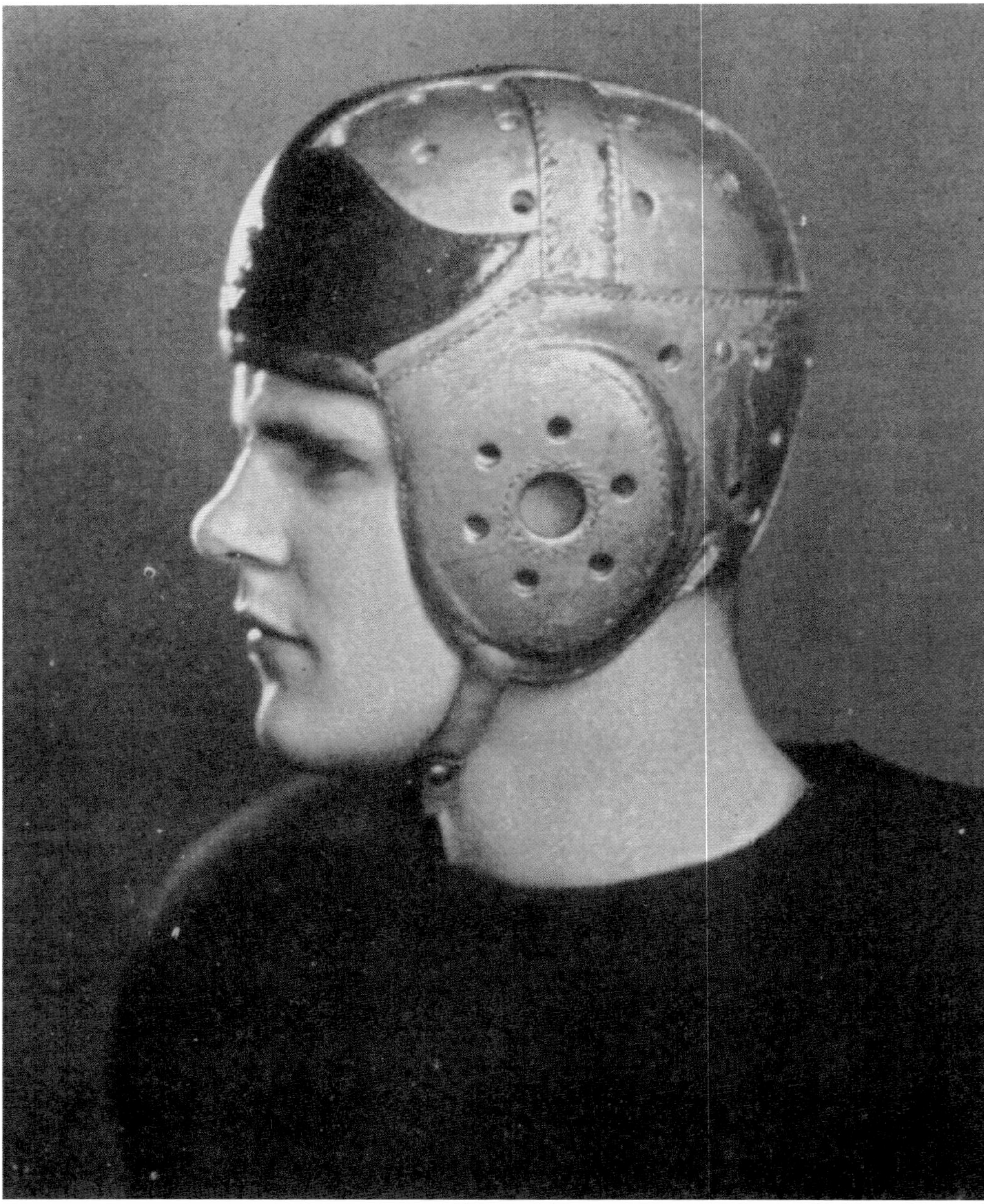

Ralph Edward Bennett Jr.

Bennett was the first Mount Clemens man killed in action during World War II. A star football player for Mount Clemens High School, Bennett attended Michigan State University where he won two letters in football and was active in campus activities. He received a commission as an army officer while a student, and was activated in March 1941, sailing for the Philippines two months later. Bennett was assigned to the 57th Infantry Regiment of the Philippine Scouts, which was tasked with the defense of the islands against Japanese invasion. Wounded in action on March 27, 1942, Bennett died of his injuries on May 6 of that year, during the fall of Corregidor. The Mount Clemens AmVets post was named in his honor. (Courtesy of Michigan State University Archives and Historical Collections.)

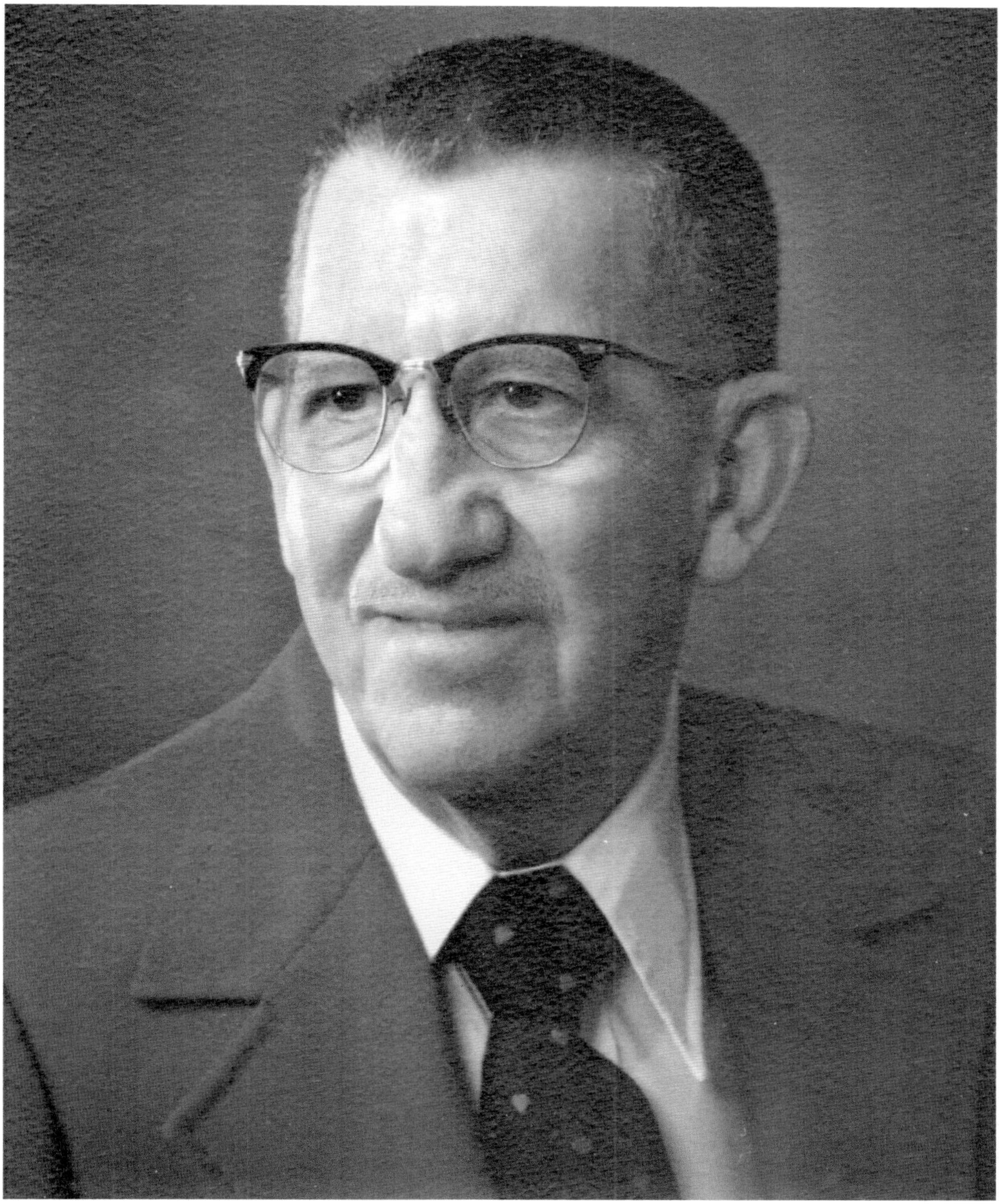

James Harlan Jewell

Jewell earned his medical degree from Western Reserve University (later Case Western Reserve) in 1934. During World War II, he served in the US Army Air Corps as a flight surgeon with the 8th Air Force in Europe, and he coordinated the method by which American wounded were airlifted from the Normandy beaches on D-Day, saving thousands of lives with his medical and organizational skills. Following the war he remained in the US Air Force Reserve, and retired with the rank of colonel in 1969. During his civilian medical practice in Mount Clemens, he served as chief of the medical staff at St. Joseph Mercy Hospital and as president of the Macomb County Medical Society. Jewell was also active in community affairs, and was a 32nd degree Mason. (Courtesy of Mount Clemens Public Library.)

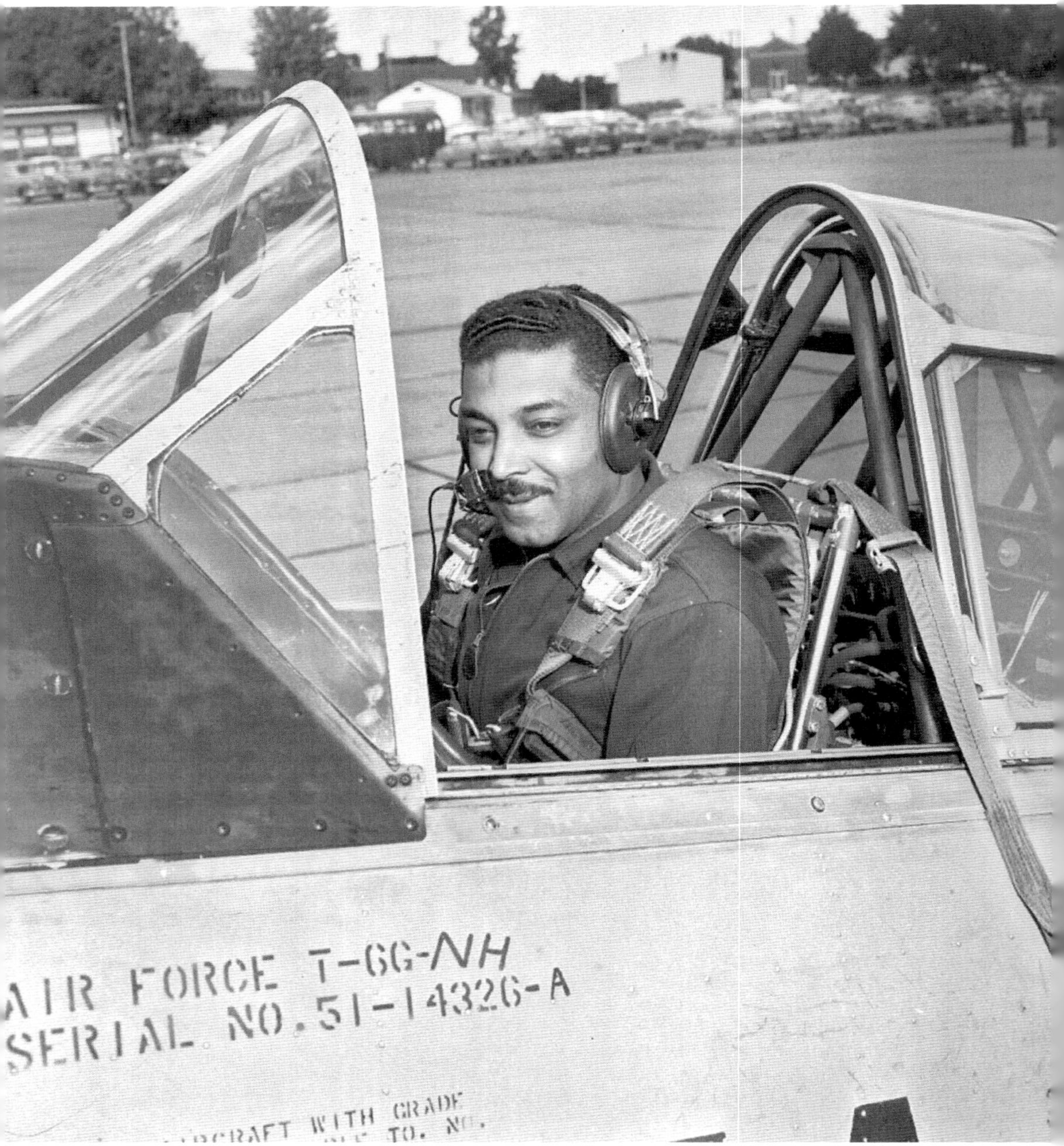

Vincent Ivor Mitchell

During World War II, Mitchell flew the P-51 Mustang fighter with the 99th Pursuit Squadron, part of the heroic organization of African American aviators known as the Tuskegee Airmen. Tasked to provide heavy bomber escort, the Tuskegee Airmen had an unparalleled reputation for seeing the bombers safely to their targets. Mitchell was a 1940 graduate of Mount Clemens High School and received his wings at Tuskegee Army Air Field in 1944. He is shown above in 1953 at the controls of a T-6G Texan, the airplane he flew after the war as a member of the Air Force Reserve's 439th Fighter-Bomber Wing at Selfridge Air Force Base. (Courtesy of the *Macomb Daily*.)

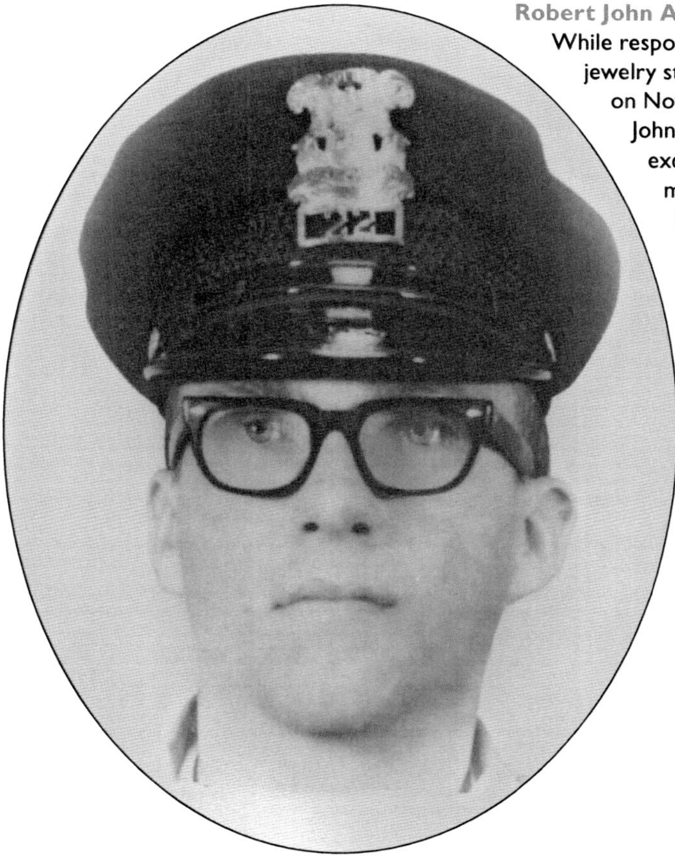

Robert John Ahrens

While responding to an armed robbery of a jewelry store in downtown Mount Clemens on November 1, 1973, patrolman Robert John Ahrens was fatally wounded while exchanging gunfire with the hold-up men. The 28-year-old father of two had served in the army before joining the Mount Clemens Police Department in 1969, and was the only officer in the history of the department to lose his life in the line of duty. Shown below are members of the Mount Clemens Police Department participating in a memorial service for Ahrens that was conducted at his gravesite on the first anniversary of his death. (Courtesy of City of Mount Clemens and the *Macomb Daily*.)

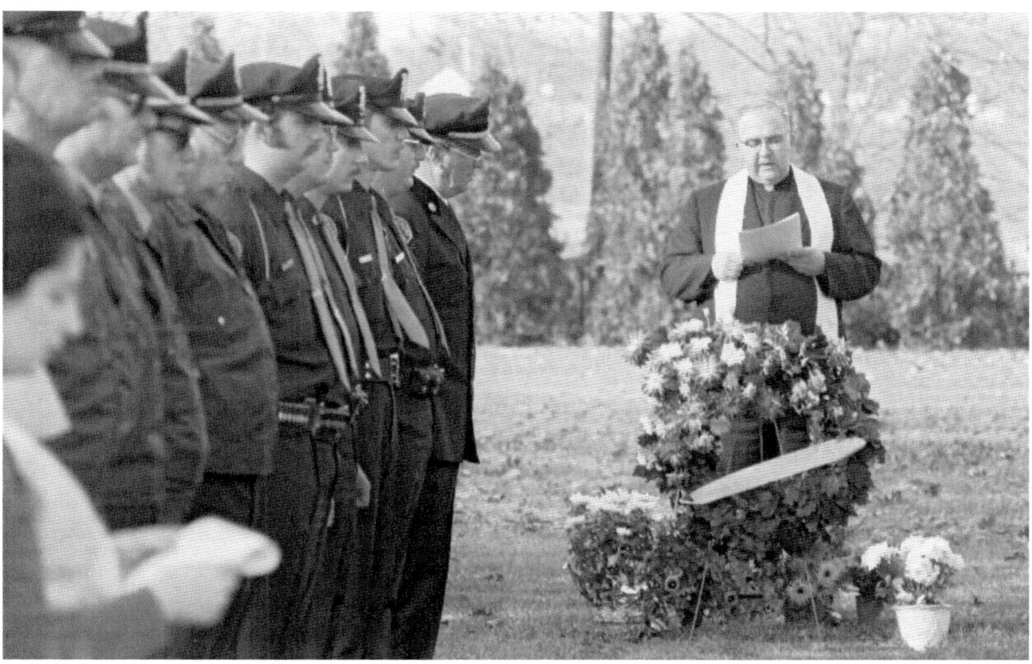

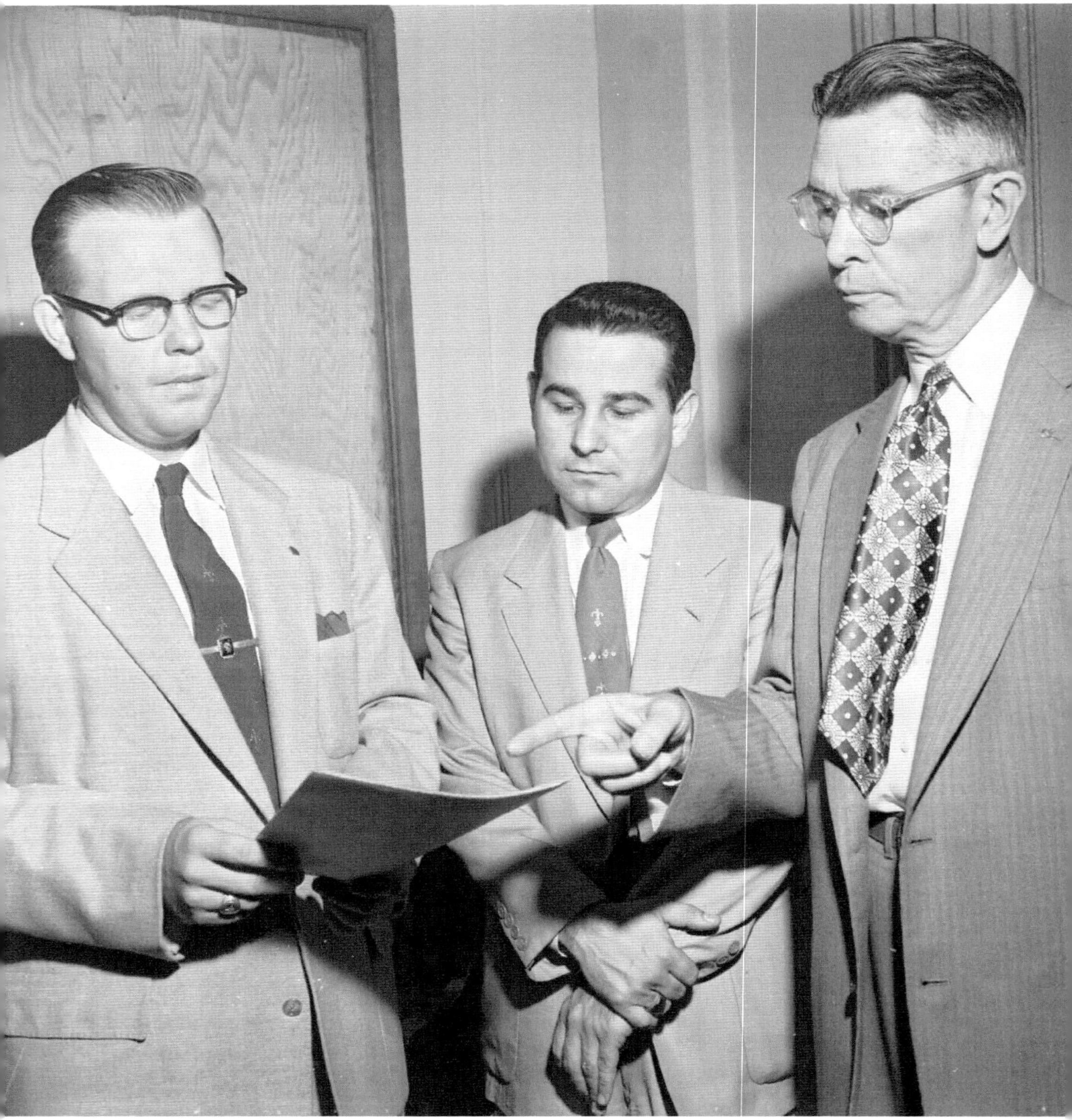

Kenneth Noble Sanborn

During the era of McCarthyism, attorney Kenneth Noble Sanborn risked his career when he agreed to assist in the defense of his former classmate, Milo Radulovich, a young Air Force officer who faced losing his commission because his father and sister were suspected communists. Sanborn and veteran attorney Charles C. Lockwood handled Radulovich's case despite the very real possibility that they themselves would be branded pro-communist. This photograph, taken during the 1953 hearing of the case at Selfridge Air Force Base, shows Sanborn (left) conferring with Radulovich and Lockwood. Far from having his legal ambitions derailed, Sanborn went on to a distinguished career as a state legislator and judge, and was awarded the Macomb County Bar Association Medal of Courage and Honor in 2006. (Courtesy of the *Macomb Daily*.)

Donald Eugene Odell

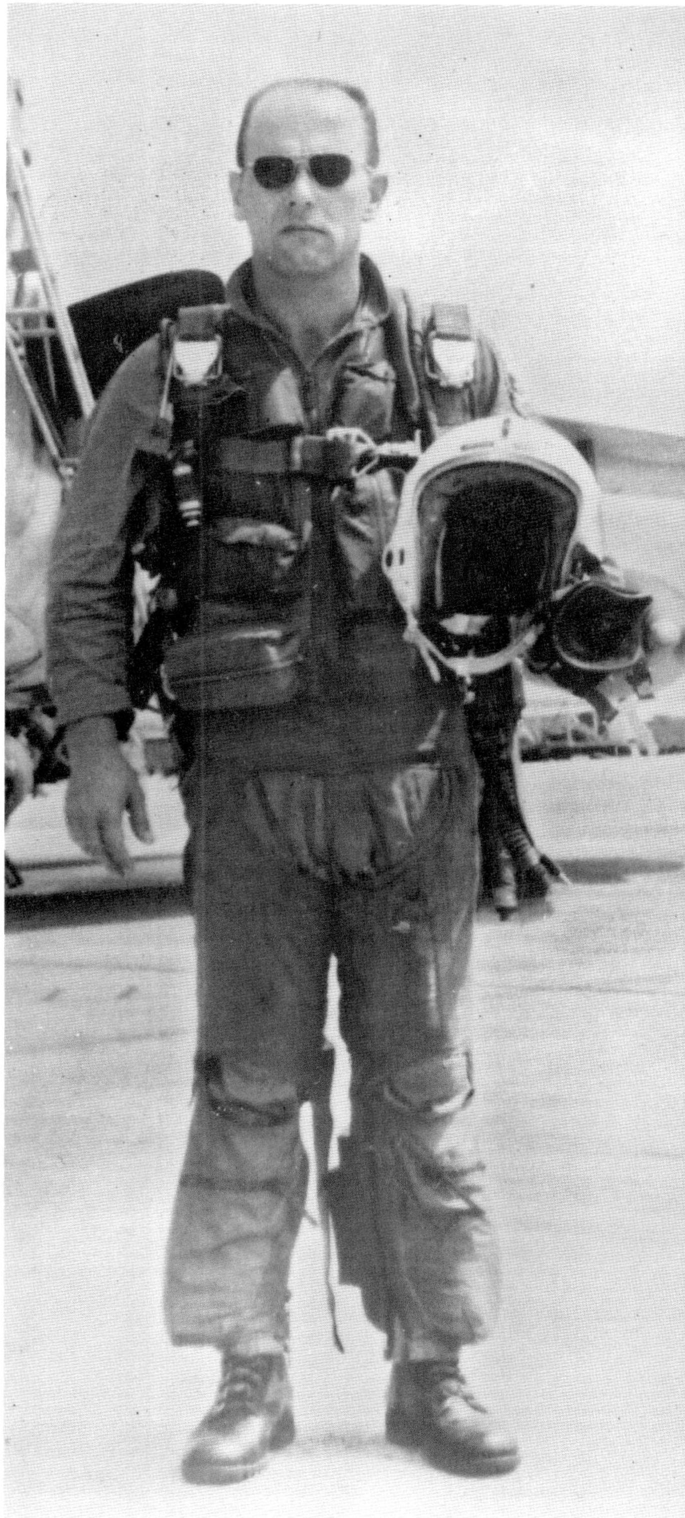

Odell served as an instructor pilot in the Air Force Pilot Training School and was assigned to the 94th Fighter Interceptor Squadron at Selfridge Air Force Base prior to training to fly the F-105 Thunderchief fighter-bomber in 1966. The following year, at the height of the Vietnam War, he was stationed with the 34th Tactical Fighter Squadron at Korat Royal Thai Air Base, Thailand, where the F-105—affectionately called the "Thud" by its crews—was being tasked as a primary strike bomber. While flying his 17th mission over North Vietnam on October 17, 1967, Odell was shot down by anti-aircraft fire as he approached his target 16 miles north of Hanoi. As his aircraft broke apart, he parachuted out and was captured by enemy forces. After a few days, Odell was transferred to North Vietnam's infamous Ho Loa prison, dubbed the "Hanoi Hilton" by those incarcerated there. He was held as a prisoner of war for five and a half years, during which time his captors employed severe torture techniques and prolonged periods of solitary confinement in an attempt to break their prisoners. Odell was released during "Operation Homecoming" as the US forces withdrew from Vietnam, and returned home on April 7, 1973. Among the many awards and decorations conferred upon Donald Odell for heroism in connection with his service are the Silver Star, Legion of Merit, and Distinguished Flying Cross with oak leaf cluster. Odell later served as the public affairs officer at Selfridge Air National Guard Base and retired from the US Air Force at the rank of lieutenant colonel. In retirement, Donald Odell has been deeply involved in community service in the Mount Clemens area through his work with the Wertz Warriors and his support of the Selfridge Base Community Council. The photograph shown right was taken just days before Odell's fateful flight in 1967. (Courtesy of Donald E. Odell.)

INDEX